D0791554

Adobe® GoLive® CS2

CLASSROOM
IN A BOOK®

www.adobepress.com

Adobe

Lesson files . . . and so much more

The *Adobe GoLive CS2 Classroom in a Book* CD includes the lesson files that you'll need to complete the exercises in this book, as well as other content to help you learn more about Adobe GoLive and use it with greater efficiency and ease. The diagram below represents the contents of the CD, which should help you locate the files you need.

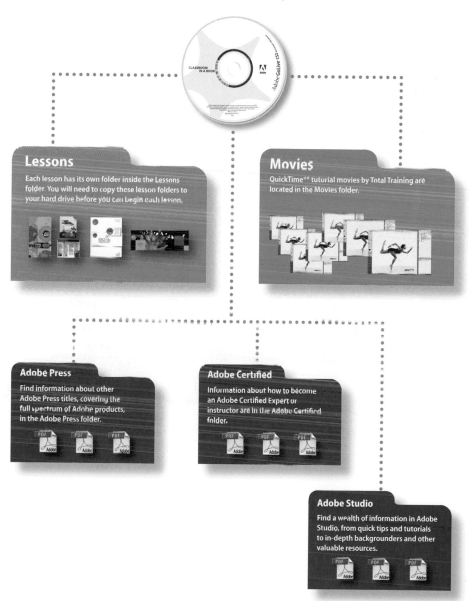

Lessons

Each lesson has its own folder inside the Lessons folder. You will need to copy these lesson folders to your hard drive before you can begin each lesson.

Movies

QuickTime** tutorial movies by Total Training are located in the Movies folder.

Adobe Press

Find information about other Adobe Press titles, covering the full spectrum of Adobe products, in the Adobe Press folder.

Adobe Certified

Information about how to become an Adobe Certified Expert or instructor are in the Adobe Certified folder.

Adobe Studio

Find a wealth of information in Adobe Studio, from quick tips and tutorials to in-depth backgrounders and other valuable resources.

** *The latest version of Apple QuickTime can be downloaded from www.apple.com/quicktime/download.*

Contents

Getting Started

About *Classroom in a Book* 1

Prerequisites 1

Installing the program 2

Copying the *Classroom in a Book* files 2

To install the *Classroom in a Book* files 2

Restoring default preferences 3

To save your current GoLive CS2 preferences 3

Windows... 3

Mac OS 4

To restore your saved settings after completing the
lessons... 4

Additional resources 4

Adobe certification 5

What's New in Adobe GoLive CS2?

Innovative visual CSS authoring 6

Helpful new tools.................................. 6

Enhanced Layer, Layer Grid and Layout Text Box tools . . 7

Liquid layouts 8

Other CSS improvements 8

Standards-based mobile authoring 9

Enhanced live rendering 9

Automated favicon creation......................... 9

Enhanced InDesign Package for GoLive 9

Collaborative asset management 10

Version Que 10

Adobe Bridge 10

Cropped components 10

Samples 10

A Quick Tour of Adobe GoLive CS2

Creating your own site 15

Adding assets to your site 16

Adding metadata to your page 18

Creating the layout of the page. 21

Adding a background image to a page. 23

Placing images onto your GoLive page. 24

Creating grid text boxes. 27

Formatting text using Cascading Style Sheets 29

Creating a second text area 32

Placing an optimized image. 34

Creating a table 35

Spanning a column 37

Creating hyperlinks 37

Using the Live Rendering feature 39

Using Cascading Styles for hyperlinks 40

1   Getting to Know the Work Area

Getting started 43

Using the View and Window menus 47

Using the Zoom tool 48

Using the Window menu to control palettes and
toolbars. 49

Customizing the workspace 49

Using the toolbox 51

Understanding the Inspector palette. 51

Helpful keyboard shortcuts for palettes 52

Separating the Objects palette from the toolbox. 53

Using the site window to link an image 55

Working with the document window 58

The Layout Editor 58

The Frame Editor 59

The Source Code Editor 59

The Outline Editor 59

The Layout Preview. 59

The PDF Preview. 60

Using the Document and Source Views 60

Using the Outline Editor. 61

Previewing your document in GoLive 63

Using the View palette 64

Previewing your document in a browser 64

Using PDF Preview. 66

Setting Preferences and Web Settings. 67

Exploring on your own. 69

Review questions. 70

Review answers 70

2   Creating a GoLive Site

What is a site? 73

Getting started 75

Creating a new blank site 76

Behind the scenes 77

web-content 78

web-data 78

web-settings 80

About the site window. 80

Understanding the Files tab 81

The Main toolbar 84

Saving a new page into the Files tab 85

Adding existing files to a blank site 86

Adding a file saved from Photoshop 87

Creating site colors 89

Adding your own site colors. 90

Adding site objects to a page. 91

Checking usage on the Files tab 96

Deleting a file 98

Closing and re-opening your site 99

Creating a GoLive site from existing files 100

Organizing the site window 103

Navigating within a site. 104

Creating a folder for pages 104

Storing Smart objects 105

Using the Navigation View 106

Exploring on your own 109

Saving files into a site 109

More on sites 109

Review questions 110

Review answers 110

3 Creating Page Layouts in GoLive

Layout grid-based designs 113

Table-based designs 114

CSS-based designs 114

What is the difference between CSS and traditional
HTML tables? 114

Getting started 114

Creating the site 116

Using the CSS-based layout grid 116

Adding images to the layout grid 118

Aligning objects on the layout grid 120

Using the target insertion point 123

Using the layout text box 124

Assigning font sets and color 127

Changing the background of a layout grid 128

Changing the background color of layout text boxes . 129

Adding an image to a layout text box 131

Converting a layout grid to a table 132

Converting a layout grid to a traditional HTML table . 133

Using HTML tables for page layout 134

Placing a table on your page 135

Adjusting cell size 136

Spanning rows and columns 138

Designing a layout using spans 140

Changing the table attributes 141

Creating and saving table styles 142

Importing text into a table 143

Applying a table style 145

Placing text and images in the table 146

Applying a Cascading Style Sheet to the cell 147

Completing the table 148

Using layers 150

Adding layers to an HTML page 150

Inserting objects into the layer 152

Aligning and distributing layers 153

Adding imagery and text 155

Organizing layers 157

Changing the Z-index 158

Using the Layers palette 159

Liquid layouts 161

Creating a page using liquid layouts 162

Exploring on your own 164

Experimenting with liquid layouts 164

Review questions 165

Review answers 165

4 Creating Navigational Links

Getting started 167

About links 168

Opening the site 169

Creating hypertext links 171

Adding links to a graphic 175

Using components 176

Adding components to a page 178

Creating a component 180

Creating anchors 182

Testing anchors 184

Using anchors within a site 185

Creating external links 186

Creating external links with the External tab 187

Creating e-mail links 189

Changing a link's color 191

Changing preferences for link warnings 192

Using the In & Out Links palette 194

Exploring on your own. 195

Review questions. 196

Review answers 196

5   Adding and Formatting Text

Getting started 199

Importing and working with text 200

Basic formatting in HTML 201

Creating lists from text 202

Setting text color 203

Using the CSS palette and editor. 204

Paragraph formatting 204

Using the CSS Editor to redefine markup elements . . . 206

Formatting the body text of your page 208

Using CSS styles to format your text. 209

Applying CSS to the body of your text. 211

Adding a CSS class style 212

Applying a CSS class style to a div. 214

Exporting an Internal Style Sheet 216

Importing an External Style Sheet 217

Exploring on your own. 217

Review questions. 218

Review answers 218

6   Working with Color

Getting started 221

Setting page background color 223

Setting page background color with CSS 224

Using the Color palette 226

Choosing CMYK and Spot colors using the Swatches palette. 229

Adding colors to your Swatches palette 232

Extracting color from an image 235

Saving the custom colors in your Swatches palette. . . 236

Loading Adobe Swatch Exchange files 236

Working with site colors. 237

Exploring on your own. 238

Review questions. 240

Review answers 240

7   Using Graphics in GoLive

Getting started 243

Understanding Web file formats 244

Creating the page 245

Placing the top image 247

Creating an image map 248

Adding alt text 251

Adding a background image 253

Smart Objects 254

Testing the Smart object 260

Using the Smart Illustrator object. 261

Using the color table. 263

Using variables 265

Text to Banner. 267

Cropping a Smart object 272

Exploring on your own. 273

Review questions. 274

Review answers 274

8   Adding Interactivity: Rollovers and Actions

Getting started 277

Setting up your rollover buttons. 278

Creating self-rollovers 280

Detecting rollover images 283

Adding a link to a rollover. 284

Creating a remote rollover 285

Adding an Open Window action 290

Creating head actions. 294

Locating and installing GoLive CS2 actions 296

Exploring on your own. 297

Creating a Close Window action 297

Review questions. 298

Review answers 298

9 Creating Forms

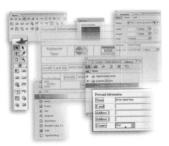

Getting started 301

About forms. 304

Adding e-mail and address fields 307

Linking labels to text fields 309

Creating a pop-up menu 310

Adding the table to the Library palette. 312

Modifying a list box. 314

Adding radio buttons 315

Adding a Submit button 318

Adding a Reset button 319

Setting the tabbing order 321

Exploring on your own. 322

Review questions. 323

Review answers 323

10 Using Stationeries, Components, Page Templates, and Snippets

What is the difference?. 325

Getting started 326

Creating a component file. 328

Placing a component 330

Editing a component 332

Cropping text in a component. 333

Using snippets 335

Placing the snippet 338

Creating a stationery file 339

Saving the stationery file. 340

Creating a page from a stationery file 341

Saving a page template file 344

Defining template regions 346

Using the page template 349

Building from the page template 350

Exploring on your own 351

Practice with components 351

Practice with snippets 351

Review questions 353

Review answers 353

11   Using Site Diagrams

Getting started 355

Creating a new site diagram 357

Anchoring a diagram to a page 359

Adding Sections, Pages, and Groups 360

Creating a group of pages   362

Adding annotations 363

Adding text and images to your diagram pages 364

Using the staging tools to create site pages 365

Recalling a diagram from a site 368

Adding common elements using the Master tab 369

Exporting and printing your diagram 370

Exploring on your own 371

Review questions 372

Review answers 372

12   Managing and Publishing Web Sites

GoLive site management and publishing 375

Getting started 376

Importing an existing site into GoLive CS2 377

Converting the site into GoLive structure 378

Correcting errors 379

Correcting the hypertext link error 383

Managing folders 384

Backing up and cleaning up your site 384

Working with Site Trash 387

Setting up GoLive for FTP 388

Configuring a publish server 388

Uploading files via FTP to your server 390

Maintaining your site 391

Synchronizing files in your site 392

Exporting a site 393

Exploring on your own 396

Review questions 397

Review answers 397

13   **Using Version Cue and Bridge with GoLive CS2**

Getting started 399

Working with Version Cue 400

Creating a new Version Cue project 400

Checking out a file for editing 402

About Version Cue Status 405

Managing existing sites 405

Adding files to a Version Cue site 407

Working offline 408

Working with Adobe Bridge 409

Navigating and viewing files 410

Index 411

Getting Started

Adobe® GoLive® CS2 is the industry-standard Web content creation program. Whether you are a designer or technical illustrator, an artist producing multimedia graphics, or a creator of Web pages or online content, the Adobe GoLive CS2 program offers you the tools you need to get professional-quality results.

About *Classroom in a Book*

Adobe GoLive CS2 Classroom in a Book® is part of the official training series for Adobe graphics and publishing software from Adobe Systems, Inc.

The lessons are designed so that you can learn at your own pace. If you're new to Adobe GoLive, you'll learn the fundamentals you need to put the program to work. If you are an experienced user, you'll find that *Classroom in a Book* teaches many advanced features, including tips and techniques for using the latest version of Adobe GoLive.

Although each lesson provides step-by-step instructions for creating a specific project, there's room for exploration and experimentation. You can follow the book from start to finish or do only the lessons that correspond to your interests and needs. Each lesson concludes with a review section summarizing what you've covered.

Prerequisites

Before beginning to use *Adobe GoLive CS2 Classroom in a Book*, you should have a working knowledge of your computer and its operating system. Make sure you know how to use the mouse and standard menus and commands, and also how to open, save, and close files. If you need to review these techniques, see the printed or online documentation included with your Windows or Mac OS documentation.

Note: *When instructions differ by platform, Windows commands appear first, and then the Mac OS command, with the platform noted in parentheses. For example, "press Alt (Windows) or Option (Mac OS) and click away from the artwork." Common commands may be further abbreviated with the Windows command first, followed by a slash and the Mac OS command, without any parenthetical reference. For example, press Alt/Option; or Ctrl/Command+click.*

Installing the program

Before you begin using *Adobe GoLive CS2 Classroom in a Book*, make sure that your system is set up correctly and that you've installed the required software and hardware.

You must purchase the Adobe GoLive CS2 software separately. For complete instructions on installing the software, see the "How to Install" Readme file on the application CD.

Copying the *Classroom in a Book* files

The Classroom in a Book CD includes folders containing all the electronic files for the lessons. Each lesson has its own folder. You must install these folders on your hard disk to use the files for the lessons. To save room on your hard disk, you can install the folders for each lesson as you need them.

To install the *Classroom in a Book* files

1 Insert the Adobe GoLive Classroom in a Book CD into your CD-ROM drive.

2 Create a folder on your hard disk.

3 Do one of the following:

• Copy the Lessons folder into the newly created folder.

• Copy only the single lesson folder you need into the newly created folder.

Restoring default preferences

The preferences file controls how palettes and command settings appear on your screen when you open the Adobe GoLive program. Each time you quit Adobe GoLive, certain command settings are recorded in the preferences file. If you want to restore the tools and palettes to their original default settings, you can delete the current Adobe GoLive CS2 preferences file. [Adobe GoLive creates a preferences file (if one doesn't already exist) the next time you start the program and save a file.]

You must then restore the default preferences for GoLive before you begin each lesson. This ensures that the tools and palettes function as described in this book. When you have finished the book, you can restore your saved settings.

If at any time you wish to return the palettes to their default position, choose Window > Workspace > Default Workspace.

To save your current GoLive CS2 preferences

Windows

1 Make sure that the GoLive CS2 application is not running.

2 On the Windows platform, locate the following file C:\Documents and Settings\ username\Application Data\Adobe\Adobe GoLive\Adobe GoLive 8 and right-click and select Cut.

3 Paste in another folder, or on the desktop, so that you can retrieve the file later if you wish to return to your previous settings.

Note: You may have to choose Folder Options from the Control panel to show hidden files to locate these preferences. From the Folder Options window, click on Views. Check the radio button to the left of Show Hidden Files or Folders.

4 Repeat step 2 with the folder inside the Adobe GoLive folder named Settings8.

These files, when removed, will be recreated upon launch of GoLive CS2.

Mac OS

1 On Mac, in your User folder, select Library\Preferences and select and drag the following files/folders: Adobe folder and the Adobe GoLive 8.0 Prefs to another folder or on the desktop. This way you can retrieve the file later if you wish to return to your previous settings.

Note: If you cannot locate the preferences file, use your operating system's Find command.

If you can't find the file, either you haven't started Adobe GoLive yet or you have moved the preference file. The preferences file is created after you quit the program the first time and is updated thereafter.

To locate and delete the Adobe GoLive preferences file quickly each time you begin a new lesson, create a shortcut (Windows) or an alias (Mac OS) for the GoLive CS2 Settings folder.

To restore your saved settings after completing the lessons

1 Exit Adobe GoLive.

2 Drag the Adobe GoLive 8.prf file from the desktop or folder in which you saved the file to the Adobe GoLive folder. Also replace the Settings8 folder with your saved folder.

3 In the warning dialog box that appears, confirm you'll replace the existing file.

Note: You can rename the preferences file with your current settings, rather than moving it or throwing it away. To restore your current settings when you have finished the lessons, change the preferences filename back. Exit GoLive, and return the renamed preferences file to the Adobe GoLive\Settings8 folder.

Additional resources

Adobe GoLive CS2 Classroom in a Book is not meant to replace documentation that comes with the program. Only the commands and options used in the lessons are explained in this book.

For comprehensive information about program features, refer to these resources:

• GoLive Help, which you can view by choosing Help > GoLive Help. (For more information, see Lesson 1, "Getting to Know the Work Area.")

• Training and support resources on the Adobe Web site (Adobe.com), which you can view by choosing Help > Online Support if you have a connection to the World Wide Web.

• The Adobe Web site (Adobe.com), which you can view by choosing Help > GoLive Online if you have a connection to the World Wide Web.

• Adobe Studio (http://studio.adobe.com), where you can find a wealth of tips, tutorials, plug-ins, actions, and other design inspiration and instructional content.

• The Adobe GoLive CS2 Users Guide, which contains most of the material included in the Help system. If the Users Guide book is not included in your GoLive CS2 Package, it is available for purchase at Adobe.com. The Help system that is already built into the application contains all the information in the User Guide, plus additional information not included in the printed version.

Adobe certification

The Adobe Training and Certification programs are designed to help Adobe customers and trainers improve and promote their product-proficiency skills. There are three levels of certification.

Adobe Certified Expert (ACE)

Adobe Certified Instructor (ACI)

Adobe Authorized Training Center (AATC)

The Adobe Certified Expert program is a way for expert users to upgrade their credentials. You can use Adobe certification as a catalyst for getting a raise, finding a job, or promoting your expertise.

If you are an ACE-level instructor, the Adobe Certified Instructor program takes your skills to the next level and gives you access to a wide range of Adobe resources. Adobe Authorized Training Centers offer instructor-led courses and training on Adobe products, employing only Adobe Certified Instructors. A directory of AATCs is available at http://partners.adobe.com. For information on the Adobe Certified programs, visit www.adobe.com/support/certification/main.html.

What's New in Adobe GoLive CS2?

GoLive CS2 introduces new features that make it easy for Web designers to use Cascading Style Sheets (CSS), preview pages for mobile devices, and edit SVG files, just to name a few. In GoLive CS2, you will find a rich environment for mobile content, and tighter integration with other applications in the Adobe Creative Suite 2.

The What's New section includes some of the features that are included in the *GoLive CS2 Classroom in a Book* lessons. You can find a complete list of new features in GoLive Help. To access GoLive Help choose Help > GoLive Help.

Helpful new tools

With the addition of the toolbox, GoLive makes selections of objects easier. Using the Object Selection tool (⬉) and Standard Editing tool (I⬉) makes it easy to select CSS containers (DIVs) and their contents.

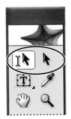

New tools make selections more precise.

The Selection tools are referenced and used throughout all of the lessons in the *GoLive CS2 Classroom in a Book*.

Enhanced Layer, Layer Grid and Layout Text Box tools

The enhanced Layer tool helps you to draw and position CSS DIVs with precision and accuracy.

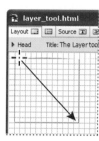

The Layer tool.

Use this tool to visually position your layers. You can be more precise by entering exact values in the new Set Position, and dimension fields in the Main toolbar. Discover more about the Layer tool in Lesson 3, "Creating Page Layouts in GoLive."

Set precision coordinates as well as width and height.

Whether using the default CSS-based layout grid or the table-based grid, you can take advantage of the new Grid Text tool.

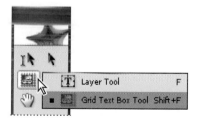

The Grid Text Box tool allows you to visually create text areas on layout grids. Simply select the tool and click and drag a text area on your grid, much like you would create a text area in a page layout application such as InDesign or PageMaker. Read more about the Grid Text Box tool in Lessons 3, "Creating page Layouts in GoLive," and 5, "Adding and Formatting Text."

Liquid layouts

GoLive CS2 offers new support for pre-built, drag-and-drop CSS block objects. You can now recreate a number of standard CSS designs in no time by dragging CSS objects onto a page. You can then customize the design by adding objects into the layouts.

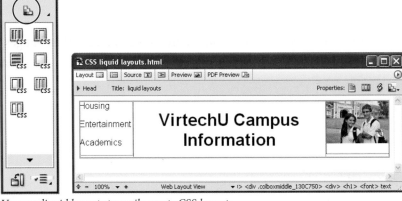

Use new liquid layouts to easily create CSS layouts.

The new CSS objects are located in the CSS section of the Objects palette and include a 3-column layout with a liquid (flexible) center as well as a standard two-column layout with a fixed left column. Read more about using liquid layouts in Lesson 3, "Creating Page Layouts in GoLive."

Other CSS improvements

GoLive CS2 also introduces other CSS enhancements such as an improved CSS Editor. The CSS Editor allows you to check source code and syntax as you edit CSS styles, provides automatic conversion of HTML styles to CSS, and provides a default external style sheet that applies to all new pages in a site. Read more about CSS used in text formatting in Lesson 5, "Adding and Formatting Text."

Standards-based mobile authoring

With the Mobile market booming in Asia and Europe, and now emerging in the United States, designers need to be prepared with the right tools for creating and editing mobile content.

GoLive delivers rich mobile authoring tools based entirely on open standards, such as CSS, XHTML, SMIL, SVG-Tiny, MPEG-4, and 3GPP.

Discover more about designing for the mobile market in "Designing for mobile devices" in GoLive Help.

Enhanced live rendering

GoLive CS2 offers live previews. As you make changes, you can see the changes immediately in the Live Rendering window. Change the settings in the Live Rendering to display a small screen by choosing SSR (Small Screen Rendering). Read more about displaying your page in the "Previewing your document in GoLive" section in Lesson 1, "Getting to Know the Work Area."

Automated favicon creation

Favorite icons let you specify an image that appears with your page's title in the Favorites or Bookmarks menu of a Web browser. You can specify an image by using the favicon feature in GoLive CS2. You can even use a Smart Favorite icon from the Smart set of the objects toolbox to specify a Smart Object as a favorite icon. For more information see "Smart Favorite icons" in GoLive Help.

Enhanced InDesign Package for GoLive

With InDesign's Package For GoLive feature, you can easily incorporate content from InDesign documents into GoLive pages and sites. From open InDesign packages, you can either drag individual text and graphic assets to Web pages or export entire InDesign layouts to HTML. If you regularly revise package assets in InDesign, GoLive automatically updates related text and images using components and Smart Objects. For more information read "Importing InDesign packages" in GoLive Help.

Collaborative asset management

Keep track of your team-based projects with Version Cue® and keep projects organized using Adobe Bridge®.

Version Que

Version Cue uses projects to store related files and folders. If you work independently, you create a project to gather all the files you need, view the files in Bridge, and use Version Cue features such as versions and alternates. In a workgroup, depending on your workflow, you can create one Version Cue project for files that everyone in your workgroup collaborates on, a different project for files that don't require collaboration, and yet another project restricted to specific users. Discover more about Version Que in Lesson 13, "Using Version Cue and Bridge with GoLive CS2."

Adobe Bridge

Adobe Bridge is the control center for Adobe Creative Suite. You use it to organize, browse, and locate the assets you need to create content for print, the Web, and mobile devices. Adobe Bridge keeps native PSD, AI, INDD, and Adobe PDF files as well as other Adobe and non-Adobe application files available for easy access. You can drag assets into your layouts as needed, preview them, and even add metadata to them. Bridge is available independently, as well as from within Adobe Photoshop, Adobe Illustrator, Adobe InDesign, and Adobe GoLive.

Cropped components

Customize text components for different audiences. The Crop Text feature allows you to delete text that resides on components on individual pages without affecting the original component file. Discover how to use the cropping feature in Lesson 7, "Using Graphics in GoLive."

Samples

Choose from predesigned pages, frame sets, scripts, style sheets, and more. For more information see, "To create a site from a site sample" in GoLive Help.

In this tour you will create Web pages using time-saving features that are unique to Adobe GoLive CS2. You will also discover how to build simple Web sites on your own.

A Quick Tour of Adobe GoLive CS2

In this tour, you will create a university Web site. Using GoLive CS2 you will create a collection of pages that are organized and appropriately linked to each other.

This is a rather fast-paced tour, so if you are not yet familiar with the work area, you may want to review Lesson 1, "Getting to Know the Work Area" first.

Before you begin, restore the default preferences for Adobe GoLive CS2. Then open the finished art file for this lesson to see the finished product.

1	To ensure that the tools and palettes function exactly as described in this lesson, delete or deactivate (by renaming) the Adobe GoLive CS2 preferences file. See "Restoring default preferences" on page 3.

2	Open GoLive CS2. If the Welcome Screen appears, choose Open Document, or choose File > Open. Navigate to the Lesson00 folder and open it. Open the lesson00_site folder and select the tour.site file. Choose Open.

A site window appears listing several items, including an index.html file, a css folder, an images folder, and a pages folder.

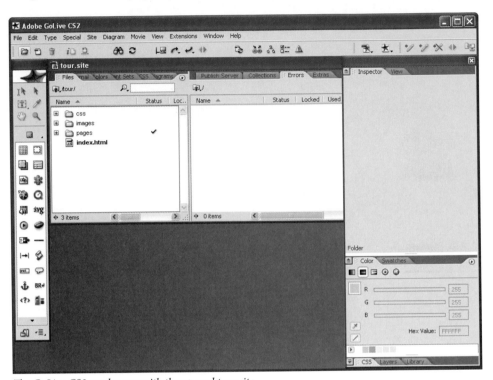

The GoLive CS2 workspace with the opened tour.site.

Notice the Objects palette with toolbar, and three palette groups in the work area. You will be using these items throughout the tour.

Note: *If your palettes do not appear as shown, choose Window > Workspace > Default Workspace.*

3 Double-click the index.html file to open the page in GoLive.

4 You will create a Web page similar to the one that appears in the GoLive document window. You can leave the file open as a reference, or choose File > Close.

Note: Always choose File > Open to open sites or individual pages in GoLive. If the files are not opened from within GoLive, they may default to opening in your browser.

5 Choose File > Close to close the tour.site window. When the Adobe GoLive CS2 window appears, click OK. You do want to close the site window.

Creating your own site

In this next section, you will create a blank site, typical if you are starting with little or few existing pages. You will then add files to the site, such as existing images and pages.

1 Choose File > New. Choose Site > Create Site and select Blank site. This creates a new Web site with a blank.html page. Use this if you have no main page created for your Web site but have images and other assets ready.

2 Click the Next button in the lower right and type the name **virtechu** in the Name text field. Choose Browse to locate the Lesson00 folder you copied onto your hard drive. Click OK (Windows) or Choose (Mac OS).

3   Click the Next button. In the "Use a Version Control System?" window, leave "Don't Use Version Control" selected, and click Next again.

4   In the "Publish Server Options" window, leave the selection for "Specify Server Later" selected. Select Finish.

A site window appears that includes a css folder for Cascading Style Sheets, and a blank index.html page.

The new blank site includes some assets to get you started.

Adding assets to your site

It is critical that you keep assets, such as images and pages, within the GoLive site window. By doing this, you can be assured that links and references do not become broken. It also helps to assure that all necessary assets make it to your FTP server when uploaded. Using a GoLive site also allows you to take advantage of the many helpful features, such as error control and automatic updating.

In this section, you will create folders for the site assets and import files into the site.

First you will create folders in the site. You can do this in the Files tab of the GoLive site window. Don't reorganize your site files using your computer's directory system. GoLive will not be aware of, and therefore not able to update, new paths to links that have already been referenced.

Before following the next steps, confirm that you see the index.html file in the site window and that all folders are closed.

1   With the virtechu site window open, click on the New Folder button in the far left side of the Main toolbar.

A folder appears, ready to be re-named. Type **images** for the folder name, and then press Return or Enter.

Note: Typically, it is best to keep all folder names, asset names, and other references in lower case. This allows for consistency and is easy to remember when referencing links.

2   Double-click to open the images folder, which is currently empty.

3   Choose File > Import > Files to Site.

💡 *You can also access this menu item contextually by right-clicking in the images folder window (Windows) or Ctrl+clicking (Mac OS), and selecting New > Add Files.*

4   Navigate to the Lesson00 folder and open the lesson00_assets folder.

5   Press Ctrl+A (Windows) or Command+A (Mac OS) to select all the imagery, and click Open (Windows) or Choose (Mac OS). You can also select the first item and Shift+click the last item to select all the imagery.

The images are now added to your site window.

Note: When you choose to import files into a site, GoLive copies the selected images to the site folder, leaving them in their original location. Learn more about sites in Lesson 2, "Creating a GoLive Site."

6   Press the Go up button (⬆) in the upper left of the site window to go up one file level; this reveals the images folder and the existing index.html page.

Navigate up from folders using the Go up button.

7   Click on the New Folder button in the upper left of the Main toolbar to create another folder. When the folder appears, type the name **pages** for the folder name, then press Return or Enter.

8   Double-click to open the pages folder and choose File > Import > Files to Site. In the Open window, browse to locate the folder named lesson00_pages in the Lesson00 folder.

9   Select the page named contact.html and Shift+click the other page named events.html. Click Open (Windows) or Choose (Mac OS). When the Copy Files alert window appears click OK.

Note: By unchecking Update in the Alert window, the paths to any links will be left unchanged, and not reference the files in the original folder.

The pages are added to the pages folder in your site window.

10   Press the Go up button in the upper left of the site window to go up one file level. You now have three folders: css, images, and pages, including the existing index.html page.

Adding metadata to your page

In this section you will work "under the hood," building the foundation of a good Web page; one that will help your page be found more easily by the viewer.

1   Double-click on the index.html page; a blank page appears.

When the page opens, notice the tabs across the top. You will use some of these later to see the page in different views. At this time you should be in the Layout tab.

Titling your page accurately is of the utmost importance. This is how your page will be labeled in the viewer's browser if saved as a Bookmark or Favorite. It also appears when the cursor is crossed over a link to the page. Many search engines display and use this information in search results.

2   To change the title of this page, click on Untitled Page to the right of Title.

3   Change the name to **VirtechU – University of the future**. Press Enter.

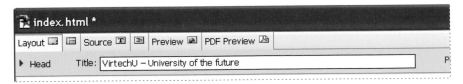

Now you will add a page description. A clear description helps search engines find your page and is frequently listed after the title in search results. If you do not provide a description, the first lines of text in your page might be used. This usually does not provide the most accurate representation of the page.

4　Click on the black arrow to the right of the Draggable Basic Objects button to show the palette menu, and select Head. The Head objects are revealed.

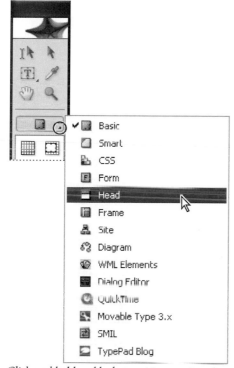

Click and hold on black arrow to see categories.

Note: *The contents of the head section is not visible to the viewer, but contains valuable information such as meta (keywords and descriptions), scripts, actions, and cascading style information. The objects in the Head category of the Objects palette are to be placed in the head section of the page.*

5   Access the head section of your page by clicking once on the Toggle Head Section arrow to the left of the word "Head."

The head section window pane appears directly below. You will see existing objects, such as the encode object (providing valuable information to the browser so it can recognize the page contents), title, cascading styles, and existing default metadata.

6   Cross over the Head objects in the Objects palette to see the tooltips. Locate and select the object named Meta and drag it to the head section of the page.

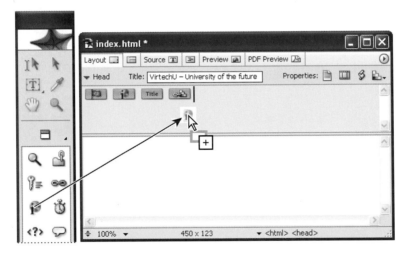

When the Meta object is selected, the Inspector becomes a Meta Inspector, displaying the Name and Content of generic.

7   Using the drop-down menu directly to the right of the first text field that states generic; choose description.

8   In the Content text field, replace the word "generic" with a more appropriate description of your page. Put the most important information first, as some search engines may truncate (cut off) part of your description. Count on approximately 15 words showing up. For this example use, **VirtechU, learn online or on campus. Discover the latest in virtual technology**.

Creating a Meta object for a page description.

9   Click on the arrow to the left of Head to close the section and choose File > Save.

Creating the layout of the page

Now that you have set up the page with the non-visual information, it is time to put the visual information together. In this section you will learn how to use the new layout grid, a feature that builds your page with Cascading Style Sheet technology. This creates a faster-loading page and is typically more compliant with accessibility programs (such as for the visually impaired).

1   Click on the Draggable Head Objects button on the Objects palette and select Basic. The Basic objects are revealed.

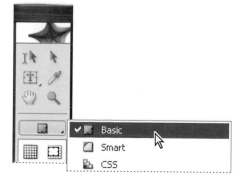

2   Position the mouse over the first object, and note that a tooltip appears, indicating that this is the Layout Grid object.

3   Drag and drop the Layout Grid object on the page. A cursor with a plus sign appears (Windows), or a hand (Mac OS), indicating that you are adding it to the page. When the mouse is released, the layout grid is positioned in the upper left of the page.

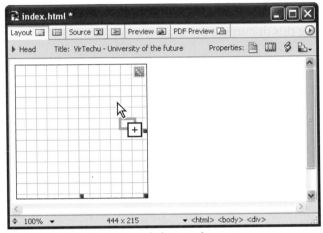

Click and drag the Layout Grid object to the page.

The layout grid gives you the ability to lay out a Web page, much like you would in a program such as InDesign or PageMaker. In Adobe GoLive CS2 the layout grid creates a CSS-based (Cascading Style Sheet-based) or table-based layout grid (your choice) that enables you to create designs by freely positioning objects anywhere on the grid. You can convert a CSS-based layout grid to a table-based layout grid with one click. You can also convert a table-based layout grid to a Hypertext Markup Language (HTML) table.

With the layout grid selected, the Inspector is a Layout Grid Inspector, giving you the opportunity to change the attributes of the grid.

4   Change the size of the grid by typing **720** in the width text field and **475** in the height text field. Press Enter.

Note: The size of your page should be determined by the needs of your viewers. A typical 14" screen is 640 pixels wide; a 17" monitor is 720 pixels wide. Choose a size and be consistent throughout your site.

5   Center the entire layout grid by selecting the Align Center button from the Main toolbar. The layout grid will now stay centered as the viewer widens or closes the browser window.

6   Choose File > Save; leave this document open.

Adding a background image to a page

You can be very creative with backgrounds. In this example, you'll add a simple stripe to the background of this page. As a default, HTML repeats a background image to fit the page. That works well in this instance but not always. Keep in mind that pages with busy backgrounds are difficult to read.

1   Choose the Show page properties button in the upper right of the page. The Inspector becomes a Page Inspector.

The Page Properties.

Use Page Properties to change standard page attributes, including the background color and image.

2   Check the box to the left of Image, then use the Browse button (🗁) to navigate to the virtechu folder you created inside the Lesson00 folder. Choose web content > images > bg.gif. Click Open. The image is now placed on the page as a background.

Note: It is important that you select the image from the images folder within the web-content folder of your site to maintain proper links.

The background may look checkered with the layout grid guides showing through. Select the Preview tab to get a better look at the background, then return to the Layout Editor by clicking on the Layout tab.

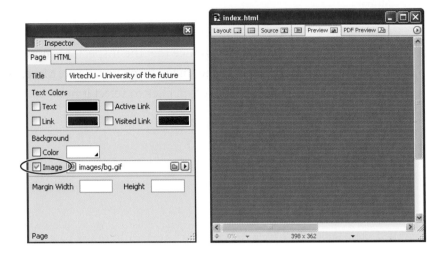

3　Choose File > Save; leave the file open.

Placing images onto your GoLive page

1　Using the palette menu of the Objects palette, choose Smart. The Smart section of the palette menu offers all sorts of incredible coding shortcuts from auto time stamping, smart favorite icons, and URL pop-ups. Choose the Smart Photoshop object. Click and drag to place it in the upper left corner of the layout grid.

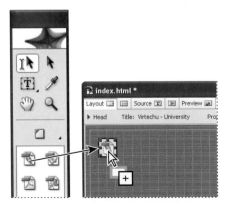

You can click and drag to reposition the Smart Photoshop object anywhere there is room on your layout grid, and it stays in place. If you understand HTML, you realize that elements typically do not stay in place unless you have a formatting element, such as a table or CSS layer.

2   If you have moved the Smart Photoshop object, click and drag it back to the upper left corner of the grid. While it is active, notice that the Inspector is now a Smart Photoshop Inspector. There are three tabs on the Image Inspector: Basic, More, and Link. If you are not on the Basic tab of the Inspector, click to select it now.

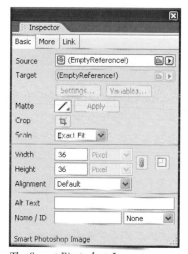

The Smart Photoshop Inspector.

So what exactly is a Smart Photoshop object, and what can it do for you? This object is probably one of the best tools to help better streamline your workflow when creating Web imagery. Using this object, you can import a native Photoshop file and optimize it for the Web directly in GoLive. This gives you the freedom to frequently change the optimization settings, image size, and even text layers without having to return to Photoshop. Read more about this feature in Lesson 7, "Using Graphics in GoLive." This feature can revolutionize the way you design your pages.

3   Choose the Browse button to the right of the Source (EmptyReference!) text field and navigate to the Lesson00 folder on your hard drive. Open the Lesson00 folder and select the image photobanner.psd. A Variable Settings window appears.

Variables allow you to overwrite existing text from the topmost Photoshop layer. This exciting option makes it easy to create buttons, navbars, and banners using GoLive.

4   In the Variable Settings window, check the box under Use, for the Topmost Textlayer.

5   In the text box that appears at the bottom of the window, type **School of thought...**, and click OK. The Save for Web window appears.

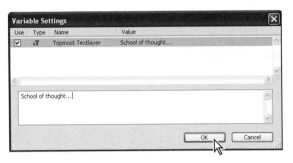

Understand that the font, alignment, and size attributes are determined in Photoshop. If you change the font in the original file, it will be updated, maintaining your variable text in GoLive.

Next you will choose the optimization settings for the image in the Save for Web window. Optimization of an image creates an image that retains its quality with a reduced file size.

6   When the Save for Web window appears, click on the 2-Up tab. This allows you to compare the original image with the image that is being optimized for Web use.

7   You can experiment with optimization settings, as well as the image size. For this example, choose the GIF 64 No Dither from the Preset drop-down menu.

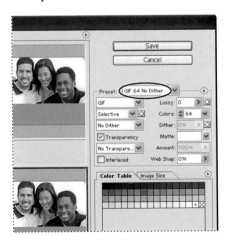

Note: You can also change these settings after the image has been placed by selecting the Settings button on the Inspector.

8   Click the Save button. In the Save As dialog window, select the Site Folder button (🗂,) at the bottom of the window and choose Root (Windows) or Root folder (Mac OS); this directs you back to the web-content folder, which contains the files you see in the Files tab of the site window.

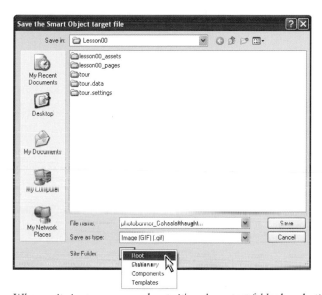

When a site is open, you can locate it's web-content folder by selecting Root.

9   The GoLive Save for Web window automatically provides your file with a unique name based upon the original file name and the variable text you entered, photobanner_Schoolofthought.gif. Click Save.

10   Choose File > Save to save your updated Web page.

Creating grid text boxes

Putting text on the layout grid is easy—even more so if you are familiar with creating text frames in popular page layout programs. In this section, you will add two layout text boxes to your grid.

1   Note that your Objects palette, in its default form, has a top tool section and then the section with the objects below. Click and hold on the Layer tool to reveal the Grid Text Box tool.

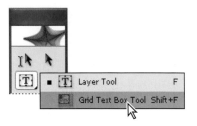

2   With the Grid Text Box tool selected, position your cursor over an open area of the Layout grid, then click and drag from the top-left corner to the lower right. This creates a grid text area. The exact size does not matter, as you will adjust it later.

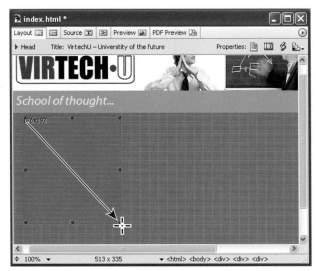

Click and drag to create a grid text box.

3   Choose the Object Selection tool (➤) and click on the anchor points to resize the text object to approximately 160 pixels wide x 240 pixels high. Use the measurement hint that displays in the Grid Text box as you adjust it. If it is not positioned on the left side of the page, click and drag to position it now.

4   Though you can type directly in GoLive, you can also open a text file, then copy and paste. Choose File > Open and locate the file named virtechu_copy.txt in the Lesson00 folder. Click Open. A new window named virtechu_copy.txt appears.

5   Select the text from Events to Site Map and choose Edit > Cut from the menu items.

6   Choose Window > index.html to bring forward the page you are creating.

7   Choose the Standard Editing tool (⟨k⟩) from the toolbar and click in the text area you created. Then select Edit > Paste. The text is now placed in the text area.

8   Choose Edit > Select All and choose the Align Left button from the Main toolbar.

Select the text.

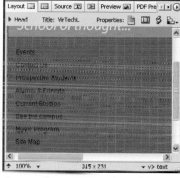

Copy and paste into grid text box.

9   Choose File > Save.

Formatting text using Cascading Style Sheets

Cascading Style Sheets (CSS) make it easy to update text properties and other attributes throughout a Web site. If a CSS style needs to be updated, you simply edit the style, and all content that uses the style automatically reflects the new properties. With style sheets, you can set text size to display more consistently across different platforms, and control the position of content on a page with pixel-level precision. An External Style Sheet can be shared by an entire site, giving your pages a consistent presence and enabling you to update the site's styles with a single file.

In this exercise you will be introduced to Cascading Style Sheets (CSS). Read Lesson 5, "Adding and Formatting Text," for more details.

1   If the index.html page in your tour.site is not open, use File > Open Recent to open it now.

2   Click on the Source tab to view the underlying code of this page. The three main components you see in the source code of a typical HTML page are the <DOCTYPE>, <head> and <body>.

The <DOCTYPE> makes the browser aware of what version of HTML to use when checking the document's syntax. The <head> section, as discussed earlier, contains essential information such as scripting, Metadata, and cascading styles. The <body> contains information visible on the page.

A clear example of a basic Cascading Style Sheet is one that takes advantage of existing HTML tags, such as <body>. The <body> tag encompasses the visible elements on a Web page. By defining an element style named body, you automatically choose styles that format the text on a page.

3   Click on the Layout tab and select the Open CSS Editor button in the upper right of the GoLive workspace.

The CSS Editor button.

4   Select the Create a Style That Applies to Markup Elements button (⬚). The window changes to show the style name (called the Selector) on the left (element). The properties of the element style are on the right. Change the element name to **body**. Press Enter. Now, when properties are changed they will apply to any contents in the <body>.

5   Click on the Font Properties tab.

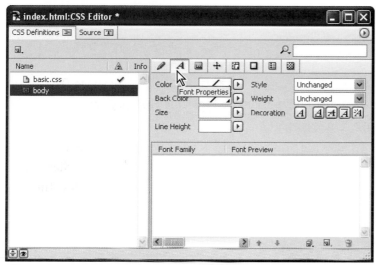

*Change element name to **body**, and choose the Font Properties tab.*

💡 *You can click and hold the Create a Style That Applies to Markup Elements button to select from a variety of common element tags.*

6   Type **12px** in the Size text box. By using px, you define your font size in pixels. This provides more consistent sizing between platforms.

7   Type **14px** in the Line Height text box. This controls the leading, which is the space between the lines of text.

8   Change the text to the Helvetica font set by choosing the Create new font family button at the bottom of the properties window. Click and hold to select the Helvetica Set. This instructs the browser to look for the Helvetica font on the viewer's system; if it is not loaded, the next font in the set will be used, and so on down the font list.

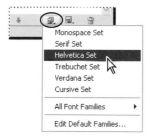

9 Close the CSS Editor; the font properties are applied to the text.

10 Choose File > Save. Leave all windows open for the next part of this lesson.

Creating a second text area

1 If the Grid Text Box tool (⊞) is not visible on the toolbar, click and hold on the Layer tool (⊤) to reveal the hidden Grid Text Box tool.

If your tools are not active, click in the existing text area once.

2 With the Grid Text Box tool selected, position your cursor over an open area of your Layout grid to the right of the existing text. Click and drag to create a new text area.

3 Switch to the Object Selection tool (➤) to resize the text object or reposition it. Make the text area approximately 240 pixels wide x 272 pixels high. Use the measurement hint that displays in the Grid Text box as you adjust it.

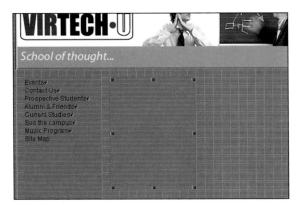

4 Choose Window > virtechu_copy.txt to bring the text window forward. If the virtechu_copy.txt window is no longer open, choose File > Open and locate it in the Lesson00 folder.

5 Select the text from the words VirtechU to community, then choose Edit > Cut. If you do not see all the text, select the Word Wrap button (⊒) at the top of the text page. Choose Window > index.html to bring forward the page you are creating.

6 Choose the Standard Editing tool (I➤) from the toolbar and click in the text box you created. A cursor appears. Select Edit > Paste. The text is now placed in the text box.

7   Using the Standard Editing tool, insert the cursor into the newly created text box and select Edit > Select All or Ctrl+A (Windows), Command+A (Mac OS). Choose the Align Left button in the Main toolbar.

8   With the text still selected, double-click on the Set text color box in the Main toolbar to open the color picker. Type **ffffff** in the #: text box. This is the hexadecimal color value for white. Click OK (Windows) or press Return, then OK (Mac OS).

Note: The Color Picker on the Mac OS requires you to confirm any entries into the Hexadecimal text field with a Return before clicking OK.

9   If the text area is not lined up next to the previous text box, pass the cursor over the edge of the Grid Text Box to reveal a hand. Click and hold while dragging to relocate the box.

Note: If the cursor does not change to a hand, click inside the text box to deselect the text then pass the cursor over the edge of the Grid Text Box to reveal the hand.

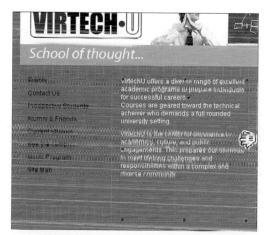

Arrange the text box on the page to allow for additional objects.

10   Select the first word in the text area, VirtechU, and choose the Strong button (**T**) from the Main toolbar. The text becomes bolder.

11   Choose File > Save. Leave the file open.

Placing an optimized image

Now you will place an image with the Basic Image object. This is the object you would use to place an image that has already been optimized for the Web.

1 If you are not in the Basic section of the Objects palette, use the palette menu to choose Basic. Select the Image object (▣) and drag it to the right of the existing text boxes.

2 Using the Image Inspector, click on the Browse button to the right of the Source text field.

3 Navigate to the virtechu folder you created and open web-content > images > building.gif. The image is now placed on the page.

💡 *You can also add an image to your page by simply dragging an image from your Site window right onto the page!*

4 With the image selected, select the Basic tab of the Image Inspector if it is not forward.

5 Type **Our building** in the Alt Text field. Alt text shows up before the complete download of the page, and also identifies the image for viewers using accessibility software.

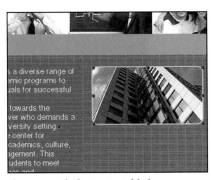

The page with the image added.

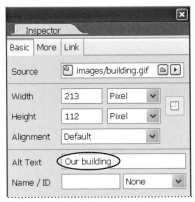

Alt text is added to identify the image.

6 Choose File > Save. Leave the file open.

Creating a table

You can use a table to format an entire page or just to clarify tab-delimited data on your page. This could be for dates, prices, or other data that would be viewed in columns and rows.

In this section, you will create a new, empty table and import tab-delimited text from a text file.

1   If you are not in the Basic section of the Objects palette, use the palette menu to choose Basic. Select the Table object (▦) and drag it to a location underneath the image of the building.

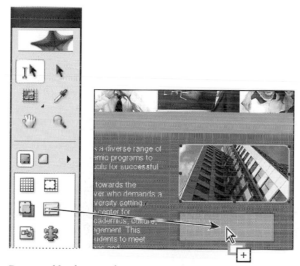

Drag a table object to the page.

2   As a default, the table has three rows, and three columns. GoLive remembers the last table configuration, so if yours is different choose Window > Inspector to see the Table Inspector. In the Table tab, change the Rows to **3** and the Columns to **3**.

3   Select any cell by positioning your cursor next to an edge of a cell and clicking, or with the Standard Editing tool (I▸), click to insert a cursor in any of the cells, and press Ctrl+Enter. (This works on both Windows and Mac OS.) The cell becomes highlighted with a dark border, signifying that it is selected.

4   Choose Edit > Select All. All cells become selected.

5   Choose Special > Table > Import tab-delimited text. In the Open dialog window, navigate to the Lesson00 folder on your hard drive and select launch.txt.

The text is automatically entered into the table, creating the necessary cells and rows.

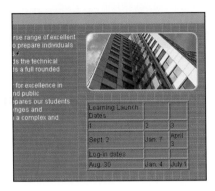

Note: If the table does not automatically expand, select the Preview tab and then return to the Layout tab of the document window. GoLive automatically recognizes tabs as new columns, and returns as new rows, when importing text into a table.

If you are a Macintosh user and plan on using this feature with your own text you must File > Open your .txt file in GoLive and then save it. Otherwise, you will not be able to select it.

6   Using the Object Selection tool (↖), hold down the Alt key (Windows) or the Option key (Mac OS) and click and drag on the cell borders. This adjusts the cells visually.

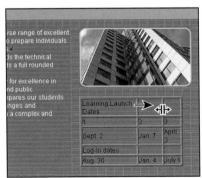

Hold down the Alt/Opt key to size cells manually.

*Make precise adjustments by selecting one cell, and then choosing Edit > Select All. With all the cells selected, choose the Cell tab of the Table Inspector and choose Percent from the drop-down menu to the right of Width, then type **33** into the Width text field. GoLive will even-out the width of the columns. Read more about controlling tables in Lesson 3, "Creating Page Layouts in GoLive."*

Spanning a column

Next, you will span, or join, a column with its neighboring columns in order to create a more efficient table.

1   Using the Standard Editing tool (⇡), select the cell with the text "Learning Launch Dates." Remember that you can insert the cursor into the text of the cell and use Ctrl+Enter (both Windows and Mac OS) to select the cell.

2   Hold down the Shift key and press the right arrow (→) twice, one time for each column that you wish to span into. The text is now spanning across three columns.

A spanned column.

3   Repeat steps 1-2 for the column containing the text Log-in dates.

4   The page design is complete. Choose File > Save. Leave the page open for the next part of this lesson.

Creating hyperlinks

A hyperlink is a function that allows viewers to navigate from one HTML file or location to another. A link can direct the viewer to an entirely different document, another location in the current document, a PDF document, an e-mail address, and more.

Now that the page is complete, you will create hyperlinks from this page to two existing pages.

1   With the index.html open, and the Standard Editing tool selected (⇡), locate and select the text labeled "Events" in the far left text area.

2   If the Inspector window is not visible, choose Window > Inspector. Click on the Create link button (🔗).

3   Replace (EmptyReference!) with a path to a page by choosing the Browse button (🗁) to the right of the reference text field. Navigate to the virtechu folder you created in the Lesson00 folder. Choose web-content > pages > events.html. Click Open. The Events text is now linked to the events.html page.

Test your link by choosing the Preview tab and clicking on the text Events. Return to the Layout Editor by choosing the Layout tab.

4   Create the second link by selecting the words Contact Us. This time, use the Fetch URL button (🎯) that is to the right of the link buttons.

Note: For all the icons to appear, GoLive CS2 must be at a display resolution of 1024 x 768 or higher.

5   Click and drag. A directional line follows your cursor as you drag. Point it to the Select window button (🗔.) in the Main toolbar. This brings the site window forward— don't let go! Continue dragging down, then point at the pages folder until it opens. Before releasing the mouse, position the cursor over the contact page. When it is highlighted, release. The page has been referenced.

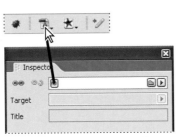

Click and drag the Fetch URL button to the Select window button in the Main toolbar.

When the site window comes forward, point at the file you wish to link to.

6   Choose Window > index.html to bring your page forward. Test your links by choosing the Preview tab and clicking on the text Contact Us.

7   Choose File > Save. Leave the file open.

Using the Live Rendering feature

If you have a large screen monitor, or don't mind clicking back and forth from one window to another, you should consider using the Live Rendering feature in GoLive.

As you build your page in the Layout Editor, changes are automatically reflected in the Live Rendering browser window.

Note: If you have multiple document windows open, the Live Rendering browser previews the currently selected document.

This section is optional for this lesson.

1   Click and hold on the Preview in Browser button ( ) in the Main toolbar.

2   Select Live Rendering and release.

3   You can preview your page as it will appear on a mobile device, by clicking the SSR button ( ) in the Live Rendering browser. Click on SSR to return to the normal page view.

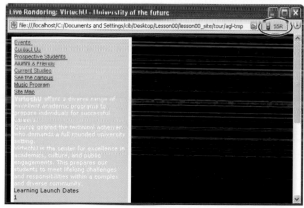

You can preview your Web page appears on a small screen in the Live Rendering window.

4   Choose File > Close to close the Live Rendering window.

5   Choose File > Save.

Using Cascading Styles for hyperlinks

Want to rid your hyperlinks of the underline, or even spice up your page with simple text rollovers? Then this section is for you!

1 Select the text Events using the Standard Editing tool (⌶▸), and switch to the Source tab of the GoLive window. Notice that GoLive keeps your text selected so that you can locate it in the source code.

The Source view maintains your selection from Layout to Source view.

Notice that the text is selected by a tag starting with an "a," followed by "href=," and then references the page that you selected as the destination page. You will use this information to build a cascading style that will affect the appearance of your hyperlinks.

2 The style you will create to change the text in the hyperlinks on this page is called an element style. To access the CSS Editor and create this style, return to the Layout view and click once on the Open CSS Editor button in the upper right of the GoLive workspace.

3 Select the Create a Style That Applies to Markup Elements button (⟨⟩). The window changes to show the style name on the left and the properties that can be altered on the right. While the Selector is selected, change the name from element to **a**. Press Enter. When properties are changed, they will apply to any contents in the <a> tag.

4   Click on the Font Properties tab on the right side. In the Decoration section, choose the No Text Decoration button. Underlines are removed from the linked text. Keep the CSS Editor open for the next part of the lesson.

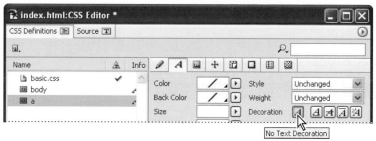

Remove underlines from your hyperlinks using styles.

Now you will create a style that affects the hyperlink when a cursor passes over the text.

5   Create a new element style, by clicking anywhere in the empty section of the left side of the CSS Editor, then choose the Create a Style That Applies to Markup Elements button (⊡).

A selector with the default name of element appears.

6   Change the element text to **a:hover,** and click on the Font Properties tab.

7   Use the arrow to the right of the Color box to select Red. The hyperlinks will now turn red when the cursor crosses over them. Close the CSS Editor.

💡 *If you want to set up the rest of the text in the text box with "dummy" links to view this effect with all the links, select each word and use Ctrl+L to create a link to an EmptyReference. Change (EmptyReference!) to a # sign. The link will look like a link, but will not go to any location when selected in the preview or on the browser.*

8   Choose File > Save.

Congratulations! You have finished the tour.

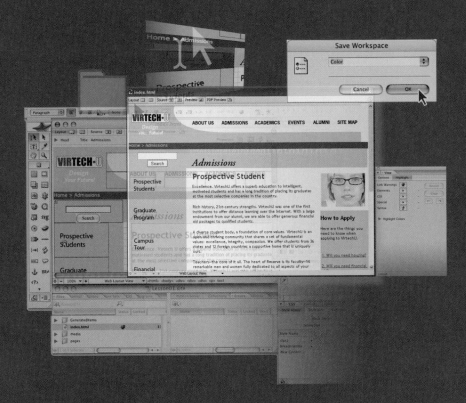

In this lesson you will learn how to customize your GoLive CS2 workspace using palettes and windows. You will also discover how to work more efficiently in GoLive by using keyboard shortcuts and by customizing preferences.

1 | Getting to Know the Work Area

In this overview of the GoLive CS2 workspace you'll learn how to do the following:

- Work with the site and document windows.
- Arrange palettes and use workspaces.
- Use the toolbars and menus.
- Use different view configurations.
- Preview Web pages.

Getting started

In this lesson, you will be working on an existing single HTML file. You will use this file to learn how to use the GoLive CS2 tools, palettes, and windows.

1 To ensure that the tools and palettes function as described in this lesson, delete or deactivate the Adobe GoLive CS2 preferences file. See "Restoring default preferences" on page 3.

2 Launch Adobe GoLive CS2. When started, Adobe GoLive CS2 displays a Welcome Screen with various options.

The Welcome Screen allows you to create a new document or open a previously existing document. You can also click on the link for Cool Extras to be linked to the Adobe GoLive CS2 In-depth Web page. Deselect the option "Show this dialog at startup" in the lower left corner if you do not wish to see the Welcome Screen again.

The Welcome Screen can be found through Help > Welcome Screen at any time.

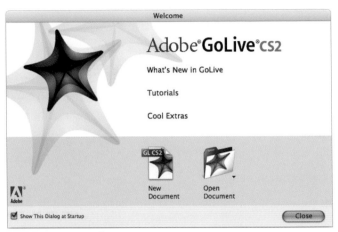

The GoLive CS2 Welcome Screen.

In this lesson, you will be working on a single Web page. To access this page, you will first open a pre-existing site file. A site file should be thought of as the master directory. The site file keeps track of all the elements in a Web site: the HTML pages, the images, and the other source files. Although sites often consist of many pages, it is possible to have a site with only one page, as in this example.

3   Click the Close button in the bottom right corner of the Welcome Screen.

4   Choose File > Open and locate the file Lesson01.site in the Lesson01 folder, located on your hard drive. Click open and the Lesson01.site window appears.

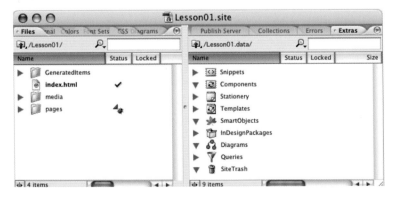

The site window provides access to all the site files and assets. In this lesson you will maintain all your source files, data, HTML files, scripts, and media in the Lesson01.site window. The site window not only helps you avoid breaking links and creating orphan files, it also gives you easy access for fixing site file errors.

This site is organized in folders, just like your directory system. You can add, delete, rename, and relocate folders easily in the site window. By making these changes in the site window, GoLive can track paths to links and update them automatically, helping you avoid lost or broken links.

Notice that the pages folder has a link warning icon (✳) to the right of the folder. A page in this folder has a broken link, or bug, which you will fix later in this lesson.

5　Double-click on the index.html page. This is the final version of what you will create in this lesson. You can leave this page open for reference or choose File > Close to close the file.

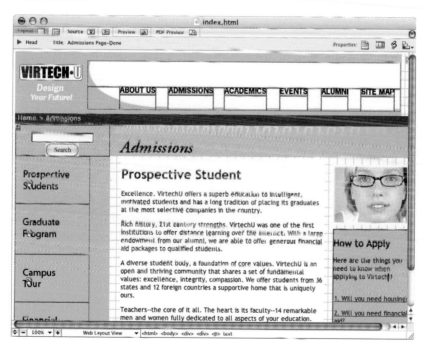

6　In the site window, double-click to open the folder named pages. Then double-click the file named lesson01_start.html. The document window containing the HTML file "lesson01_start.html" appears in the center of your screen.

7 Choose File > Save As and name the file **admissions.html**. Select the Site Folder button (📁,) from the bottom of the Save As window, and select Root (Windows) or Root folder (Mac OS). This directs you to the site's root directory. Open the pages folder, and click Save.

The GoLive work area

The GoLive work area includes the site window (one for every site project), document windows for each open Web page, and a variety of editors, toolbars, and palettes for working with everything in your site. You can stack or tile windows on your screen, and group, ungroup, or rearrange palettes, as well as save custom workspaces.

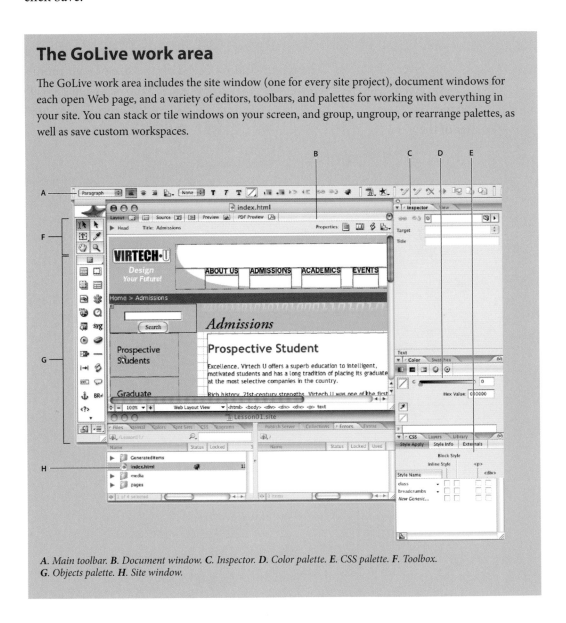

A. Main toolbar. B. Document window. C. Inspector. D. Color palette. E. CSS palette. F. Toolbox.
G. Objects palette. H. Site window.

Using the View and Window menus

GoLive CS2 allows you to have precise control over the display of your workspace and documents using the View and Window menus. In general, commands in the View menu will give you control over your document, while commands in the Window menu will give you control over your workspace.

1 Choose View > Zoom Out to view more of your Web page, or click on the minus sign in the lower left of your document window. Based on the size of your monitor, you may not be able to view your entire Web page on your screen; working at 75% allows you to view more of your Web page. You can see your zoom value in the bottom left corner of the document window. Our zoom value is 75%.

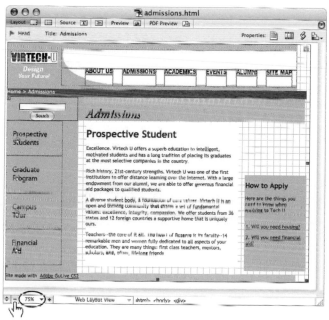

Use the Zoom controls to zoom in and out of your Web page.

2 Click on the black plus sign to the right of the zoom value in the document window to zoom in to 100%.

3 Use the horizontal and vertical scroll bars in the document window, if necessary, to scroll through your page so the logo in the top left corner is visible.

Note: *You can zoom from 8.33%-1600%.*

Using the Zoom tool

In addition to the View commands, you can use the Zoom tool to magnify and reduce the view of artwork. Use the View menu to select predefined magnification levels or to fit your artwork inside the document window.

1   Click the Zoom tool (⌕) in the toolbox to select the tool, and move the cursor into the document window. Notice that a plus sign (+) appears at the center of the Zoom tool.

2   Position the Zoom tool anywhere on the page and click once. The artwork is displayed at a higher magnification.

3   Click two more times; the view is increased again, and you'll notice that the area you clicked is magnified. Next you'll reduce the view of the artwork.

4   With the Zoom tool still selected, hold down Alt (Windows) or Option (Mac OS). A minus sign (-) appears at the center of the Zoom tool.

5   With the Alt/Option key still depressed, click in the artwork twice. The view of the artwork is reduced.

A much more controlled and effective zoom is achieved by dragging a marquee to magnify a specific area of your artwork.

6   With the Zoom tool still selected, hold down the mouse button and drag over some body copy on the page; watch as a marquee appears around the area you are dragging, then release the mouse button. The area that was included in the marqueed area is now enlarged to fit the size of the document window.

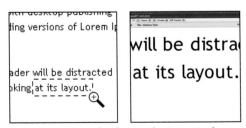

Control your zoom level using the Zoom tool.

The percentage at which the area is magnified is determined by the size of the marquee you draw with the Zoom tool—the smaller the marquee, the larger the level of magnification.

Using the Window menu to control palettes and toolbars

Palettes and the Main toolbar are part of your main interface with GoLive CS2.

1   Choose the Window menu to view the list of windows. In GoLive, windows which are currently visible on-screen have a checkmark next to them. Hidden or unopened windows have no checkmark.

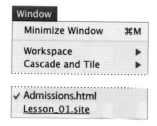

2   Choose Window > Tools to remove the toolbox and Objects palette from view. Choose Windows > Tools again to return the toolbox and Objects palette to view.

3   Choose Window > Actions to bring the Actions window into view. This window allows you to add JavaScript to your pages. Read more about Actions in Lesson 8, "Adding Interactivity: Rollovers and Actions."

4   Close the Actions window by clicking the Close button. You also could have closed the Actions window by selecting Actions in the Window menu.

Customizing the workspace

Upon first opening a project, GoLive will attempt to fit all the windows and palettes in the available space on your monitor. However, windows and palettes can be moved and resized according to your needs. If you have a specific arrangement of windows and palettes that you consistently want to use, GoLive CS2 allows you to create and save workspaces by using the Workspace command.

Note: Depending upon your screen resolution you may not see the GoLive palettes. If this is the case, choose Window > Workspace > Default Workspace.

1 On the right side of your screen, click on the Inspector palette tab and drag it all the way to the center of your screen, then release your mouse. The Inspector palette separates from the window.

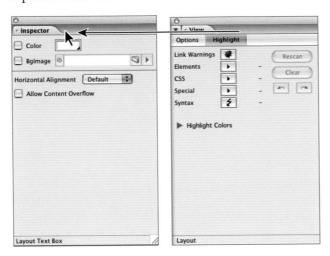

2 Choose Window > Workspace > Default Workspace. The Inspector palette will snap back to its original location. This can be useful whenever you need to restore your palettes.

3 Place your cursor over the Color palette tab and click and drag it to the left to separate it from the window. Choose Window > Workspace > Save Workspace. In the Save Workspace window that appears, type **Color** and click OK. Now you can switch between workspaces when needed.

4 Choose Window > Workspace > Default Workspace to return to the default GoLive configuration.

Using the toolbox

The toolbox, located on the left side of your screen, holds the tools and objects, which can be separate palettes, although they are, by default, joined together. The tools in the toolbox are used to select objects and modify them. Objects are added to your page by dragging them from the Objects palette to your page.

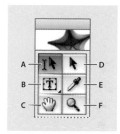

The toolbox.
A. Standard Editing tool.
B. Layer tool.
C. Hand tool.
D. Object Selection tool.
E. Eyedropper tool.
F. Zoom tool.

1   Place your cursor over the Standard Editing tool (↕) and let the cursor sit for a moment; a tooltip appears with the name of the tool and the letter S in parentheses. S is the keyboard shortcut to access that tool.

2   Click on the Standard Editing tool and then click on the VirtechU logo in the upper left corner to select it. Now, using the same tool, click and drag over the text "How to Apply." This tool allows you to select an object as well as edit text, if desired.

Understanding the Inspector palette

The Inspector palette is a contextual palette, the contents of which change depending upon which object is selected.

1   If the Inspector is not visible, choose Window > Inspector.

2   With the Standard Editing tool (↕), click on the VirtechU logo in the upper left of the document window. The Inspector changes to an Image Inspector. The attributes listed in the Inspector pertain to values and attributes that relate to images, such as Source (where the image file is located), Width, Height, Alignment, and Alt Text. Read more about these attributes and values in Lesson 7, "Using Graphics in GoLive."

3   Still using the Standard Editing tool, double-click the word "Excellence" to select it. It is the first word in the body copy under "Prospective Student." The Inspector is now a Text Inspector and the options are fewer.

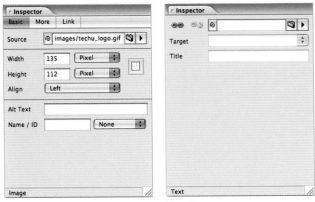

Image Inspector.   *Text Inspector.*

While creating pages in GoLive, keep the Inspector palette open at all times to access the options relating to your active selection.

Helpful keyboard shortcuts for palettes

You will find that there are certain palettes that should be open most of the time. Use these keyboard shortcuts to view the most popular palettes. Also use the keyboard shortcuts to show and hide the palettes.

Function	Windows	Macintosh
Show/hide Inspector palette	Ctrl+1	Command+1
Show/hide Objects palette	Ctrl+2	Command+2
Show/hide Colors palette	Ctrl+3	Command+3

Note: If the selected palette is docked to other palettes, they will all show and hide.

Separating the Objects palette from the toolbox

As a default, the Objects palette is docked to the toolbox. Throughout the lessons the Objects palette and toolbox in their default view will be referred to as the Objects palette. Tools in the toolbox are referred to individually as needed.

If you prefer to separate the Objects palette from the toolbox, click on the Separate tools and objects button (⬚) at the bottom of the Objects palette.

Use the Join tools and objects button (⬚) in the upper right of the Objects palette to join the Tools and Objects palettes together again. For this lesson, keep the palettes in the joined position.

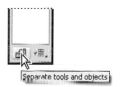

Click to separate the Objects from the toolbox.

As mentioned earlier, objects are elements that you can add to a page. They are separated into categories: Basic, Smart, CSS, Form, Head, Frame, Site, Diagram, QuickTime, Movable Type 3x, SMIL, and TypePad Blog. In this part of the lesson, you will add an Image object from the Basic category to your page and then link it to an image.

1   Click and hold down the Draggable Basic Objects button on the Tools palette. A palette menu appears with a list of the different categories of objects available in GoLive. Each category contains related objects. Confirm that you have the Basic group of objects selected by releasing on Basic. The objects belonging to the Basic group appear in the Objects portion of the palette, under the toolbox.

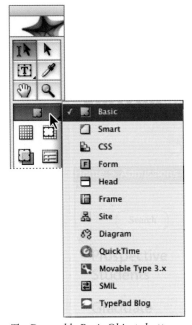

The Draggable Basic Objects button.

2   Place your cursor over the Image object (⊠) in the first column. Look for the tooltip to appear to verify that you are over the Image object.

3 Click and drag the Image object from the Objects palette to your document window. Your final destination will be directly above the blue column on the right side of the page with the heading "How To Apply." Release the image object. Once you release the image object, it becomes an image placeholder.

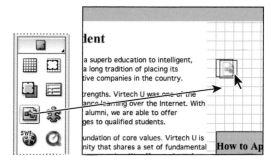

4 Using the Set Position fields in the upper left of Main toolbar, enter **596** into the Horizontal position and **208** into the Vertical position.

💡 *You can also place an object on a page by inserting your cursor where you want the object, then double-clicking the object in the palette. The object is inserted.*

Note: The layout grid was previously added to this document, making the repositioning and aligning of the image object possible. You will learn how to create layout grids in Lesson 3, "Creating Page Layouts in GoLive."

Using the site window to link an image

Now that you have an image placeholder in your page, you'll link it to the source image file using the site window. There is more than one way to do this, but you will be using GoLive's point-and-shoot method in combination with the site window. As you will discover, the site window is an integral part of the GoLive workflow, as it provides a central location of all the assets used in your document, such as HTML files, media files, images, and more.

You will learn how to create a site and use the site window in greater depth in Lesson 2, "Creating a GoLive Site."

1   First, make sure your site window is available. Choose Window > Lesson01.site. If the site file is not listed at the bottom of the Window menu, choose File > Open and choose the Lesson01.site file in your Lesson01 folder on your hard drive. Click Open and the site window appears on your screen. Click and drag the site window to the bottom of your screen.

Note: You can also choose File > Open Recent to find files, including pages and site files, that were recently opened.

2   In the Main toolbar at the top of your screen, click and hold down on the Select window button (⊞). Do not release your mouse button. A menu appears listing the two available windows: admissions.html and Lesson01.site. Use this button to easily switch from one page to another in GoLive, or bring forward your site or page window.

3   Select the admissions.html option in the menu to make sure your document window is forward.

4   If necessary, click on the image object you added in the last exercise to select it. In the Inspector palette, make sure the Basic tab is selected. In the Source location of the Basic tab, place your cursor over the small spiral (⬙) in the EmptyReference! field. This is GoLive's Fetch URL button, sometimes referred to as the pick whip. It allows you to point to objects to link them.

5   If you are in your pages folder of the site window, click on the Go up button (⬙) in the upper left of the Files tab to go up one directory level. The media folder should be visible in the site window.

6   Click and drag the Fetch URL button to the site window. Do not let go of the mouse, but point to the media folder, it will open. Release the mouse when the image a_student_photo.jpg becomes highlighted.

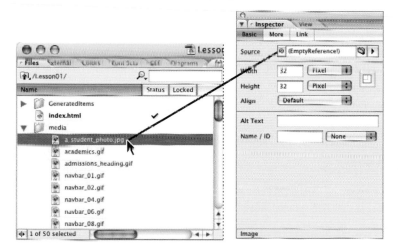

The student photo is now linked with the image object and appears in your document.

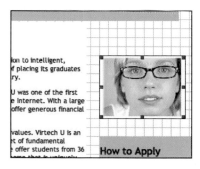

7   If necessary, choose the Object Selection tool (➤). Click and drag the image to reposition it over the column.

8   If the Image Inspector is not visible, choose Window > Inspector or use the shortcut Ctrl+1 (Windows) or Command+1 (Mac OS) to show the Inspector palette.

9   Type **student** in the Alt Text field. Alt Text specifies alternate text that is rendered when the image cannot be displayed. The Alt Text is also conveyed to reader software that helps the disabled understand relevant information about an image they may not be able to view.

10   Choose File > Save to save your document. Leave the document window open for the next part of the lesson.

Working with the document window

The site and document windows have equally important roles in GoLive. The site window gives you a bird's-eye view of your entire Web site, whereas the document window allows you to view and work with the objects on a single page.

Within the document window are six separate tabs which allow you to view your Web page in different ways. There is the Layout Editor, the Frame Editor, the Source Code Editor, the Outline Editor, the Layout Preview, and the PDF Preview.

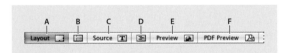

*A. Layout Editor. **B**. Frame Editor. **C**. Source Code Editor.
D. Outline Editor. **E**. Layout Preview. **F**. PDF Preview.*

The Layout Editor

The default view, the Layout Editor allows you to manually position objects on a page such as CSS layout objects, images, tables, GoLive layout grids, and text boxes. When you are in this view, GoLive writes all the source code of your page for you. When you add text and select the Strong (**T**) button from the Main toolbar, for example, GoLive generates the code automatically as you type in the Layout View. This view is sometimes referred to as WYSIWYG or "What you see is what you get." It is important to note that this view may be similar to what you will see in a Web browser, but it is not identical. Certain elements such as the layout grid or image icons will be visible in the Layout Editor but not in the Web browser.

The Frame Editor

The Frame Editor is similar to the Layout Editor in that it allows you to manually position objects on a page. However, the Frame Editor requires a frameset to be created first. Frames allow you to load two or more Web pages at the same time into a single screen.

Frame sets are available from the Frames Object category and can be dragged onto a page when in the Frame Editor.

The Source Code Editor

This view allows you to view and edit the source code of your Web page. HTML is a tag-based language, and before the advent of programs such as GoLive, working in a text editor to edit was the primary method for creating Web pages. Working with the source code is a much different experience than working in the Layout Editor. Source code requires a better understanding of tags, but it also offers a designer finer control over the objects in a Web page. Certain users may prefer to work more frequently with the source code, others not at all. GoLive allows the user to work in either mode, provides an easy way to switch between modes, and even allows you to work in both modes at the same time using the split view. Split View is discussed later in this lesson.

The Outline Editor

The Outline Editor allows you to view the HTML elements of a Web page in a structured, hierarchical view. Working in this view allows users to create code in their Web page without having to type. Additionally, users can perform other operations in this view, such as check the source code for missing links or visually identify code which may be incorrect.

The Layout Preview

The Layout Preview offers a quick way of previewing your page as it will appear in a Web browser. Whereas the Layout Editor and the Source Code Editor allow you to edit and rearrange the objects on your pages, the Layout Preview is there simply to display the pages. Additionally, functionality, such as image rollovers, will not work in the Layout Editor but will work in the Layout Preview.

The PDF Preview

The PDF Preview allows you to view your Web page (and then export it if desired) in Adobe's Portable Document Format (PDF). This process allows you to repurpose content designed for the Web into a print-based format.

Using the Document and Source Views

1   You should currently have the admissions.html page open and be in the Layout Editor. If you are not, click on the Layout tab at the top of your document window.

2   In the toolbox, if not already selected, click on the Standard Editing tool (ɪ★) in the Tools palette and place your cursor after the text "Prospective Student" and click once. You will see a blinking insertion point; type the letter **s** to modify the text. While in the Layout Editor, you can add and delete text, among other things.

3   Quickly click three times in the heading "Prospective Students" in order to select the entire line of text.

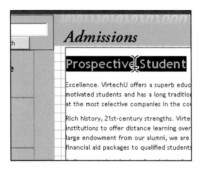

4   Click on the Source tab at the top of your document window to switch to the Source Code Editor. You will see the following line of code highlighted: <h1 align ="left">Prospective Students</h1>. This is the source code which corresponds to the Heading in the Layout Editor. Objects selected or highlighted in the Layout Editor are automatically selected or highlighted in the Source Code Editor (and vice-versa).

5   Choose View > Document Mode > Layout to return to the Layout Editor. You can also use the View commands to switch between modes.

6   In the bottom left corner of the Document window, click on the Show/Hide split source button. This will split your screen with the Layout Editor on top and the Source Code Editor on the bottom.

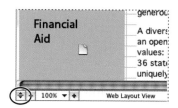

7   If necessary, use the scroll bar on the right side of the document window and scroll to the top of the page until you can see the navigation bar at the top of the screen. In the Layout Editor, click on the button labeled "About Us" and notice how the corresponding code is highlighted in the Source Code Editor. This can be useful when you want to modify code by hand or simply learn how GoLive generates code automatically.

8   Press Ctrl+Y (Windows) or Command+Y (Mac OS) to return to the Layout Editor.

Using the Outline Editor

The Outline Editor is useful for those who are familiar with source code but would like some automatic features as well. If you're unfamiliar with the concept of HTML, don't be put off by the apparent complexity of this exercise; GoLive is a powerful tool because it can accommodate beginner, intermediate, and advanced Web users

1   Click on the Outline Editor tab (▣) in the area at the top of the Document window. This allows you to view your page in a hierarchical view. Because the "About Us" button is still selected from the last exercise, you see the button's relationship to the rest of the document.

2   Use the scroll bar on the right side of the page and scroll up until you see the top of the page. Right-click (Windows) or Ctrl+click (Mac OS) on the second element at the page marked "html" to reveal a contextual menu.

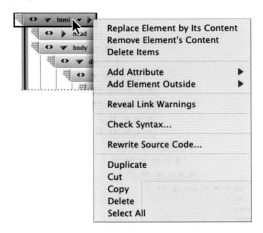

3   From the list of options in the contextual menu, choose Reveal Link Warnings. The form element of your page should be highlighted. This is GoLive's visual indicator that this particular form (which is the search box in the upper left corner of the page) has no link associated with it, and therefore would not work. Right-click or Ctrl+click on the "html" element again and deselect the Reveal Link Warnings option.

4   Click on the Layout tab to return to the Layout Editor.

5   Select the Show link warnings button (✳) in the Main toolbar. The Form is again highlighted. This is how you view link errors when in the Layout Editor.

6   Click on the Form object symbol (▣) in the upper left of the Search form. The Inspector now changes to a Form Inspector.

7   Replace the words (EmptyReference!) with a # (pound sign), and press Return or Enter. This produces a null link. It will not take the viewer anywhere, but will eliminate the link error.

Note: This is the field into which you would enter a script location or e-mail address to make the form active.

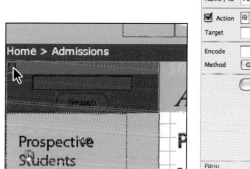

Click on the Form icon (■) in the Search form to see the Form Inspector.

8   Choose File > Save.

Previewing your document in GoLive

The Layout Editor is helpful when designing Web pages; however, as the author or editor of a page you will also need to see the page from the perspective of the user. GoLive allows you to do this with the Layout Preview.

1   Click on the Preview tab at the top of your document window to enter the Layout Preview. Place your cursor over the navigation at the top of the screen and notice the black text turns to orange when the cursor is over it. This rollover behavior is visible in the Layout Preview and in a browser, but not in the Layout Editor. Additionally, the tools in the Main toolbar are greyed out because objects are not editable or movable when in Layout Preview.

2   Click on the Layout tab to return to the Layout Editor.

Using the View palette

The View palette allows you to configure the look of your GoLive page as well as define which areas of your document you would like to investigate. For example, if there are areas of your document, such as an image, a link, or a form, which do not have links assigned to them, the View palette allows you locate those areas with a visual highlight.

1   Click on the View tab, docked with the Inspector palette, in the window at the right-hand side of your page. You could also choose Window > View. The View palette appears.

2   Click on the Options tab of the View palette, then deselect the option "Show Invisible Items" to turn off this selection. Seeing invisible items is useful when authoring your Web pages; however, there may be times when you want to turn them off.

3   Select the "Show Invisible Items" option to turn them back on.

Previewing your document in a browser

The Layout Preview is useful for quickly determining the look and functionality of your pages. However, because the user will be viewing your pages in a Web browser, you should get into the habit of using a browser to determine how your site looks. Furthermore, the same page may look different in different browsers; GoLive CS2 allows you to specify what browser is being used and allows you set default and alternative browsers based on what's available on your system. The default method for previewing a page is GoLive's Live Rendering browser.

1   In the Main toolbar at the top of your screen, click and hold down on the Preview in Browser button (✸.). A menu appears with various options. As a default, GoLive CS2 has Live Rendering and Small Screen Rendering options.

Note: If the browser preferences in GoLive have been previously configured, your button may appear with a browser icon, such as the logo for Internet Explorer or Safari. The options may be different as well.

2   Choose the Edit option to open the Preferences screen. You will now instruct GoLive to locate all browsers on your system and add them to your browser list.

3   Click the Find All button at the bottom of the preferences screen. It may take a few moments for GoLive to scan your system, but all browsers visible by GoLive will be added to the list.

You can add browsers that GoLive may not have found by clicking the Add button and browsing your hard drive. Alternatively, older or duplicate browsers on your system can be removed from the list by clicking on the browser name and clicking the Remove button.

You can also choose which browsers you would like to designate as the default browser (or browsers) when previewing your pages.

4   Click on the checkbox to the left of the browser you would like to use as your default browser. For this lesson, we chose Safari, the default browser for Mac OS X. If you are on a PC, you may wish to choose Internet Explorer or alternative browsers on your list. Checking multiple browsers on the list will force multiple browsers to open when you click on the Preview in Browser button. When you are done, click OK to commit the change.

5   Click and hold on the Preview in Browser button. Based on your system, you should see the list of browsers your system found in step 3. Selecting any browser from the list will preview your page in that particular browser.

6   Choose your default browser and place your cursor over the navigation at the top of the screen. Similar to the Live Rendering option, rollovers are visible in the browser, but they are not visible in the Layout Editor.

7   Close your browser and click on the Layout Editor tab to return to this mode.

You can also use keyboard shortcuts to preview your pages. Press Ctrl+T (Windows) or Command+T (Mac OS) to preview your page in the Live Rendering browser. Press Shift+Ctrl+T (Windows) or Shift+Command+T (Mac OS) to preview your page in the default browser(s).

Using PDF Preview

GoLive CS2 allows you to convert Web pages to Adobe's PDF format. PDFs traditionally have provided a standard form for storing and editing documents for print publishing. Documents saved in .pdf format retain the author's formatting and can easily be seen and printed by users on a variety of computer and platform types. PDF files are typically created with Adobe Acrobat; however, GoLive will also make a PDF based on your open document.

1   Click on the PDF Preview tab to enter this mode. It may take a few moments for GoLive to create the preview page. When it is finished, you will see the GoLive default preset for converting Web pages to 8.5" by 11" documents (standard letter size). Based on your layout, this may not be the ideal format for print, as Web pages are usually designed for computer screens, which are often wider than a standard letter page. GoLive's default behavior is to scale a page to the document size, but these parameters can be changed in the Inspector palette.

2   In the Inspector palette, click on the Landscape button (🏠) to the right of the Size drop-down menu. Also, check the Use Single Page layout box. Selecting these two options will place your page on a landscape-oriented letter page and force all the content onto a single page.

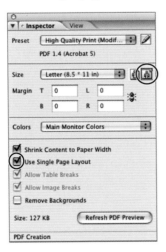

3 Click the Refresh PDF Preview button in the Inspector palette to view the new layout. Each time you make a change to the settings, you must click the Refresh button to see the new layout.

4 Click on the Save as PDF button (⊡) in the top left corner of your Main toolbar. This will open the Export PDF File window. Navigate to your Lesson01 folder and click Save to save the .pdf file. After saving, the admissions.pdf file will open in GoLive. Scroll to the bottom of the document, if necessary, to locate the hyperlink site made with Adobe GoLive CS2. Place your cursor over the link, but do not click. A pop-up will preview the URL of the hyperlink. Links created in GoLive are translated to links in the PDF.

5 Close the admissions.pdf file by clicking the Close button.

💡 *You can also print a PDF by clicking on the Print PDF button in the toolbar, and e-mail a PDF by clicking on the E-mail PDF button.*

Setting Preferences and Web Settings

GoLive allows you to set a number of preferences which give you control over many aspects of the program. As you become more advanced with the program, you may find that you need to change the way the program functions. One simple example might be to open your documents in Source view, if you are more comfortable working in code. Although these settings are generally more useful for advanced users or those familiar with source code, it's a good idea to know where to access them.

1 Choose Edit > Web Settings (Windows) or GoLive > Web Settings (Mac OS) to open the Web Settings window. This window allows you to change some of GoLive's code writing abilities. There are five separate tabs: Global, Markup Language, Characters, Browser Profiles, and File Mappings. Close the Web Settings window by clicking on the Close button.

2 Choose Edit > Preferences (Windows) or GoLive > Preferences (Mac OS) to open the preferences window. On the left side of the window is a list of the different categories of preferences. Click on General preferences if not currently selected. In the Default Mode section, click on the menu to view the various options available. Advanced users might want to open all documents in the Outline Editor, for example. Make sure the default Layout option remains selected. Click OK.

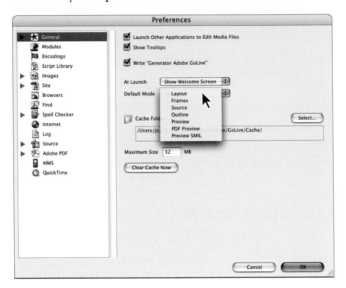

3 Save your file and close this document.

Congratulations! You have finished the tour of the workspace.

Exploring on your own

1   Using the View and Window menus, practice zooming in and out of a page.

2   Highlight an image or some text in your final document and switch between the Layout Editor and Source Code Editor using the tabs at the top of your document window. Delete or modify objects in the Layout View and note how the associated code in the Source view is affected.

3   If you have more than one Web browser on your system, preview your Web pages on different browsers. Doing this will help you understand how differently the same Web page appears on older or alternative browsers.

Review

▶ **Review questions**

1 What is a workspace and how can you change and reset workspaces?

2 What is a site in GoLive and how do you open an existing Web site in GoLive?

3 What is the source code of a Web page and how would you view it?

4 Which palette do you use to add an image placeholder to your page? Which palette do you use to link an image placeholder to an image file?

5 What's the recommended method to preview a site or page that you've created in GoLive?

▶ **Review answers**

1 A workspace is the layout of the windows and palettes in Adobe GoLive CS2. You can always restore the default workspace by choosing Window > Workspace > Default Workspace. You can also create custom workspaces by rearranging your palettes and windows, and then choose Window > Workspace > Save Workspace.

2 A site is GoLive's way of collecting and keeping track of all the elements used in your Web site, including the individual pages, images, and any other assets. One way to open a pre-existing site is to choose File > Open and locate the site document with the .site extension.

3 The source code of a Web page is the tag-based HTML that GoLive generates when the user adds text, images, or other objects while in Layout Editor. However, the source code is not visible unless the user chooses to see it. To view a Web page's source code, either click on the Source tab in the document window to enter the Source Code Editor, or choose View > Document Mode > Source.

4   You use the Basic set of the Objects palette to add an image placeholder to your page and the Inspector palette to link the placeholder to an image file.

5   You can use GoLive's internal preview option by clicking the Preview tab in the document window. However, you will also want to get into the habit of previewing your pages on at least one Web browser, perhaps more, based on your target audience. You can quickly preview your pages by clicking on the Preview in Browser button in your top toolbar.

Discover how to organize your site—save time and keep your Web site consistent. You will also find out how to update your site easily by taking advantage of GoLive's site tools.

2 | Creating a GoLive Site

Some of the best features come together in the site creation and management tools in GoLive CS2. A Web site is a collection of pages, images and other resources that are linked in a way that makes it easier for the viewer to find the information they need. The site features in GoLive CS2 allow you to organize these files and maintain valid links to your resources.

In this lesson, you'll learn how to do the following:

- Create a new blank site.
- Create new pages for a site.
- Add files to a Site Folder.
- Save an image file from Photoshop into the web content folder.
- Close and re-open a site window.
- Create a site from existing files.
- Organize a site.
- Create a site color palette.

What is a site?

A site is a location on the World Wide Web. Each Web site contains a home page, which is the first document users see when they enter the site. The site might also contain additional documents and files that are linked using hyperlinks to the home page.

In GoLive you can take advantage of features to help assure that an organized site is created and posted to the World Wide Web.

A GoLive site mimics how the structure will appear when the site is posted—a structure that includes navigation links from the main home page to other pages, and other assets that can include image, PDF, Flash, QuickTime, and other types of files.

These are some of the benefits of working in a GoLive site:

• You can keep site assets, such as images and HTML pages, organized and accessible to the creator. New Folders can be created, as well as renamed, in the site window.

• The GoLive site window tracks changes and automatically updates any link name or location changes.

• The site window keeps you informed of unreferenced files. The Used column in the site window shows which assets are being referenced by html pages in the site.

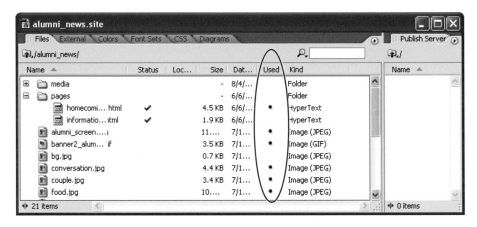

• You can keep the look of a site consistent and make updating easier by using features available only when working with site files. See Lesson 10, "Using Stationeries, Components, Page Templates, and Snippets" for more information.

- You can use site tools such as the In & Out Links palette that can track which files and links are being used, and by which pages.

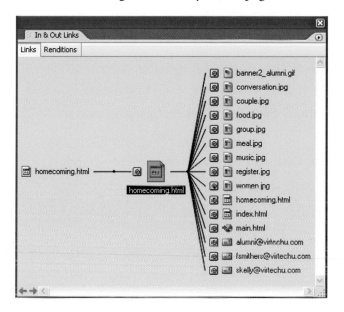

- The Color tab of the site window can help you to be more consistent by defining a color palette to be used throughout the site.

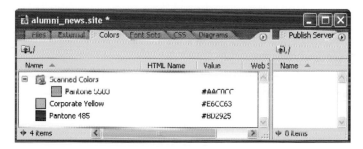

Getting started

In this lesson, you will create a site using two methods: one without an existing home or main page, and one with an existing home page. The latter could be from a previously created site residing on your computer or on a server.

Creating a new blank site

In this first example, you will create a blank site and import images. You will then use the site window to help you understand the organizational tools available when using a GoLive site.

1   To ensure that the tools and palettes function exactly as described in this lesson, delete or deactivate (by renaming) the Adobe GoLive CS2 preferences file. See "Restoring default preferences" on page 3.

2   Start Adobe GoLive CS2. Close the Welcome Screen if it appears.

3   Choose File > New to open the New options window.

4   Choose Site > Create Site and select Blank Site. Click Next.

5   In the Specifying a Site Name and Location window, type **alumni** in the Name text field.

6   Click on the Browse button beneath the Save To text field and locate the Lesson02 folder on your hard drive. Click OK (Windows) or Choose (Mac OS), then click Next.

7   The "Use a Version Control System?" window appears. Choose "Don't Use Version Control." Click Next. You can find out more about Version Cue in Lesson 13, "Using Version Cue and Bridge with GoLive CS2."

8   In the "Publish Server Options" window, choose "Specify Server Later." Click Finish. The alumni.site window appears.

The GoLive site window.

The index.html page is bolded, indicating that it is the home page, upon which all other navigation and links are based.

Note: You can make any page your home page by selecting it in the Files tab and choosing the Page tab of the File Inspector. Check the Home Page checkbox. The selected page is bolded, indicating that it is now the home page for this site.

A GoLive site includes many parts. In the site window, you see the index.html page and a css folder. As a default, the index.html is a blank page. Cascading Style Sheets can be an integral part of Web sites. GoLive CS2 provides you with a few initial CSS selector names ready for you to customize. Cascading Style Sheets are discussed briefly in this lesson, but you can discover more in Lesson 5, "Adding and Formatting Text."

9 Leave the site window open.

Behind the scenes

Beyond what you see in the site window, GoLive created three folders and a .site file within a project folder in your directory system. Notice that GoLive provides backups for the site file in case of corruption. The folders reside in the Lesson02 folder on your hard drive, into which you saved the alumni site.

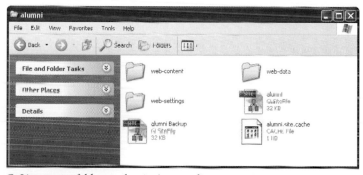

GoLive creates folders and a site in your directory system.

The .site file is the file you select to open a site. It contains important information about your site and should always be open when you are working on pages that are part of a Web site.

web-content

The web-content folder contains the files that you see in the Files tab of the GoLive site window. This includes the contents of your site, such as pages, images, PDFs, and Flash files. These are the source files that are typically loaded to the FTP server when the site is complete. Save files to this folder when adding new assets to your site.

web-data

The web-data folder is where you will find GoLive Extras. When in a site window, these items are found on the Extra tab on the right side. They are found in your directory system inside the named site folder. Many of these items will be used throughout the book.

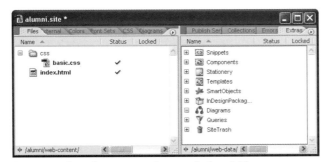

Site extras show the contents of your web-data folder.

What are the Extras?

The **Extras** tab contains all the files and folders in the site's web-content folder and web-data folder. The web-data folder contains four types of reusable objects: components, stationery pages, snippets, and page templates. The Extras tab also contains diagrams, Smart Objects, InDesign packages, queries, and files moved to the Site Trash.

The **Snippets** folder stores reusable portions of source code, text, images, and other objects from pages in GoLive or documents in other applications. Read more about Snippets in Lesson 10, "Using Stationeries, Components, Page Templates, and Snippets."

The **Components** folder stores HTML source files that can be used for buttons, logos, headers, mastheads, or other common navigation elements that you want to use throughout your site. When you add a component to a page, the component remains linked to its source file until you detach it.

(Continued on the next page)

What are the Extras? *(continued)*

The **Stationery** folder stores .html files that can be used as templates for creating new pages. Unlike page templates, stationery has no dynamic link with the pages created from it. Changes you make to a stationery file do not affect pages already created from that file. Read more about Stationery files in Lesson 10, "Using Stationeries, Components, Page Templates, and Snippets."

The **Templates** folder stores any page designated as a Page Template. Page Templates allow you to establish editable regions within a page. Any part of the page template that is not marked as an editable region is automatically locked so that when you or others on the same site project create new pages from the template, only the editable regions can be changed. Pages created from a Page Template maintain a dynamic link to the original Template file. Read more about Templates in Lesson 10, "Using Stationeries, Components, Page Templates, and Snippets."

Use the **Smart Objects** folder to hold native images such as native Photoshop and Illustrator files, and then use GoLive's Save For Web feature to create web-optimized images. Read more about Smart Objects in Lesson 7, "Using Graphics in GoLive."

The **InDesign Package** folder stores packages exported from InDesign. With InDesign's Package For GoLive feature, you can easily incorporate content from InDesign documents into GoLive pages and sites. From Open InDesign Packages, you can either drag individual text and graphic assets to Web pages or export entire InDesign layouts to HTML. If you regularly revise package assets in InDesign, GoLive automatically updates related text and images using components and Smart Objects.

Use the **Diagrams** folder to store diagrams. A diagram lets you lay out the structure of a site before you create real pages, and helps you manage the site creation process. You can use multiple prototype diagrams as you build and revise a site, creating and testing designs as you need them. You can present diagrams in print or online in Adobe PDF or SVG format. When you are ready to work with live pages, you submit a diagram, converting its pages to actual pages in the site. Read more about Diagrams in Lesson 11, "Using Site Diagrams."

Use the **Queries** folder to store saved Query results. The Queries window lets you search for files using a wide range of criteria. You can search in open sites and collections, in a user-defined list of files, or in a result list; and you can view the results in the Query Results window. You can define nested queries to perform complex searches, or use GoLive's predefined queries for simple searches. Use the Query Editor to edit predefined queries or create new queries. Save queries to use with application-wide searches, or save site-specific queries in the Queries folder of the Extras tab. You can also save query results as collections in the Collections tab.

The **Site Trash** folder contains any file that you choose to throw away. When you delete a file or folder from the site, you send it to a Site Trash folder or to the system Recycle Bin or Trash. The default destination is Site Trash, but you can select the Recycle Bin or Trash as the destination in the Site preferences.

web-settings

The web-settings folder is used to store settings you make in the site window and the Site Settings dialog box.

As a default, your site window is in split view. If at any time during this lesson you prefer to see more of the Files tab, you can click on the Toggle split view button in the lower portion of the site window, or uncheck Show Split View from the Site palette menu.

The Toggle split view button.   *Result.*

About the site window

GoLive organizes a site into ten tabs to handle different aspects of site management. Listed below are brief descriptions of each tab and its function.

Files—Contains HTML, XHTML, XML, media, and other files, as well as folders that you can use to organize the files. This tab will be discussed in detail throughout this lesson.

External—Displays external URLs and e-mail addresses referenced by the site files. This tab is discussed at the end of this lesson.

Colors—Contains a collection of colors used in your site. You will use the Colors tab in this lesson to create a site color palette.

Font Sets—Contains a collection of font sets used in your site. The font sets are lists of alternative fonts that you use to override the browser's default display font settings. Font sets are discussed in Lesson 5, "Adding and Formatting Text."

CSS—Contains a list of the External Style Sheets, classes, and identifiers (IDs) used in your site. The CSS tab also lists the number of times a style sheet, class, or identifier is defined in the site and how many times it's used. Learn more about Cascading Style Sheets in Lesson 5, "Adding and Formatting Text."

Diagrams—Contains diagrams with a graphical view of possible site implementations. Diagrams are discussed in detail in Lesson 11, "Using Site Diagrams."

You can also show and hide the right pane of the site window that contains these additional tabs:

Publish Server—Displays the site on a remote server while GoLive is connected to a publish server (an FTP, WebDAV, or local file server). You will discover how to publish your site in Lesson 12, "Managing and Publishing Web Sites."

Collections— Displays custom sets of one or more files that you select manually or define as a result of a query, syntax check, or find operation.

Errors—Contains missing files, orphan files, Smart Object warnings, and files that have a name that doesn't meet your file name constraints. An orphan file is referenced in a link, but GoLive can't find it if the file is outside the web-content folder. If you manage files in the site window, you can avoid creating orphan files. Click a file in the Errors tab to open the Error Inspector.

Extras—As discussed earlier in this lesson, the Extras tab contains all the files and folders in the site's web-content folder and web-data folder.

Understanding the Files tab

The default tab that you see in your site window is the Files tab. It may look similar to the directory system of your computer. Use the Files tab when updating file names, creating new folders and deleting files. GoLive alerts you if a file is being used, and where it is located, and it can even update link names and locations in any pages using the changed files.

Now that you have created a site, you will create pages and add them to the Files tab of the site window.

1   Make sure that the new alumni.site window you created earlier is still open. If not, choose File > Open Recent and choose alumni.site. Select the Files tab. You can also choose File > Open and navigate to Lesson02 > alumni > alumni.site.

2   Choose File > New. The New options window appears.

3   Choose Web > Pages > HTML page. Click OK. A new, blank HTML page is created.

With the site window forward you can automatically add a blank page by choosing the Create new Page button ( ) in the Main toolbar. A page appears in the Files tab, ready for you to type an appropriate page name.

4   Click the cursor in the upper left of the page window and type **Homecoming information coming soon!** and then choose the Center Align button ( ) from the Main toolbar.

Add text and center align it on the blank page.

5   Click the arrow to the left of Head to see that any new pages created while the alumni site window is open, are automatically linked to the external styles stored in the Files tab of the site window. This feature can be deactivated. Read more about CSS and how this may affect your page in Lesson 5, "Adding and Formatting Text."

Creating a site without a default CSS file

If you do not want all of your pages within a site to be linked to the basic.css file, or want to use another .css file as the default, follow these steps:

1 In your site window open the css folder.

2 Click once on the basic.css.

3 In the File Inspector, click on the Page tab.

4 Uncheck the Default CSS checkbox.

5 If you have another .css file that you would prefer to use, select the file and check the Default CSS checkbox.

6   Double-click on the External CSS link in the head section to access the style sheet and make a change. The basic.css window appears.

7   Click on the style selector named body. The right side of the window updates to show attributes for the contents that are in the body tag.

Note: The <body> tag contains the visible section of an HTML page; any changes to this style will apply to the text you add to the new page. Since you are editing an external style, any changes made in the basic.css window will reflect on every page within your site. See how this can be overridden with an Internal Style Sheet in Lesson 5, "Adding and Formatting Text."

8   Click on the Font Properties tab (**A**) on the right side of the basic.css window. Specific attributes for the font appear.

9 Type **14 px** in the Size text field. Press Enter. The text changes to 14 pixels.

10 Click and hold on the Create new font family button (▦) and select the Helvetica Set. The text changes to a sans serif face.

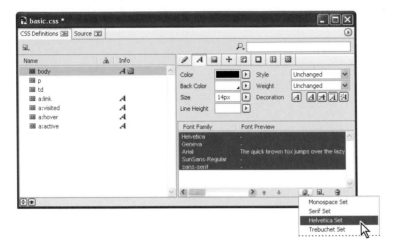

11 Click the Close box in the basic.css window, and choose Yes (Windows) or Save (Mac OS) to save the changes you made.

12 Keep the untitled HTML page open for the next part of the lesson.

The Main toolbar

The Main toolbar is contextual. The options change depending upon whether you have a page or site window forward. Choose the Window menu item. Notice that you can select any open pages or sites from the list at the bottom. You can also use the Select window button from the toolbar to toggle between the page and site window.

The toolbar as it appears when an HTML page is forward.

The toolbar as it appears when a site window is forward.

Saving a new page into the Files tab

When creating sites, you must be very careful to keep your site content together. Otherwise, you may create a page whose links are not current when uploaded to the server. GoLive helps you to keep the files together by providing you with options in the Save As window.

1   Choose File > Save. In the Save As window, type **homecoming** in the File name text field.

2   Click on the Site Folder button (📁,) and choose Root (Windows) or Root folder (Mac OS) from the drop-down menu. By choosing Root, you are navigated automatically to the web-content folder for the alumni site.

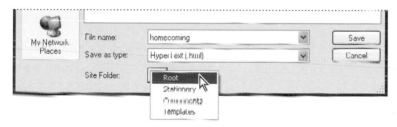

Note: *If the Site Folder button is not visible at the bottom of the Save As window, your site window has been closed.*

3   Choose Save.

GoLive recognizes that you have not provided this page with a title. A Set title alert window appears.

4   In the Enter a new title text field, type **VirtechU Homecoming**, then press Set. The page is now titled correctly, and the file is saved. It also appears in the Files tab.

5   Choose File > Close to close the saved page. Your alumni.site window should still be open.

Adding existing files to a blank site

Though you are creating a new site, there could be many assets for the site that are already created. This might include logos, images, or even existing HTML pages that are to be incorporated into this site. In this part of the lesson, you will add them to the Files tab.

1 Make sure the alumni.site window is still open and choose File > Import > Files to Site. The Add to site window appears.

Note: Click in the Files tab of the alumni.site window if Files to Site is grayed out.

2 Navigate to the Lesson02 folder on your hard drive. Open the folder named add_to_blank. There are two files in this folder.

3 Click on the first file, banner_alumni.gif, and Shift+click on the other file, gathering.html to select the files. Click Open (Windows) or Choose (Mac OS).

4 A Copy Files alert window appears, indicating that the gathering.html is going to change the reference for a link when the file is relocated. Click OK.

The files are added to the files tab of the alumni.site window.

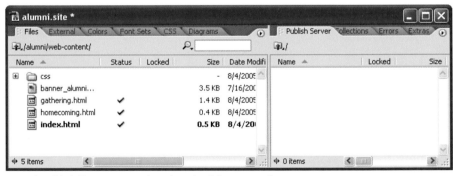

Properly added files appear in the Files tab of the site window.

Note: When importing files into a GoLive site, they are copied into the site, leaving the original files in their same location.

💡 *You can also drag files from your desktop into a GoLive site, or copy and paste files from one GoLive site window to another.*

5 Leave the alumni.site window open.

Adding a file saved from Photoshop

When working in other applications, you may wish to add files directly to your Files tab. In this section you will use Photoshop, or any other application capable of re-sizing an image and saving it as a JPEG. If you do not have an image editing program, read this section without doing the steps.

1   Launch Adobe Photoshop or any other editing program able to save a JPEG. Choose File > Open. Navigate to the Lesson02 folder on your hard drive and open the file named incharge.jpg.

2   In Photoshop, re-size the image by selecting Image > Image Size. Make sure Resample Image is checked and the method selected is Bicubic.

3   Change the number in the Pixel Dimension Width text field to **125** and click OK.

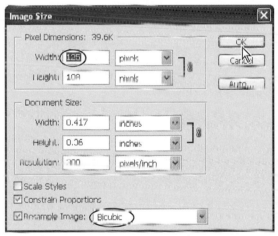 

Resize the Photoshop image before saving it.

Note: *Resolution does not affect the image when used for on-screen presentation. What is important is the Pixel Dimension area in the top portion of the Image Size window.*

After resizing the image, you will apply the Unsharp Mask filter. The Unsharp Mask filter makes an image crisper. This next step can be skipped if your image editing program does not have an Unsharp Mask feature.

4   Double-click on the Zoom tool (🔍) to zoom the image to Actual Pixel size. It is best to preview filters in Photoshop when an image is at its actual pixel size.

5 Choose Filter > Sharpen > Unsharp Mask. Enter these settings:

Amount, **200**; Radius, **1.0**; Threshold, **10**. The Threshold setting allows the image to become crisp without adding sharpening to areas that should remain smooth. Click OK.

Image prior to Unsharp *Settings.* *Result.*
masking.

6 Choose File > Save for Web. The Save for Web window appears. Click on the 2-up tab to compare the original image (left) to the optimized image (right).

7 Since this is a continuous tone image, it is best saved as a JPEG. From the Presets drop-down menu, choose JPEG Medium, then Click Save.

8 In the Save Optimized As window, locate the Lesson02 folder on your hard drive. Inside the Lesson02 folder is the alumni project folder created when you created the site. Open the alumni folder and then the web-content folder.

9 Confirm the File Name is "incharge" and click Save.

10 Choose File > Close. Choose "Don't Save" when the Adobe Photoshop alert window appears.

11 Exit Photoshop and return to GoLive. The file is listed in the Files tab of the alumni.site window

The Refresh view button.

Note: *When you save files from another application into the web-content folder of a site,*
you may need to click the Refresh view button (◯) in the Main toolbar. This can also be
done if you unexpectedly quit GoLive to rescan and update the Files tab.

12 Leave the site window open for the next section.

Creating site colors

Keep your site consistent by using a standard color palette for your pages. By using the
Colors tab of the site window, you can access, rename, and change colors site-wide.

Before starting this lesson, open the file gathering.html by double-clicking on it in the
Files tab. Note that this page has a cell colored blue. GoLive will start the site colors with
this color.

GoLive can scan for any colors used in a site.

1 If the site window is not forward, choose the Select window button (▤). Choose
the Colors tab.

2 Select Site > Update > Add used > Colors. A Scanned colors folder appears with the
colors used on the gathering.html page.

The colors can be renamed to help you identify and select colors more easily. The
hexadecimal value for the colors (what is used for the source code) is listed to the right
of the name.

3 Select the untitled light blue color. If the Inspector is not visible, choose Window > Inspector. In the Name text field, rename the file **corporate blue** and press Enter to update the named color.

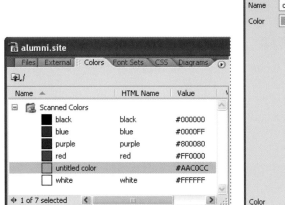

Provide logical names for site colors by changing the name in the Color Inspector.

Adding your own site colors

1 Choose Site > New > Color. An untitled color appears in the Colors tab.

2 Choose Window > Swatches, the Swatches palette appears.

3 From the Swatches palette menu (⊙), choose Open Swatch Library. Scroll and release on Web Named Colors.

The Web Named Colors palette appears.

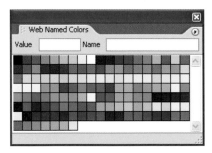

4   Using the Web Named Colors palette menu, choose List View to view the names of the colors.

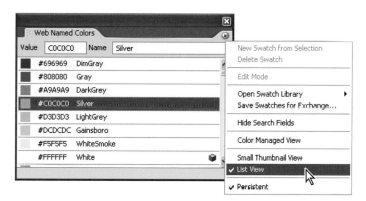

5   Choose the color named Silver. The untitled color in the site window is assigned the silver color. Click on untitled color and use the Inspector to change the name to **corporate silver**. Click Return or Enter to confirm the name.

As you create a site, you can access all site colors on their own palette by choosing Open Swatch Library > Site colors from the Swatches palette menu. This helps you to consistently use the same colors throughout the entire site. Read more about colors in Lesson 6, "Working with Color."

6   Click the Close button on the Web Named Colors palette and return to the Files tab of the alumni.site window.

Adding site objects to a page

One of the benefits of using a GoLive site is that it monitors and tracks the usage of each file. In this lesson, you will create some simple links from the index.html page to the gathering.html page. You will also place some of the provided images.

1   With the alumni.site window open, click on the Files tab and double-click on the index.html page. A blank index page appears.

2   Select the Title text field and type **VirtechU Alumni**. Press Enter.

Change the title of the page.

3   If the Objects palette is not visible, choose Window > Objects, or use the keyboard shortcut Ctrl+2 (Windows), Command+2 (Mac OS). Choose CSS from the palette menu.

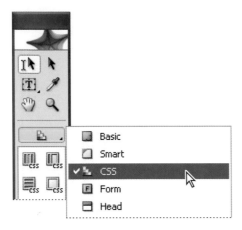

You will create a simple CSS layout before elements are added to this page.

4   Select the Padded Box object (⬚) and drag it to the blank index.html page. A CSS object is added to the page.

5   Now select the Two Columns: Fixed Left object (⬚) and drag and drop it onto the index.html page.

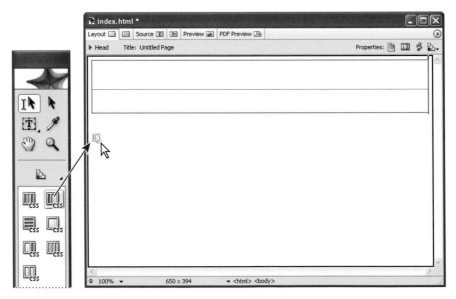

6   Use the Select window button (🖼.) in the Main toolbar to bring the alumni.site window forward so that you can see the named items on the Files tab. If the window is maximized, resize it so that you can see the index.html page behind it.

7   Select the file named banner_alumni.gif and drag it to the top CSS padded box you created on the page.

There are many methods that you can use to place images on a GoLive page. Read Lesson 7, "Using Graphics in GoLive," for more information.

8   Click on the index.html page to bring it forward.

9 Using the Standard Editing tool (👆), click in the left column of the Two Columns:
Fixed Left CSS object you dragged on to the page. Type the following:

VirtechU Home

Homecoming

Send us an email

10 If the Inspector palette is not open, choose Window > Inspector, or Ctrl+1
(Windows), Command+1 (Mac OS). Select the word Homecoming; the Inspector is
now a Text Inspector palette.

11 Click on the Fetch URL button (◎) in the Inspector and drag to the Select window
button in the Main toolbar. Don't let go! This brings the alumni.site window forward.

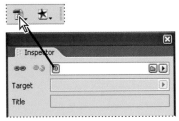

*Point the Fetch URL to the Select
Window button.*

12 Continue dragging the Fetch URL path down over the Files tab and point to the page named gathering.html. Release. This creates a link from the highlighted text to that page.

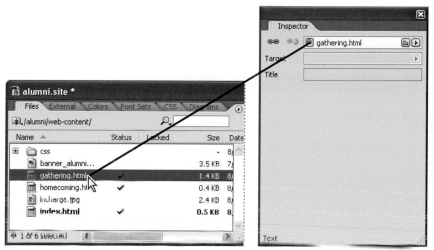

When the site window is brought forward, point the Fetch URL button to gathering.html.

13 Make sure that the index.html page is forward, then choose File > Save. Choose File > Close.

You can also Option+click (Windows) or Command+click (Mac OS) and drag directly from text or an object on the page to use the Fetch URL feature without the Inspector.

Checking usage on the Files tab

Make sure that the alumni.site is open and that the Files tab is active.

1   If you are in split view, click on the Toggle split view button (◀▶) to expand the left side of the site window.

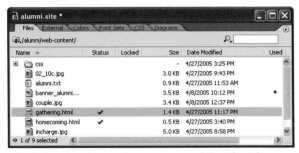

Use the Toggle split view button to expand the Files tab.

Notice that you can use the scrollbar at the bottom of the site window to see more information about each file. There is a black dot under the Used column if the file is being used in the site.

Another method to find out whether a file is used is to utilize the In & Out Links palette.

2   Select the index.html file and choose the Open In & Out Links palette button (🔛) from the Main toolbar. The Links tab of the In & Out Links palette appears.

The In & Out Links palette.

Incoming links to the file appear on the left side of the In & Out Links palette, and outgoing links or file references from the file appear on the right. For non-file items, the files that reference or use the selected item appear on the left. As you move the cursor over a file in the In & Out Links palette, a tooltip appears showing information about the file.

Using the In & Out Links palette to view links

The In & Out Links palette is a powerful link management tool that graphically shows you the links or file references to or from a selected file or item in the site window. It is especially useful for troubleshooting link errors listed in the Errors tab of the site window, and showing all the pages linked to a missing file. You can also create a site map by printing the contents of the In & Out Links palette.

You can use the In & Out Links palette with any file or non-file item in the web-content folder—that is, with any file or item listed in the Files, External, Colors, Font Sets, CSS, Extras, Collections, or Errors tabs in the site window. For example, you can use the In & Out Links palette to show the files that use a color listed in the Colors tab, or use a Cascading Style Sheet located in the CSS tab. You can also use the In & Out Links palette with a file in the navigation and links views, or with a diagram in the Design tab in the diagram window.

You can use the Renditions tab of the In & Out Links palette to view implied (not actual) links between files. For example, the Renditions tab displays the implied link between a Smart Object source file and its target file, or between a file and its duplicate (created by choosing Edit > Duplicate).

—From GoLive Help

3   Close the In & Out Links palette, and select the file named gathering.html in the Files tab of the site window.

4   Using the File tab of the File Inspector palette, change the name gathering.html to **social.html**. Press Enter.

5   A Rename File alert window appears, indicating that the source code on the index.html page needs to be updated to maintain the link to the page. Click OK.

The file name has been changed and the link on the index page has been changed to look for the file named social.html.

Deleting a file

As a default, a file deleted from a GoLive site is stored in a separate GoLive Trash folder. This is helpful if you ever need to retrieve a file.

1   Select, by clicking once in the alumni.site window, the file you created named homecoming.html.

2   Click once on the Delete selected item button (🗑) in the upper left of your Main toolbar.

A GoLive CS2 alert window appears, verifying that you want to delete the selected file. Click Yes (Windows) or Move (Mac OS).

3   Choose Extras from the Site palette menu (⊚). The Extras appear on the right side of the site window.

4   Open the SiteTrash folder to reveal the location of any deleted files. You can choose to delete again to put the file in your system trash, or drag the file back into the Files tab if you discover that it is needed. For this example, you will leave the file in the SiteTrash.

Note: If you would rather send your deleted files directly to your system's Trash, choose Edit > Preferences (Windows) or GoLive > Preferences (Mac OS), then select Site. In the When Removing Files section, choose Move Them to the System (Windows) or Finder (Mac OS) Trash radio button. Click OK.

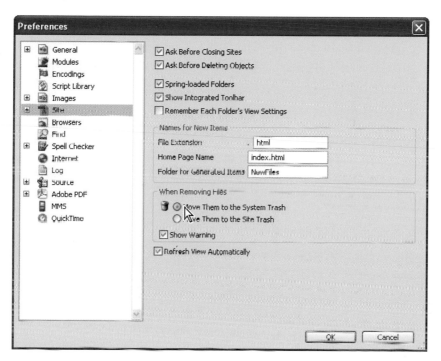

Closing and re-opening your site

Once a site file is created, you should have it open as you create new pages or modify existing pages. It helps to eliminate errors and provides access to all your site assets in one location. In this lesson, you will close the site file and re-open it.

1   Choose the close box on the site window or choose File > Close when the alumni.site window is forward.

2   An Adobe GoLive CS2 alert window appears, verifying that you want to close the site file. Choose OK.

3   To re-open the alumni site, you can choose File > Open Recent. Site files are listed in the upper section, pages are listed in the middle, miscellaneous files such as CSS, SVG, and others are listed at the bottom. Choose alumni.site.

Note: If your .site file is not available from the Open Recent folder, choose File > Open, navigate to your project folder, in this case the alumni folder inside of Lesson02, and open the file named alumni.site.

4   Choose File > Close to close this site. Click OK on the Adobe GoLive CS2 alert window. If social.html is still open choose File > Close to close that document.

Creating a GoLive site from existing files

Perhaps there is no existing GoLive site file due to the fact that the site was not originally created in GoLive or that you are creating the site from files of an existing site. In this section you will create a site file for an existing site that already includes an index.html page.

1   Choose File > New. The New options window appears.

2   In the Site Creation Wizard, choose Site > Create Site. Select "Site from Existing Content." Click Next.

3   In the "Creating a Site from Existing Content" window, choose "From a Local Folder of Existing Files." Click Next.

4   In the "Selecting a Local folder of Existing Files" window, select the top Browse button under the heading of Folder. Navigate to the Lesson02 folder on your hard drive and select the folder named **alumni_news.** Select OK (Windows) or Choose (Mac OS), then click Next.

Note: If you do not have an index file, you can select the top Browse button under Folder. GoLive will then automatically create a blank index.html file for the site.

5 In the "Specifying a Site Name and Location" window, click Finish. As a default, the necessary folders discussed earlier in this lesson are added at the same directory level as the containing folder.

The site window appears with the files from the containing folder.

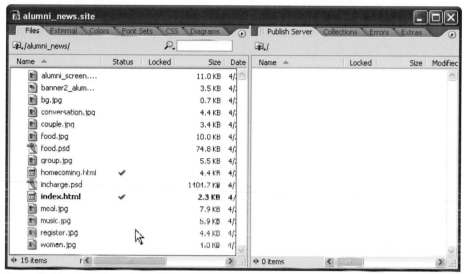

A new GoLive site using existing files.

Importing sites from FTP or HTTP servers

Using the Site Creation Wizard, you can import an entire Web site into GoLive, including every linked page that branches out to multiple HTTP servers and every source file (such as images) referenced by the pages. Because large sites can take a long time to download, you can restrict the number of page levels in the page-link hierarchy to import.

Note: If you already have an ongoing workgroup project that employs version control, and you wish to continue the collaboration, connect to the existing site instead of using this procedure.

1 *Choose File > New.*

2 *Select Site > Create Site.*

3 *Select Site From Existing Content, and click Next.*

4 *Select By Downloading Files From A Remote Server, and click Next.*

5 *Choose the server type (FTP or HTTP) from the Type Of Server menu.*

6 *If you are downloading from an HTTP server, specify the home page URL of the server in the URL box and then do one of the following:*

• To download only the pages that are located in the same folder (or a subfolder) that contains the home page URL, select Only Get Pages Under Same Path.

• To download only those pages that are on the same server as the home page URL, select Stay On Same Server. GoLive downloads from other servers any source files that are referenced by the pages it downloads, whether or not this option is selected.

7 *If you are downloading from an FTP server, enter the FTP server information. Click Advanced to set security and passive mode options.*

8 *Click Next, and then specify a name and location for the downloaded files. To specify how the new site will handle encoding and case sensitivity checking in URLs, click Advanced.*

9 *Click Finish.*

GoLive imports only the pages on the levels you specify and the source files for images and other objects on those pages. GoLive converts any remaining page links that go to other levels into external URLs, and lists them in the External tab of the site window. After you create the site, you can individually download the pages from these external URLs by choosing Download from a URL's context menu.

—From GoLive Help

Organizing the site window

In this next part of the lesson you will create new folders and organize the files in the site window.

1   With the alumni_news.site open, select the Create new folder button (⬚) in the Main toolbar. An untitled folder appears in the Files tab.

2   Name the folder **media**. Press Enter.

3   Select the file named alumni_screen.jpg and drag it on top of the media folder to place it inside.

4   A Move Files alert window appears, indicating that the image is used on the index.html page and that the source code needs to be revised. Click OK. The reference to the new location of the image file is updated on the index.html page.

5   Hold down the Ctrl (Windows) or Command (Mac OS) key to select the remaining nine JPEG files and one GIF file in the site window.

Do not select the two Photoshop images (food.psd and incharge.psd), as we will put these files in a dedicated folder.

6   With the ten files selected, drag them into the media folder. Click OK when the Move Files alert window appears.

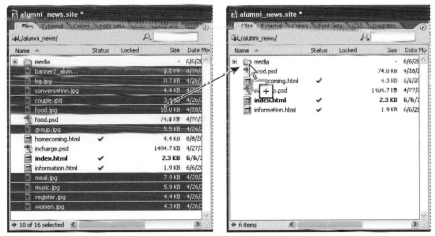

Select files.   *Drag into media folder.*

Navigating within a site

When a folder contains data, a plus sign (+) (Windows) or an arrow (▶) (Mac OS) appears to the left of the named folder.

1   Click on the plus sign, or arrow, to the left of the media folder to show the contents of the folder in the site window.

2   Double-click on the media folder to open the folder and reveals its contents.

Close Folder.

Folder when expanded.

Folder when opened.
Use the Go up button to
exit the folder.

3   Click the Go up button (🔁) to go up one level in the folder structure.

4   Click on the minus sign (Windows), or arrow (Mac OS), to the left of the media folder to hide the contents of the folder in the site window.

Creating a folder for pages

1   Click on the Create new folder button (📁) on the Main toolbar. Change the folder name from untitled_folder to **pages**. Press Enter.

2   Select the file named homecoming.html and Ctrl+click (Windows) or Command+ click (Mac OS) on the file named information.html. Drag the selected files into the pages folder.

3   When the Move Files alert window appears, click OK.

Storing Smart objects

You were introduced to Smart Objects in the Tour lesson. Smart Objects are native files to which you want to keep an active link, but they do not need to be part of your Files tab. They will not be uploaded to your FTP server when the site is complete.

As mentioned earlier in this lesson, a Smart Objects folder was automatically created, and resides in the Extras tab of the GoLive site window.

1   Click on the Extras tab on the right side of the GoLive site window. The site extra folders are shown, including the Smart Objects folder.

2   In the Files tab of your site window, select the files named food.psd and incharge.psd.

3   Click and drag the selected files on top of the Smart Objects folder in the Extras tab. The Smart Objects are now accessible but no longer in your active Files tab.

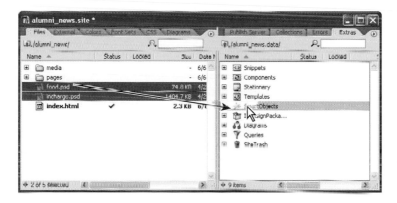

Your site is now organized. Keep the alumni_news site window open for the next part of this lesson.

Using the Navigation View

Use the Navigation View to investigate the site as a map. This can help you to keep track of the organization of the entire site.

With a new imported site, the Navigation View shows the structure of the site as a tree-like hierarchy descending from the home page. With a new blank site, the Navigation View shows a single home page.

The hierarchy comprises logical pair relationships between pages in which a page is either a child, a parent, a previous sibling, or a next sibling. A typical parent-child relationship is between a home page and the pages it links to.

1   With the alumni_site window open, choose the Open Navigation View button (⚬⚬⚬) in the Main toolbar.

The alumni_news.site Navigation palette appears.

2   Click on the plus sign to expand the view and see the navigational links that are established in this Web site. As a default, links to internal and external references, such as other Web sites and e-mail addresses, show up in the window.

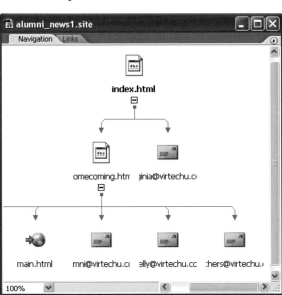

Expand the Navigation view by selecting the plus sign.

3   Choose Window > View. When you have the Navigation view open, you can change the visible details using the View palette.

4   Click on the Display tab of the View palette and experiment with different
display options. In our example below, frames and the page title were options
selected.

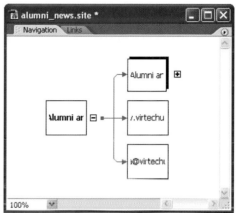

5   Click on the Filter tab of the Navigation palette. Use this tab to turn off
the view of objects you do not want visible in the hierarchy. In our example, we
selected the Toggle Links button to show only the pages within the
alumni_news.site.

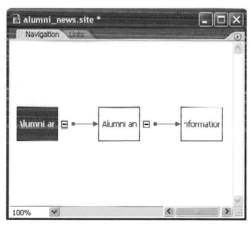

To help you plan future and manage present links, you can choose to print the Navigation View.

6   Choose File > Print Preview to see how the Navigation View will print on a page with your present settings.

Note: If you do not have the Print Preview option choose File > Print.

7   If you want to change the settings, close the Print window and choose File > Page Setup.
In the Page Setup window you can change the orientation and size of your page and select a printer. For this example, you will select only a printer.

8   If you have a printer connected, select the Printer button in the lower right of the Page Setup window. Select the printer to which you wish to print your Navigation View, and click OK to exit the printer Page Setup window and OK again to exit the Page Setup window.

9   Choose File > Print, and click Print.

Congratulations! You have finished the lesson.

Exploring on your own

You have discovered that GoLive's Site controls contain powerful organizational tools for you to take advantage of. Experiment with the site window by trying the following on your own.

Saving files into a site

1   Create site assets, such as a .jpg or .gif, in Illustrator or Photoshop and save them into the alumni_news.site web-content folder.

2   Return to the Files tab in GoLive and use the Refresh button (🔁) from the Main toolbar if the items are not automatically listed.

3   Open a page and drag one of your new images onto the page. Choose File > Save and Choose Root or Root folder to save the page in the web-content folder of the site.

4   Using the Files tab, create a new folder and drag the image you placed into the folder.

More on sites

The Site Features in GoLive are so powerful that they are covered in several lessons. In this lesson you learned how to create and organize your site. The site tools will be referenced throughout the lessons as they relate to each topic. When you are ready, you can read about taking your site to the publishing stage in Lesson 12, "Managing and Publishing Web Sites."

Review

▶ **Review questions**

1   Explain some of the benefits of working in a GoLive site.

2   When would you create a New Blank Site in GoLive?

3   You relocate an asset, such as an image, into a new folder and want all pages referencing the image except one to update the reference, how do you control which links are updated?

4   What does the Fetch URL button do?

5   How do you change which items appear in your site Navigation View?

▶ **Review answers**

1   There are many benefits of working in a GoLive site, including:

- A GoLive site window helps to keep site assets organized and accessible by the creator. New Folders can be created as well as renamed in the site window.

- If you are relocating assets within the GoLive site window, changes are tracked automatically and updated automatically using the Change Links window.

- The site window keeps the site free of unused files. The Used column in the site window shows which assets are being used. No dot in this column means that the asset is not referenced.

- GoLive tracks which references are being used by utilizing the In & Out Link palette.

- GoLive helps the designer to use consistent colors. GoLive provides the ability to create a Site Color list in the Color tab of the site window.

2   A GoLive Blank site would be created if you have no existing index page. You can import other assets such as existing pages and images into the blank site once it is created.

3   Control what pages update references by unchecking the pages you do not want updated in the Move Files alert window.

4   Use the Fetch URL button to click and drag directly to assets listed in your site window. This creates a link from the selected object to the assets you indicated.

5   With the site Navigation View forward, choose Window > View. Select the Filter tab of the View palette and uncheck the items you do not wish to see.

GoLive provides extensive control over the placement and sizing of graphics and text. In this lesson you'll learn how to use GoLive to create pages that look great.

3 | Creating Page Layouts in GoLive

In this lesson you will discover how to create HTML page layouts using a variety of GoLive methods, including the new GoLive CS2 layout grid, HTML tables, CSS (Cascading Style Sheets) layers, and liquid layouts.

In this lesson, you will learn how to do the following:

- Use the layout grid as a style sheet object.
- Use the layout grid as a table object.
- Use traditional tables for page layout.
- Use the Table palette.
- Span rows and columns.
- Create and save table styles.
- Import and export table data.

The Layout Editor in the document window provides the work area on which you create layouts for your page. GoLive layout grids, tables, layers, and new CSS liquid layouts provide the containers for holding and positioning text, images, animations, and movies.

Layout grid-based designs

GoLive CSS-based or table-based layout grids enable you to create designs by freely positioning objects anywhere on the page. You can convert a CSS-based layout grid to a table-based layout grid. You can also convert a table-based layout grid to an HTML table.

Table-based designs

All Web browsers can display HTML tables, so they are often used for page layouts. You can position images, text, and other objects on the page by placing them in table cells. You can create custom tables using the Table Object in GoLive, or convert the layout grid to a table-based object.

CSS-based designs

You can take advantage of the new CSS-based layout grid or use the new CSS layout objects that allow you to create liquid layouts. These are layouts that resize to accommodate the viewer's screen settings. Liquid layouts offer designers and viewers more flexibility than table-based designs. In GoLive, you can instantly create a liquid layout by simply dragging a CSS layout object from the CSS tab of the Objects palette to a page.

What is the difference between CSS and traditional HTML tables?

By creating objects on your page using either tables or CSS, you can accurately control size and placement of your text and objects on a Web page.

Tables, on the other hand, can contain more source code to achieve the same basic layout, and don't offer as many options. Also, keep in mind that there are issues regarding the use of tables and accessibility. According to the W3C's (World Wide Web Consortium) CSS Techniques for Web Content Accessibility Guidelines, it is recommended that CSS-based layouts be used instead of HTML tables for page layout.

In this lesson you will learn both CSS and HTML table methods, as some older browsers may not support CSS-based technology.

Getting started

In this lesson, you will create a new blank site and add provided images to the site window. You will then use the new Layout Grid object to create a page layout.

GoLive layout grids make it easy to create CSS-based and table-based designs for your Web pages. Instead of hand coding CSS or setting up table cells, you can add a single layout grid to the page, draw text boxes or layers, or drag objects anywhere on the grid. GoLive adjusts the properties of the layout grid as you add content and reposition it.

Using layout grids, you can position multiple objects on your page with 1-pixel accuracy.

Before starting, open the finished file to see what you will create using the layout grid.

1   To ensure that the tools and palettes function exactly as described in this lesson, delete or deactivate (by renaming) the Adobe GoLive CS2 preferences file. See "Restoring default preferences" on page 3.

2   Start Adobe GoLive CS2. Close the Welcome Screen if it appears.

3   Choose File > Open.

4   Navigate to the Lesson03 folder, and open the lesson03_site_folder. Select the lesson03.site file and choose Open.

The site window appears.

5   Double-click to open the index.html page.

The index page of this site was created using the Layout Grid object with the Layout Text box. You will create a page similar to this in this lesson. You can leave this page open for reference, or choose File > Close.

6   Click on the site window and choose File > Close. When the Adobe GoLive CS2 alert window appears, click OK; you do want to close the site "lesson03."

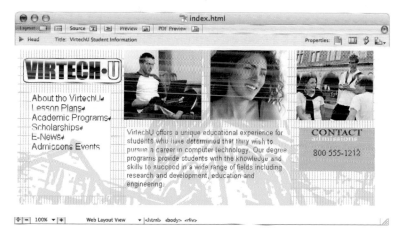

Creating the site

Now you will create your own Web site by following the steps in this lesson.

1   Choose File > New to open the New options window.

2   Choose Site > Create Site and select Blank Site. Click Next.

3   In the Specifying a Site Name and Location window, type **student** in the Name text field.

4   Choose the Browse button beneath the "Save To" text field and locate the Lesson03 folder. Click OK (Windows) or Choose (Mac OS), then click Next.

5   The "Use a Version Control System?" window appears. Choose "Don't Use Version Control." Click Next. Read about Version Cue in Lesson 13, "Using Version Cue and Adobe Bridge with GoLive CS2."

6   In the "Publish Server Options" window, choose "Specify Server Later." Click Finish.

7   Keep the site window open.

Using the CSS-based layout grid

1   Double-click on the index.html page to open the blank document.

2   Start this page by assigning a proper title. Select the text, Untitled Page to the right of Title: in the top portion of your document window. Replace the text with **VirtechU Student Information**. Press Enter.

3   If the Objects palette is not visible, choose Window > Objects, or use the keyboard shortcut Ctrl+2 (Windows) or Command+2 (Mac OS). Click on the Palette options button in the lower right to verify that the Basic objects are visible.

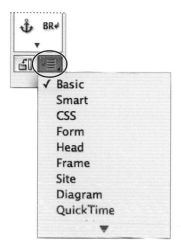

4   Select the Layout Grid object (▦) and drag and drop it to the open index page. The Layout Grid object falls into place in the upper left-hand corner.

5   If the Layout Grid Inspector is not visible, choose Window > Inspector or use the keyboard shortcut Ctrl+1 (Windows) or Command+1 (Mac OS).

6   Type **675** in the Width text field and **400** in the Height text field. Press Enter. If necessary, expand the document window to show the entire layout grid.

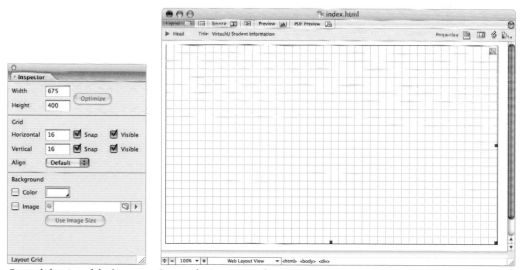

Control the size of the layout grid using the Layout Grid Inspector.

Adding images to the layout grid

Now you will import images to your GoLive site and place them on the layout grid.

1   Click on the Select window button (🖼.) in the Main toolbar to bring the student.site window forward.

2   Make sure the Files tab is forward. Choose File > Import > Files to Site. Browse to locate the Lesson03 folder. Open the folder named lesson03_images. Select the first listed image in the window and Shift+click the last item to select all the images in this folder. You can also use Ctrl+A (Windows) or Command+A (Mac OS). Click Open (Windows) or Choose (Mac OS).

The eight images are added to your site window.

3   Position the student.site window so that you can see part of the index.html page. Select image_1 and Shift+click on image_2 and image_3 in the Files. Click and drag the three image files directly to the layout grid on the page. Exact positioning at this point is unnecessary.

Note: If the images overlap, they may appear red. The red error alert will disappear after the images are repositioned.

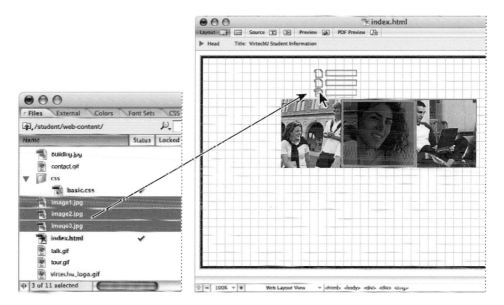

4   Click on the Select window button in the Main toolbar to bring the index.html page forward.

5 Using the Object Selection tool (↖), click and drag to separate the three images. Also, drag the images down, as you will be aligning them above their current location. Arrange the images so that image_1 (student on laptop) is the leftmost image, image_2 (female student) is the center, and image_3 (group of students) is the rightmost image. Again, exact positioning is not important at this point.

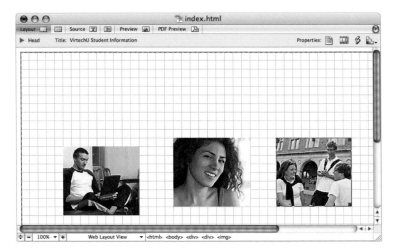

Note: If you do not know which image each object is referencing, select the image and read the Source text field in the Basic tab of the Image Inspector. The Inspector should be left open at all times; if you do not see it, choose Window > Inspector.

You will now use the rulers and grid to guide the placement of your images.

Aligning objects on the layout grid

Using the layout grid, you can precisely position objects on the grid as well as take advantage of align and distribute features.

1 Choose View > Show Rulers, or use the keyboard shortcut Ctrl+R (Windows) or Command+R (Mac OS) to show rulers on the left and top side of your document window.

2   Using the Standard Editing tool (⬧), click and drag any one of the three images; note the light guide lines that appear in the ruler. Also, notice that as you drag, the object snaps to the grid lines in the layout grid.

Note: Image objects on a layout grid cannot overlap, so there may be some restrictions as you click and drag.

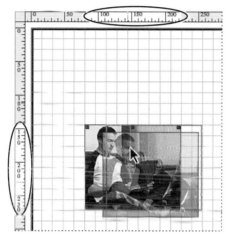

*Use the ruler guides and grid to help
reposition objects on the layout grid.*

3   Still using the Standard Editing tool, click on the layout grid. The Inspector changes to a Layout Grid Inspector. Under the Grid section, change the Horizontal Grid to **5**. The grid lines running horizontally are now closer together. You can also control the visibility and snap of the grids in the Inspector. For this example you will leave them checked.

4   Using the Standard Editing tool, select image_1 (student on laptop). Click and drag the image to the top of the layout grid. Using the Horizontal ruler, click and drag the image object until you see the white guide space start at approximately the 200 pixel mark.

Use rulers to position the image.

5   Now select image_3 (group of students) and position it at the top of the layout grid and at approximately the 525 pixel mark on the horizontal ruler.

6   You will use image_1 and image_3 to set the boundary of all three images when you use GoLive's distribute feature. Image_2 can be positioned below, but should be between image_1 and image_3.

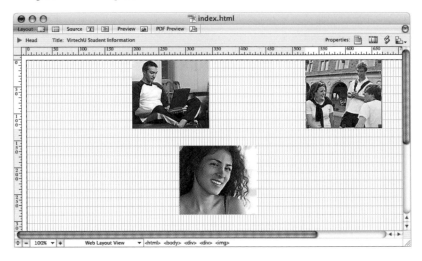

7   Still using the Standard Editing tool, Shift+click on any unselected images; all three images should be selected.

8   Select Window > Align. The Align palette appears. This palette can be used to align and distribute selected objects on the layout grid.

9   In the Distribute Objects section of the Align palette, choose Horiz. align centers (Windows) or Horiz. distribute center (Mac OS). Then choose Align tops (⬚) from the Align Objects section. If one or both of these choices are grayed out, the items are already aligned and/or distributed evenly.

Using the Align palette.   *Result. The objects are now aligned and distributed.*

10 Click the Close button on the Align palette.

11 Choose File > Save.

Using the target insertion point

GoLive provides a target insertion point to make it easier to place objects precisely on a layout grid. You will use this feature to place the VirtechU logo on the page.

1 Using the Object Selection tool (↖), click on the layout grid one grid line from the top left and two grid lines in from the left. A blinking target insertion point appears.

2 In the Basic section of the Objects palette, double-click on the Image object (🖼). It is placed precisely where the blinking target insertion point appeared.

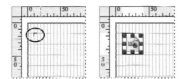

Click on the grid to insert a target insertion point. Double-click on the Image object.

3 With the Image Object still selected, choose the Browse button (📁) to the right of the Source text field in the Inspector palette. Navigate to the student folder created in your Lesson03 folder when the student.site was created. Open the student folder and the web-content folder. Select the image named virtechu_logo.gif and click Open.

The VirtechU logo is placed in the page.

4 Choose File > Save; leave the file open for the next part of this lesson.

Using the layout text box

Next you will place text on the layout grid using the Layout Text Box object.

1   Select the Layout Text Box object (▭) in the Basic section of the Objects palette.

💡 *If you need to pull the Objects palette forward, use the toggle keyboard shortcut, Ctrl+2 (Windows) or Command+2 (Mac OS). This hides or shows the Objects palette.*

2   Click and drag the Layout Text Box object to the area beneath the VirtechU logo.

3   Using the Set position text fields in the Main toolbar, enter the value of **25** in the Horizontal Position text field and **80** in the Vertical Position text field. Press Enter.

4   Using the Standard Editing tool (I⭢), use the handles to click and drag the right middle handle to expand the text box to 150 px wide. Then use the bottom middle handle to expand the height of the box to 192 px high. Use the pixel values displayed in the text box for more accuracy. You can also use the Set width/height text fields in the Main toolbar.

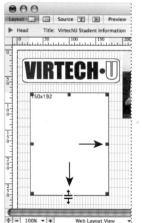

Pixel values in the empty text box.

Pixel values in the Set width/height text fields.

5   The text that is to go into this layout text box is saved as a .txt file. Choose File > Open and navigate to the Lesson03 folder. Select the file named student.txt and choose Open.

6   Click and drag to select the text above the dotted line. Choose Edit > Copy.

7   Click and hold down on the arrow to the right of the Select window button on the Main toolbar, and select index.html.

Note: When you click and hold down on the Select Window, you can choose to bring any open document forward.

8   Using the Standard Editing tool (ɪ⁎), click in the text box. A blinking text insertion point appears. Choose Edit > Paste. The text is now in the text box.

You will now create a larger text area in the center of the page.

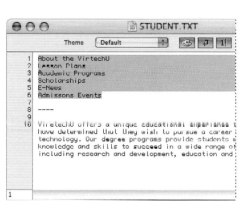
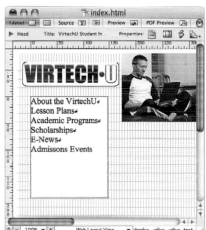

Select the text.   Paste into Layout Text Box.

9   Click and drag another Layout Text Box object onto the page, anywhere under the image_1 (student on laptop).

10   Using the top middle handle, expand the new text box to start one grid line under the images. Then use the handles to expand the text box to start at the same grid line as image_1 and end on the right side of image_2. Notice the guide lines that appear as you drag the handles to help you resize and position the text box more accurately. Using the handles, make the width and height approximately 310 pixels wide x 128 pixels high.

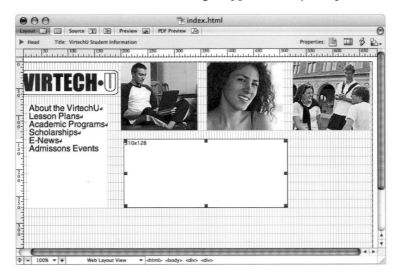

11   Click and hold down on the arrow to the right of the Select window button (⊞.) on the Main toolbar and select student.txt. The text file is brought forward.

12   Select the text underneath the dashed line and choose Edit > Copy, then choose Window > index.html to return to the index.html page. Using the bottom of the Window menu is another method for selecting which document is forward.

13   Using the Standard Editing tool, click in the large text box to insert the cursor. Then choose Edit > Paste.

14   Return to the student.txt file and choose File > Close.

Assigning font sets and color

In this section you will use traditional HTML coding to assign a font set and color to your text in the text boxes. Text attributes can also be changed using Cascading Style Sheets. Read more about Cascading Style Sheets in Lesson 5, "Adding and Formatting Text."

1   Using the Standard Editing tool (ɪ↖), click in the text box on the left side of your page. Choose Edit > Select All, or use the keyboard shortcut Ctrl+A (Windows) or Command+A (Mac OS) to select all the text.

2   Choose Type > Font > Helvetica Set. The text is changed to a sans serif typeface.

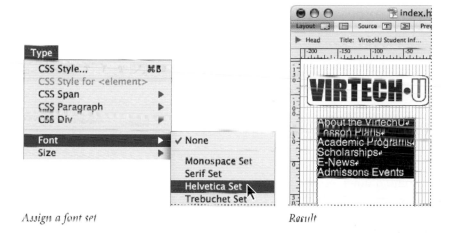

Assign a font set   *Result*

Now you will change the text in the text box in the center of the page.

3   Still using the Standard Editing tool, click inside the text box in the center of the page.

4   Choose Edit > Select All.

5   Choose Type > Font > Helvetica Set.

6 Assign a smaller text size by choosing 2 from the Set font size drop-down menu on the Main toolbar. Read more about text formatting in Lesson 5, "Adding and Formatting Text."

7 With the text still selected, change the text color by double-clicking on the Set text color box (⬜) in the Main toolbar. When the Color Picker window appears, type the hexadecimal value of **555555** (dark gray) in the hexadecimal color text field, then press the Tab key. Click OK.

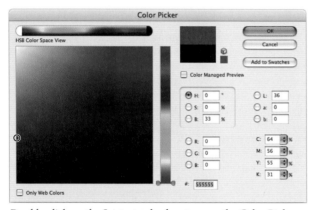

Double-click on the Set text color box to open the Color Picker.

8 Choose File > Save. Leave the page open.

Changing the background of a layout grid

In this part of the lesson you will add a background image to the layout grid.

1 Using the Standard Editing tool (⯅), click on a blank area of the layout grid.

2 If the Layout Grid Inspector is not visible, choose Window > Inspector. Check the box to the left of Image in the Background section of the Layout Grid Inspector.

3   Using the Browse button (📁) to the right of the Image text field in the Inspector, locate the image named building.jpg in the web-content folder of your site.

The image is added as a background.

Changing the background color of layout text boxes

Now you will change the background color of the individual Layout Text Box objects.

1   If the Objects palette is not forward, choose Window > Objects. The Basics section should still be visible.

2   Select the Layout Text box object and drag it from the Objects palette to the right side of the large text box, underneath image_3.

You can reposition the Layout Text box object manually by crossing the edge of the text box; when a hand appears (👆), click and drag.

In this example, you will use the positioning tools on the Main toolbar.

3   Using the Set Position text fields in the Main toolbar, enter the value of **530** in the Horizontal Position text field and **144** in the Vertical Position field. GoLive will not allow you to input numbers that cause overlap of elements on the grid. If you cannot use the numbers in bold, use the closest value possible.

4   Using the Set width/height text fields in the toolbar, enter **144** in the Width text field and **80** in the Height text field. Press the Return or Enter key.

Enter values in the Set Position and Set width/ height text fields.   *Result.*

5   With the Layout Text Box still selected, double-click the box to the right of Color in the Inspector. The Color Picker window opens.

Note: *If the first click brings your Color palette forward and blocks the Color Picker from appearing, drag the Inspector to a location clear of any other palettes.*

6   Enter the hexadecimal value of **cccc99** in the hexadecimal text field, to the right of the # sign. Press Tab, then click OK.

7   Choose File > Save. Keep the file open.

Adding an image to a layout text box

Next you will change the default alignment of the layout text box and add an image and text.

1   Using the Standard Editing tool ( ), click to insert the cursor in the new colored text box. Click on the Align Center button ( ) in the Main toolbar.

2   With the cursor still in the layout text box, double-click on the Image Object in the Basic section of the Objects palette. An Image object appears where the cursor was located.

You will use the Fetch URL button ( ), sometimes referred to as the pick whip, to link to an image. The Fetch URL button is located to the left of the Source text field in the Image Inspector.

3   Click and hold on the Fetch URL button. Do not release, but drag the directional line up to the Select window button (.) in the Main toolbar or directly to the site window. The site window comes forward. Do not release—drag the directional line over to the Files tab and release when the image contact.gif is highlighted. The image is placed inside the Layout Text Box.

4   Using the Standard Editing tool, click to the right of the image you just placed, staying inside the same layout text box. A blinking cursor appears. Press the Return key to create a new line. Type **800 555-1212**.

As a final step you will optimize the layout grid. Optimizing a grid automatically reduces the size of the grid to its minimum size, fitting around the outer borders of all the objects.

5   Using the Object Selection tool (⬉), click on a blank area of the layout grid, then press the Optimize button on the Layout Grid Inspector.

Use the Optimize button to minimize the size of the layout grid.

💡 *You can Shift+click the Optimize button to reduce the width only and Alt+click (Windows) or Option+click (Mac OS) the Optimize button to reduce the height only.*

6   Choose File > Save. Leave the index page and student.site open for the rest of this lesson.

You are finished with the layout of this page; now you will learn how to take advantage of GoLive's table features.

Converting a layout grid to a table

Up until this section, you have used the default CSS-based layout grid. In this section you will convert your CSS layout grid to a table-based layout grid.

1   With the index.html file open, choose File > Save As. Type **table_grid** for the file name.

2   Click on the Site Folder button (🗀) at the bottom of the Save As window and choose Root (Windows) or Root folder (Mac OS) from the drop-down menu. This directs you to the web-content folder of the student.site. Press Save.

Now you will convert this page version to a table-based layout grid.

3   Using the Standard Editing tool (ɪ⬉), click on a blank area of the layout grid.

4   Right-click (Windows) or Ctrl+click (Mac OS) to show the contextual menu, choose Convert to Table based Grid.

You may not initially notice a difference in your file, but if you were to click on the Source tab of the document window you would see that the code creating this page is now table-based. Also, in the Layout view, the icon in the upper right corner of the layout grid changes from a CSS icon (▦) to a table icon (▤). This icon is behind image_3, so you will not see it unless you extend the grid to the right.

If you have switched to the Source view, choose the Layout tab to return to the working page view.

Converting a layout grid to a traditional HTML table

You will now take this layout grid one step further toward looking more like a traditional HTML table.

1   Using the Object Selection tool (▶), click on a blank area of your layout grid.

2   Choose Special > Convert > Layout Grid to Table.

3   When the Convert window appears, leave at the defaults and click OK.

The layout grid is now replaced with a traditional table. Rows and columns are automatically created based upon placement of your text and images.

The layout grid when converted to a traditional HTML table.

Note: *Your results may be different depending upon how objects align on your page. To achieve the best results, align as many objects with each other before converting to a table. If you need to fix your file, choose Edit > Undo, align your objects and try converting again.*

4 Choose File > Save, then File > Close. Keep your student.site window open for the rest of this lesson.

Using HTML tables for page layout

Now you will discover how to use HTML tables. Tables are useful for organizing large amounts of data, and can be used for traditional layouts.

First you will open an existing page to see the final Web page.

1 Choose File > Open.

2 Browse to the Lesson03 folder, and select the table_finish.html page. Select Open.

A page created with an HTML table appears. Notice the page layout was created by a number of cells organized in rows and columns.

A page created with a table.

3 You can leave this page open for reference, or choose File > Close.

4 Make sure that you still have your student.site window open from earlier in this lesson. If you do not, choose File > Open Recent and select student.site, or choose File > Open > Lesson03 > student.site.

Placing a table on your page

To start the next page, you will open an existing page on which to build your table.

1   Choose File > Open. Select the file named table_start.html in the Lesson03 folder and click Open.

2   Choose File > Save As. Type **table1** for the file name.

3   Click on the Site Folder button (📁) at the bottom of the Save As window and choose Root (Windows) or Root folder (Mac OS) from the drop-down menu. This directs you to the web-content folder of the student.site. Press Save.

4   Make sure the Objects palette is open and the Basic Objects are visible. If the Objects palette is not visible, choose Window > Objects.

5   Select the Table Object (▦) and drag it to the page. A default table appears on your page and the Inspector is now a Table Inspector. The Table tab of the Inspector should be forward.

6   In the Table Inspector, change the Rows text field to **4** and the Columns text field to **2**.

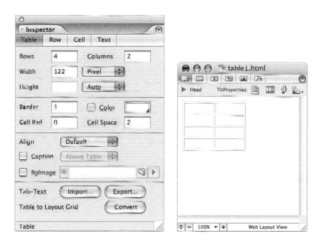

7   In the Table Inspector, select the Width drop-down menu and select Pixel. Enter **600** into the Width text field. In the Height drop-down menu leave the height at Auto. Press Enter.

💡 *Always set the number of rows and columns before setting the table size. Otherwise you will get unexpected results.*

What makes a table?

Tables are made of many parts, including borders, rows, columns, and other features that can create a unique appearance to each table.

Refer to the illustration below as you progress through this lesson.

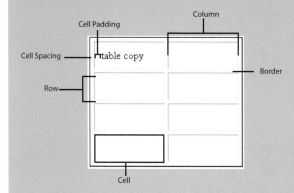

Note: Cell Spacing affects the size of the border.

Adjusting cell size

As a default, table cells are set to automatically adjust as you add content or text to the individual cells. To fix the size, you will assign a pixel dimension to all the cells at one time. The dimensions can be changed later.

1   Using the Standard Editing tool (I⬉), click inside the top left cell. The blinking cursor appears.

2   Ctrl+Enter (Windows and Mac OS) to select the top left cell, not the text area inside. The cell becomes highlighted with a dark border.

3   Select the Cell tab of the Table Inspector and select the Width drop-down menu; change it from Auto to Pixel. Then type in the value of **145**.

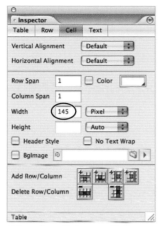

Select the cell. Enter cell size.

4   Using the Standard Editing tool, click in the top right cell. Choose Special > Table > Select Cell to select the cell.

5   In the Cell tab of the Table Inspector, change the Width drop-down menu from Auto to Pixel, then type the value **441**.

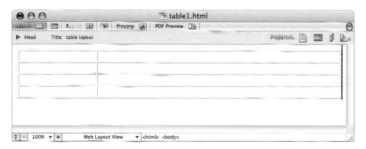

6   Choose File > Save.

Spanning rows and columns

At this point your table is in the standard grid pattern of a table. In this section you will find out how to span rows and columns to create larger areas that expand over several rows or columns.

Before you span rows and columns on your page, you will open a practice file.

1   Leave the file table1.html open and choose File > Open. Open the file named table_practice in the Lesson03 folder.

A page with a simple table appears.

You will now discover how to use the Table & Boxes palette to easily select cells.

2   Insert your cursor into any cell, then choose Window > Table & Boxes. The Table & Boxes palette appears. Make sure you are on the Select tab.

The Select Tab of the Tables & Boxes palette provides you with a frame, or outline, of the table. You can use this outline to select cells, rows, and columns. You can also use the Select parent table button (▦) in the lower left to zoom into and out of tables within tables. This button is grayed out since there are no tables placed inside of this table.

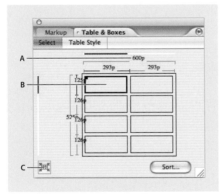

A. Pixel value. B. Selected cell.
C. Select parent table button.

Note: *The Select tab of the Table & Boxes palette lets you review the size and units of every row and column within a table, as well as those of the entire table. This tab also lets you identify and quickly fix conflicts in your column, row, and table sizes. These conflicts can occur when the dimensions of content within a table exceed the table properties, or when the table properties do not add up properly. To fix a conflict, click on any pixel values shown highlighted in red.*

3   In the Table & Boxes palette, click on the top left cell to select that cell.

Practice by clicking on other cells. You can Shift+click to select multiple cells using this palette.

Note: By positioning the cursor on the outer edge of a row (side) or column (top), you can select an entire row or column. Just click when the cursor changes into an arrow.

If you selected other cells, select only the upper left cell.

4   Locate the Table Inspector. Choose the Cell tab and type **2** in the Row Span text field.

The cell now spans two rows.

5   With the same cell still selected, type **2** in the Column Span text field, press Return or Enter. The cell is now expanded to the size of four cells.

6   Type **1** in both the Row Span and Column Span text fields to bring the cell back to its original size. Press Enter.

Next you will use keyboard shortcuts to span rows and columns.

7   Using the Table & Boxes palette, select the upper left cell again.

8   Hold down the Shift key and press the right arrow key (→). The cell is spanned to two columns.

9   Now select the right cell in the second row.

10 Press Shift+Down arrow (↓) to span the row to two rows. Repeat this again to span three rows.

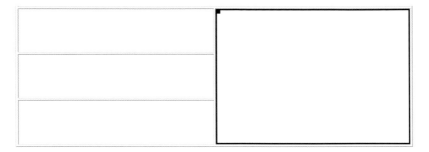

11 Now practice undoing the row and column spans by pressing Shift+Left arrow (←), and then Shift+Up arrow (↑). You can also undo spans by changing the Row Span and Column Span text fields in the Cell tab of the Table Inspector.

12 Choose File > Close and do not save. You will now apply what you practiced on this page to your table_layout.html page.

Note: You cannot expand rows upwards or columns from right to left.

Designing a layout using spans

Now apply column and row spans as part of your layout.

1 Return to the table1.html page and using the Object Selection tool (↖) select the upper left cell. Press Shift+Right Arrow (→) one time. The column now spans the entire table.

2 Now select the right cell in the second row and press Shift+Right Down Arrow (↓) . Repeat this one more time. The cell is now spanned three rows.

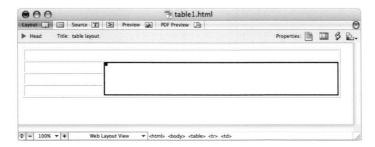

3 Choose File > Save. Leave this file open.

Changing the table attributes

In this section you will add color to some table cells.

1   If your Table & Boxes palette is not open, choose Window > Table & Boxes.

2   In the Select tab of the Table & Boxes palette, click to select the first cell in the second row. Then, Shift+click to select the two cells directly underneath.

3   In the Cell tab of the Table Inspector, click the lower right corner of the Color field and choose the Web Named Colors library from the drop-down menu. Click the corner again, and select the color #A9A9A9 DarkGrey from the swatches displayed above the list of swatch libraries. GoLive displays the swatches from the swatch library you chose.

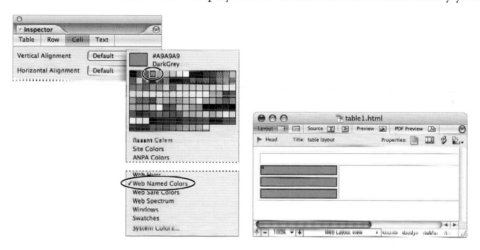

💡 *You can also double-click on the Color box to open the Color Picker in GoLive.*

4   In the Table tab of the Table Inspector, eliminate the border on this table by typing **0** in the Border text field, and pressing Return or Enter.

5   Create some padding by typing **10** the Cell Pad text field. This adds a 10-pixel margin around the interior of all cells.

6   Eliminate the spacing between the cells by typing **0** in the Cell Space text field. Press Return or Enter.

Creating and saving table styles

Make it easy to recreate tables by saving table attributes such as: Border, Color, Cell Pad, and Cell Space, Vertical Alignment, Horizontal Alignment, and Color.

1   If not visible, choose Window > Table & Boxes. If not already selected, click the Table Style tab.

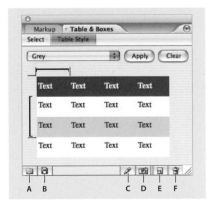

*A. Import Table Style. **B**. Export Table Style.*
*C. Rename Table Style. **D**. Grab Table Style.*
*E. New Table Style. **F**. Delete Table Style.*

2   Make sure the table is selected by inserting the cursor in any cell. Then, click on the word <table> in the line of source code that appears in the document bar at the bottom of the screen. This is a hierarchical display of your source code, and is yet another way of selecting a table in GoLive.

3   Click on the New table style button (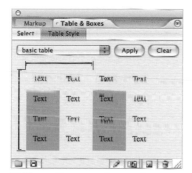) in the Table Style tab of the Table & Boxes palette. Type in **basic table** in the New Table Style dialog window and click OK.

The table attributes are captured and a preview is visible in the Table Styles tab.

Table attributes can be saved
as a table style.

Later in this lesson you will apply an existing style to a table.

Importing text into a table

Typing directly into table cells is relatively simple. You type data directly into a cell and then press Tab to position the text cursor in the next cell and so on. A more efficient way to add text is to import a .txt (text) file directly into a table. In this part of the lesson, you will import data into a new table and then apply an existing table style.

1   Using the Standard Editing tool (↖), click in the large cell in the right side of the table. The blinking insertion point appears in the cell. This is the cell that spans three rows.

2   Double-click on the Table object (▦) in the Objects palette. The table is inserted into the cell.

3   Using the Table Inspector, change the rows value to **3**, if it's not already.

Note: When text is imported into a table, rows and columns are automatically added if needed.

4   Using the Standard Editing tool, click on the upper left cell in the new table.

5   Click on <td>, furthest to the right, in the source code hierarchy in the document bar at the bottom of the page.

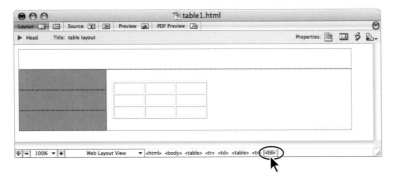

6   Choose Special > Table > Import Tab-delimited text. When the Open dialog window appears, browse to locate the Lesson03 folder and choose the text file named tour.txt. Select Open.

The text is automatically input into appropriate rows and columns. The default setting is that each tab stop is automatically read as a new column, and each paragraph return is read as a new row.

Tour the Campus		
May	20-21	9 am - 4 pm
June	17-18	4 pm - 9 pm
July	7-8	2 pm - 7 pm
August	20-21	9 am - 4 pm
Registration is required.		

You can change this default in the CoL Separator drop-down menu in the Open dialog window as you import the text. Other choices are Comma, Space, and Semicolon.

Note: You can also export text from a GoLive table by selecting Special > Export > Tab-Delimited Text.

7   Position your cursor over the right border of the table. When you see the double arrow icon (◄▮►) click and drag to make the table wider. A specific size is not necessary, just adjust the table to be larger and allow a better fit for the text.

 Hold down the Alt (Windows) or Option (Mac OS) key when adjusting individual rows and columns in a table to get independent control over width and height.

8   Insert the cursor into the cell containing the text "Tour the Campus," then choose Special > Table > Select Cell.

9   Press Shift+Right arrow twice, to span the column. Span the bottom left cell containing the text "Registration is required" using the same method.

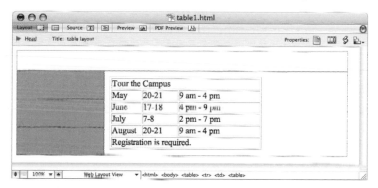

10   Choose File > Save and leave the file open for the next part of this lesson.

Applying a table style

You will now apply a table style to your new table.

1   Select the top cell of the table.

2   If the Table & Boxes palette is not visible, choose Window > Table & Boxes.

3 From the Style drop-down menu, choose Blue. Then click Apply.

The Blue table style is applied to the cells of the table.

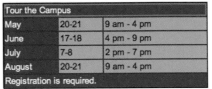

Note: While you can apply a Style to an entire table, you can also select portions of a table to apply a style to.

You can resize the blue bracket so that it marks the desired rows or columns to contain repeating styles. To resize a blue bracket, drag either end of it. The resizable area of the bracket is marked by blue lines at both ends of the bracket.

Placing text and images in the table

Now that you have a table, you will add images to the layout.

1 Using the Standard Editing tool (I↖), click in the upper left cell of the large table. This is the table created to form the layout of the Web page. The blinking insertion point appears in the cell.

2 Double-click on the Image Object (⊞) located in the Basic section of the Objects palette. The Image Object appears where the insertion point was located.

3 If the Inspector palette is not visible, choose Window > Inspector or use the shortcut Ctrl+1 (Windows)/Command+1 (Mac OS). Using the Basic tab of Image Inspector, click on the Browse button (▣). When the Open dialog window appears, locate the image named virtechu_logo in the web-content folder inside the student folder you created when the site was created. Click Open.

The Image object is replaced with the VirtechU logo.

4 Using the Standard Editing tool, click on the VirtechU logo and choose Middle from the Alignment drop-down menu in the Basic tab of the Image Inspector.

5 Using the Standard Editing tool (ɪ↖), click after the VirtechU logo to insert the type cursor. Press the spacebar once and type **The place to learn technical skills**.

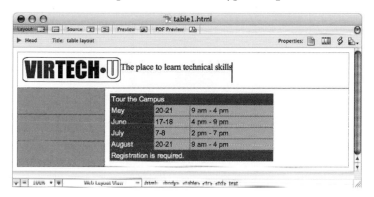

Applying a Cascading Style Sheet to the cell

1 Select the cell containing the VirtechU logo and headline text.

2 If you do not see the CSS palette, choose Window > CSS to display the CSS palette. It may be docked below the Inspector. There are two class styles already created in this document. For more information about creating a CSS class style, see Lesson 5, "Adding and Formatting Text."

Since you have a cell selected, it gives you only one option: to apply the style to the entire cell. In the source code, a table cell is represented by the tag <td>, which stands for table data.

3 Check the <td> checkbox to the right of headline. The text in the cell is now changed to represent the attributes assigned to the headline class style. You may have to undock the CSS palette in order to see the checkbox.

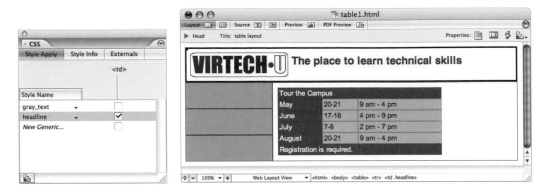

Completing the table

In this next section you will add the remaining imagery and text to complete this page.

1 Position the site window so that you can see the list of files at the same time as your page. Then drag image_1.jpg from the site window to the second cell down on the left.

2 Drag image_2.jpg into third cell down on the left.

3 Drag image_3.jpg into last cell down on the left.

4 Choose File > Open. When the Open dialog window appears, browse to locate and select the file named student.txt in the Lesson03 folder. Click Open.

5   Select all the text under the dashed line on the text document and choose Edit > Copy. Choose File > Close to close the document.

6   Return to the table1.html file. Using the Standard Editing tool (⬈), click to the right of your "Tour the Campus" table, a large cursor appears. Press Return.

7   Choose Edit > Paste. The copy appears under the table.

8   With the cursor still blinking, press Ctrl+Enter (Windows and Mac OS). This selects the table cell.

9   If the CSS palette is not already open, choose Window > CSS, and the CSS palette appears.

10   Check the <td> checkbox to the right of the class style named "gray_text." The text changes to the style attributes assigned to the gray_text class style.

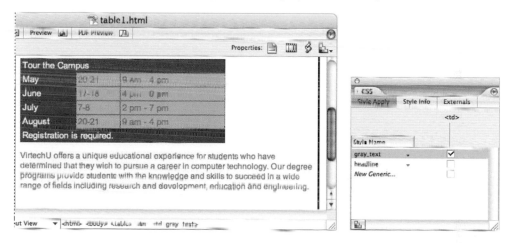

11   With the cell still selected, choose the Cell tab of the Table Inspector. Choose Top from the Vertical Alignment drop-down menu.

You can also assign class styles to a table cell using your contextual menu. With the table cell selected, right-click (Windows) or Ctrl+click (Mac OS).

You have completed the section of the lesson that pertains to layouts using tables. Read on to see how you can use Cascading Style Sheets for layout.

12   Choose File > Save, and then File > Close.

Using layers

You can use layers to divide your page into rectangles that can be formatted and positioned individually, much as you can with a traditional page layout application like Adobe InDesign. Layers can contain any HTML element that a page can contain, such as an image or simple HTML text with formatting. You use the Layer tool and the Layers palette to add and manage multiple layers on the page.

Note: Viewers may not be able to see CSS layout objects if their browser doesn't support CSS, the browser's CSS support has been turned off, or the browser is set to override page styles with a CSS file supplied by the viewer. Web browser support for CSS varies greatly between browser vendors and browser versions.

Adding layers to an HTML page

For this document you will create a layout similar to the table lesson, but use layers.

Make sure that the student.site window is still open. If it is not, choose File > Open Recent Items and locate the student.site file, or choose File > Open and browse to locate the saved student.site file in Lesson03 > student folder.

1 Choose File > Open. Browse to locate the file named layout_finish.html in the Lesson03 folder. Press Open. The finished layer file appears.

This is the page you will create using layers. You will learn how to create, name, and arrange stacking order of the layers along with other layer features.

2   Choose to leave this file open as a reference, or choose File > Close.

3   Choose File > Open and browse to locate the file named layout_start.html in the Lesson03 folder. The start page appears.

4   Choose File > Save As. Keep the name the same and click on the Site Folder (🗀.) and select Root (Windows) or Root folder (Mac Os). Click Save.

5   Begin this page by selecting the Layer object (🔲) from the Basic section of the Objects palette.

6   Click and drag the Layer object to the layer_start.html page.
A layer appears in the upper left of the page.

7   If the Inspector is not visible, choose Window > Inspector. While the layer is selected, the Inspector is a Layer Inspector.

> 💡 *If you need to reselect the layer, cross the cursor over any side of the layer; when the hand icon (✋) appears, click.*

8   Change the name from layer1 to **logo** in the Name text field; press Return. This will help you identify the layer later.

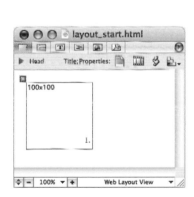

9 Drag the right center handle to the right to make the layer approximately 600 pixels wide. As you drag, observe the value in the Width text field in the Main toolbar. You can also type the value of **600** into the Width text field. Type **62** in the Height text field.

Use the Main toolbar for accurate layer coordinates and size controls.

*A. Horizontal Position. **B.** Vertical Position. **C.** Width. **D.** Height.*

Inserting objects into the layer

Now you will insert an image and text into the layer.

1 Using the Standard Editing tool (⟨↖⟩), click to insert the blinking cursor inside the layer.

2 Double-click on the Image Object in the Basic section of the Objects palette. The image Object appears in the layer.

3 Using the Image inspector, click on the Browse button (▣) to the right of (EmptyReference!) When the Open dialog window appears, navigate to locate the image file named virtechu_logo.gif in the web-content folder of the student folder inside of Lesson03. Choose Open. The logo appears inside the layer.

4 Using the Standard Editing tool, click once on the VirtechU logo image. Use the Alignment drop-down menu in the Basic tab of the Image Inspector to change the alignment to Middle. Alignment determines the position of the text that follows the image.

5 Click to the right of the logo; a large blinking cursor appears. Press the spacebar once and type **The place to learn technical skills**.

6 Position the cursor over the edge of the layer. When the hand icon (⬬) appears, click to select the layer.

Just as with table cells, you can apply a class style to the contents of a layer.

7   Choose Type > CSS Style for <div> select headline. The text is changed to red.

You can use the Select tab of the Table & Boxes palette to navigate in CSS layout objects. Click the Select Parent Table tool (▦) to select the parent CSS layout object, or click in a row or column of a CSS layout object in the tab to place an insertion point.

Aligning and distributing layers

In this next section, you will add the imagery in three separate layers which you will then align and distribute.

1   Click and drag a Layer object from the Basic section of the Objects palette to your HTML page. Make sure that you do not drag the new layer into the existing layer.

Note: You can tell if you have dragged one layer into another by referencing the yellow layer marker (▣). If the marker is not loose in the upper left corner, it is probably nested inside an existing layer. You can choose to Edit > Undo, or drag the marker out of the layer to an open area of your page.

2   Reposition the new layer by positioning the cursor over the edge of the layer. When a hand icon (☜) appears, click and drag to move the layer beneath the logo layer. Use the grid that appears to align the left sides of the two layers. Type **100** in the Vertical Position text field of the Main toolbar.

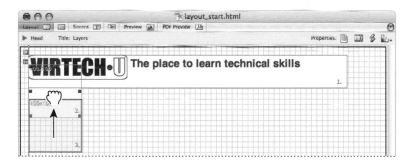

3   Select Edit > Duplicate to duplicate this layer and put a copy directly on top of the existing layer.

4   Choose Edit > Duplicate again. This will provide you with three layers, all positioned on top of one another.

You can also clone a layer by dragging and holding down the Ctrl (Windows) or Option (Mac OS) key.

5   Using the Object Selection tool (▸), click on the topmost layer and drag it to the right of the page. Then select the next layer and position it in between the left and right layer. Exact positioning is not important.

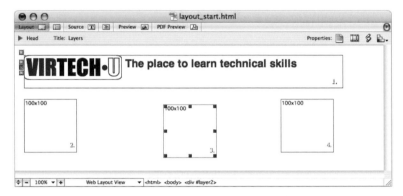

Note: *Grid rules appear as you drag layers to help you with alignment. You can use these as an aid, or use the Align palette as directed in the next part of this lesson. If you prefer not to see the grid, choose Window > Layout and select Layout Grid Settings from the Layer's palette menu. Uncheck "Visible when Dragging," click OK.*

6   Using the Object Selection tool, select the left layer and type **laptop** in the Name text field of the Layer Inspector.

7   Select the center layer. Type **female** into the Name text field in the Layer inspector.

8   Select the right layer. Type **group** into the Name text field.

9   Using the Object Selection tool, select the first layer, now named laptop. Hold down the Shift key and click on the layer named female and the last layer named group. All three layers are selected.

You can also select multiple layers by selecting the Object Selection tool and dragging a marquee around the layers you wish to select.

10 Choose Window > Align. The Align palette becomes visible. Select Horiz. align centers (Windows) or Horiz. distribute center (Mac OS) from the Distribute Objects section of the Align palette. Then select the Align Tops button under Align Objects.

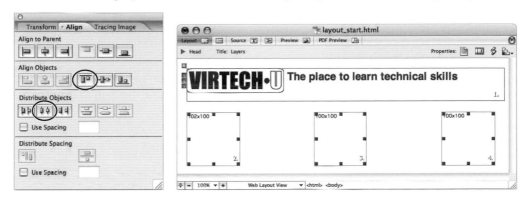

Note: If any of the options are grayed out, the item is already aligned, or distributed evenly.

11 Choose File > Save. Leave the file open for the next part of this lesson.

Adding imagery and text

1 Position the student.site window so that you can see it at the same time as the layout_start.html file.

2 Click on image_1.jpg and drag it into the leftmost layer.

3 Drag image_2 into the middle layer.

4 Drag image_3 into the rightmost layer.

You will now add another layer that will be used for text.

5   Make sure that the Basic section of the Objects palette is visible. Select the Layer object () and drag it to an empty spot on your layout_start.html page, making sure that you do not drag the new layer into an existing layer. It is positioned in the upper left of the page.

6   After placing the Layer object, cross your cursor over the side and click when you see the hand icon (✋). This selects the layer. Use the position and size text fields in the Main toolbar for an accurate-sized layer. Enter **18** for the Horizontal Position and **240** for the Vertical Position. Enter **475** in the Width text field and **150** in the Height. Press Enter.

| ┤ 18 | 280 | ┌ 475 | 150 |

7   With the layer still active, type **text** into the Name text field in the Layer tab of the Layer Inspector. Press Enter.

8   Choose File > Open. When the Open dialog window appears, browse to locate the file named student.txt in the Lesson03 folder, and choose Open.

9   Select the paragraph text located under the dashed line and choose Edit > Copy. Then choose File > Close.

10   Return to the layer_start.html file, and using the Standard Editing tool (ι↖), click inside the new text layer you created. Then choose Edit > Paste.

11   Choose Type > CSS DIV select gray_text. The text is changed to gray.

12   Choose File > Save. Leave the file open.

Organizing layers

In this next section you will create a new layer with a colored background. Since layers' default stacking order is such that this layer will cover the existing layers, you will learn how to change the stacking order.

1   Select the Layer object (▣) from the Basic section of the Objects palette and drag it to an empty spot on your layout_start.html page, making sure that you do not drag the new layer into an existing layer. The new layer is positioned in the upper left of the page.

2   After placing the layer object, select it and use the position and size text fields in the Main toolbar. Enter **-5** for the Horizontal Position and **-5** for the Vertical Position. Enter **675** in the Width text field and **150** in the Height. Press Enter.

3   With the layer still active, type **background** into the Name text field in the Layer tab of the Layer Inspector. Press Enter.

4   Click on the Background tab of the Layer Inspector and double-click on the color box. Enter **9F9F9F** into the hexadecimal text field. Press the Tab key and then press OK.

Note: For the Color Picker to appear, you may have to position the Inspector away from your other palettes.

The background of the new layer is now gray.

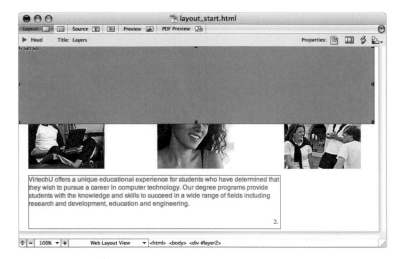

The newly created layer is covering the existing layers. To change this, you need to understand the concept of layer arrangement using Z-index.

Changing the Z-index

1   Choose Window > Layers to make the Layers palette visible.

2   In the Layers palette, select the background layer.

3   With the background layer selected, type **0** in the Z-index text field located in the Layer tab of the Layer Inspector. Press Enter.

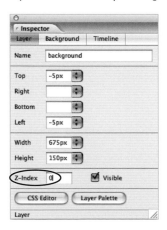

Changing just this layer will not affect where it appears in the stacking order until we also change the other layers' Z-index values. To make selecting the layers easier, you will use the Layers palette.

Using the Layers palette

You can use the Layers palette (Window > Layers) to quickly select multiple layers for alignment and grouping. You can also use the Layers palette to temporarily lock, hide, or show a layer as you work. (Unlike similar settings in the Layer Inspector, lock, hide, and show settings in the Layers palette do not affect the display of layers in the browser.)

Note: *Some settings in the Layers palette are only temporary and will be overridden when you switch document views.*

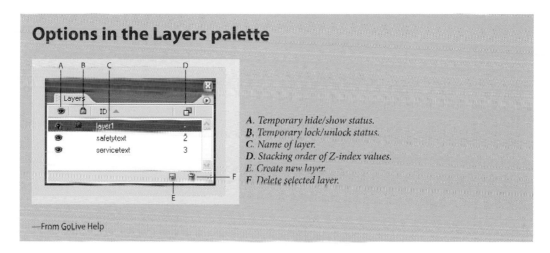

Options in the Layers palette

A. Temporary hide/show status.
B. Temporary lock/unlock status.
C. Name of layer.
D. Stacking order of Z-index values.
E. Create new layer.
F. Delete selected layer.

—From GoLive Help

1   Click on the layer "logo" in the Layers palette. This selects the layer and allows you to make changes in the Layer Inspector. In the Z-index text field, type **5**, then press Return or Enter. This brings the logo layer in front of the background layer.

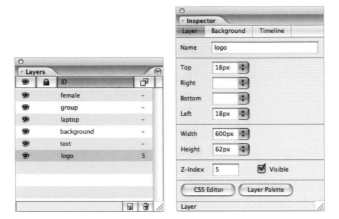

2   Select the layer named laptop and type **5** into the Z-index text field.

3   Individually select the layers female and group, and type **5** into the Z-index field. Press Return or Enter.

With the layers' Z-index assigned to higher numbers, they are now forward of the background layer.

💡 *Experienced programmers use Z-index values that increase by 5. This makes it easier to insert layers where you want them later without having to change all other values.*

4   Choose File > Save and File > Close. Leave the student.site window open for the next part of this lesson.

Liquid layouts

GoLive lets you add a predesigned CSS layout object, based on layers, to a page, and then add text and objects to the layout just as you would in any other page. CSS layout objects are liquid layouts—they adjust to accommodate the viewer's screen settings. You don't need to know how to code CSS to create CSS layout objects, but you can customize them by using the CSS Object Inspector and the CSS Editor.

1   Choose File > Open and double-click on the page named liquid.html located in the Lesson03 folder. A page using liquid layouts appears.

2   Select the Preview tab in GoLive and drag the document window to a larger size, then smaller. Note that the liquid layout feature used to create this page allows the CSS elements to adjust to the size as needed.

3   You can leave this page open for reference or choose File > Close.

Creating a page using liquid layouts

In this next section you will create a simple page using the liquid layout feature.

1   Create a new page by selecting File > New. When the New dialog window appears, choose Web > Pages > HTML Page, then click OK.

2   Choose File > Save As. When the Save As dialog window appears, type the name **liquid_virtechu**. Click on the Site Folder button (,) and select Root Windows) or Root folder (Mac OS), then choose Save.

3   When the Set Title dialog window appears, type the title **liquid layout**, then press Set.

4   Choose the CSS section of the Objects palette and select the Padded Box object (padded); drag and drop it on the page.

5   Now select the Three Columns: Scaling Center object (3col) and drag that into the lower section of the Padded box object already placed on your page.

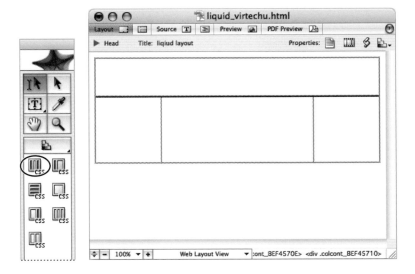

6   Position the liquid_virtechu page so that you can see the Files tab of the student.site.

7   Select virtechu_logo.gif and drag and drop it to the top box in the liquid layout.

8   Click to the right of the VirtechU logo, and then using the Standard Editing tool ( ), select the VirtechU logo. In the Basic tab of Image Inspector, select Left from the Alignment drop-down menu.

9   Click to the right of the VirtechU logo to insert the text cursor. Press the spacebar once and type **Tour the campus this summer**.

10   Choose File > Open. When the Open dialog window appears, browse to locate the text file named student.txt in the Lesson03 folder.

💡 *If you recently opened this file for the previous part of this lesson you will find the student.txt file located in File > Open Recent.*

11   When the student.txt file opens, select the text above the dashed line and choose Edit > Copy. Return to the virtechu_liquid.html page and insert the cursor into the lower left cell and choose Edit > Paste.

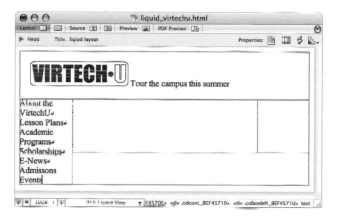

Note: Don't forget that you can easily navigate from one document to another using the file list at the bottom of the Window menu.

12   Return to the student.txt file and select the text beneath the dashed line. Choose Edit > Copy. Return to the virtechu_liquid.html page and insert the cursor into the lower center cell and choose Edit > Paste.

💡 *When referencing frequently used artwork or text, you can choose to save the elements as Snippets, making it easy to retrieve the elements frequently. Read more about Snippets in Lesson 10, "Using Stationeries, Components, Page Templates, and Snippets."*

13   Position the liquid_virtechu page so that you can also see the Files tab of the student.site.

14   Select tour.gif and drag and drop it to the box on the right in the liquid layout.

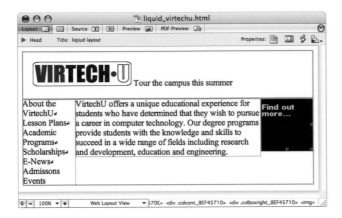

15   Choose File > Save.

16   Choose the Preview tab and drag the document window larger, then smaller to see how the page you created dynamically changes to fit the available space.

Note: If your text doesn't look accurate in the GoLive Layout Preview window, click on the Preview in Browser button (⬛.) on the Main toolbar.

Congratulations! You have finished the lesson.

Exploring on your own

In this section you can open existing files to experiment with additional table and CSS options.

Experimenting with liquid layouts

1   Choose File > Open and open the document named liquid.html.

2   Choose Window > CSS to open the CSS palette.

3   Notice the named CSS elements that are included as part of the liquid layouts on this page. Double-click on .colboxmiddle; the CSS Editor is displayed. Experiment with the various attributes to discover how each box in a liquid layout can be unique and contain many custom attributes.

4   Choose File > Save.

Review

▶ Review questions

1 As a default, what is the underlying code structure of a layout grid?

2 What are three methods for selecting a table cell?

3 What are three attributes that a table style will save?

▶ Review answers

1 Layout grids are based on CSS, but can be easily changed to use standard HTML table code.

2 Select a table cell with any of these three methods:

• Using the Standard Editing tool, click to insert the cursor into a cell. Then Press Ctrl+Enter. Pressing Ctrl+Enter again will select the table that the cell is in.

• Choose Window > Table & Boxes. Use the Select table to activate cells, rows, and columns.

• Using the Standard Editing tool, click to insert the cursor into a cell. Use the Document bar at the bottom of the window and locate the tag <td> in the source code hierarchy.

3 Table styles will save the following:

• In the Table tab of the Table Inspector: Border, Color, Cell Pad, and Cell Space.

• In the Row tab of the Table Inspector: Vertical Alignment, Horizontal Alignment, and Color.

• In the Cell tab of the Table Inspector: Vertical Alignment, Horizontal Alignment, Color, Header Style, and No Text Wrap.

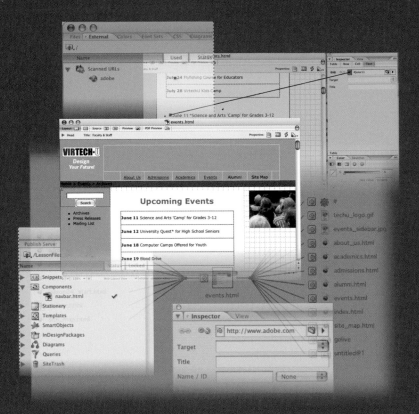

Linking Web pages to each other is the basis of the World Wide Web. GoLive CS2 allows you to easily jump from text or graphics on one page to areas on the same page, to other pages in the site, or to other sites.

4 | Creating Navigational Links

In this overview of creating links on Web pages, you will specifically learn how to do the following:

- Add hypertext links to a page.
- Create and add components.
- Edit links and anchors.
- Add navigational links to graphics on a Web page.
- Add anchors that act as targets for links within a page.
- Verify that a link is working.
- Fix broken links and change link preferences.

If necessary, copy the Lessons/Lesson04/ folder onto your hard drive from the Adobe GoLive CS2 Classroom in a Book CD. For more information, see "Copying the Classroom in a Book files" on page 2.

Getting started

In this lesson, you will be adding links from the main page of a University Web site to other sections of the site. You'll also be adding image maps to a graphic.

1 To ensure that the tools and palettes function as described in this lesson, delete or deactivate the Adobe GoLive CS2 preferences file. See "Restoring default preferences" on page 3.

2 Launch Adobe GoLive CS2; close the Welcome Screen if it appears.

3   Choose File > Open and locate the file lesson04_end.site in the lesson04end folder inside the Lesson04 folder on your hard drive. Click Open and the site window appears.

4   In the site window, double-click on the file named "events.html." The document window containing the HTML file events.html will appear in the center of your screen.

5   Preview the events.html document in your Web browser by clicking on the Preview tab in your document window. Click on the links to see how they work. You can refer to the pages in this site if you need to check your work throughout this lesson. When you are finished, click on the Layout tab.

6   Choose File > Close to close the events.html page and then choose File > Close to close the lesson04_end.site. When the GoLive CS2 alert window appears, click OK.

About links

Based on previous lessons, you should be familiar with the concept of GoLive's site window. The contents of the site window reflect HTML pages, images, and other elements of your Web site. When you create new pages, they are added to the site and you can reference images and objects to their source files using resource links. In this lesson, you will learn how to create a navigational system which allows the user to jump from one page to the next within your site; you will also add links which reference external links such as a search engine. When you add new links to your pages, GoLive will automatically update the site and verify that the link is valid.

Opening the site

Follow these steps to open the Lesson04.site window and begin the lesson. For the purpose of this lesson, the basic navigational structure of the site has been laid out for you, but not all links have been created. You will be adding the remaining links yourself.

1   Choose File > Open and navigate to the Lesson04 folder, then open the lesson04start folder. Choose the Lesson04.site file located in your Lesson04/lesson04start folder and click Open. The site window for lesson04.site appears.

Note: You will see link warning icons that appear as bug icons. These indicate that the pages have broken links. You will repair the links later in this lesson. Disregard them at this time.

As mentioned in Lesson 2, "Creating a GoLive Site," when new sites are created in GoLive, a folder named "web-content" is created. Inside this folder are all the basic HTML, CSS, and image files that are needed to create the site. Currently there are seven files that will make up the structure of the site: about_us.html, academics.html, admissions.html, alumni.html, index.html, and site_map.html. There is also the lesson04_start.html file; however, this file is used only for the purposes of this lesson and is not part of the site.

2   Double-click the lesson04_start.html file in the site window. Choose File > Save as and rename the file **events.html**. If for some reason you need to start the lesson over, you can return to the original start file. Click on the Site Folder ( ) at the bottom of the Save As window and select Root (Windows) or Root folder (Mac OS). Choose Save.

At the top of the page is a navigation bar with the six categories of the site. The first four navigation headings have been linked for you. You will now get some practice by linking the last two.

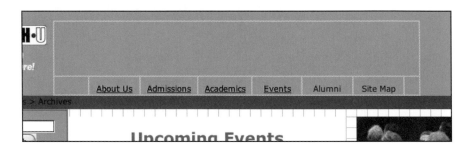

3   Click on the Select window button ( ) at the top of the Main toolbar. This brings the site window to the front. Click on the Select window button ( ) again to return to the index.html file. This button will be useful later when creating hyperlinks.

4   Select your lesson04.site window again and drag it toward the bottom of your screen. Creating links is often faster using the site window and it will help if the window is visible at the bottom of your screen.

Working with a site window can be easier if it is positioned under the document window.

Creating hypertext links

You have been using hyperlinks in the previous chapters, yet now you'll create hypertext links using some of GoLive's automatic site management features.

1   Click on the events.html page to bring it forward. Click once anywhere within the text of the first link "About Us." In the Table Inspector, the Text tab should be selected.

The first field in the Inspector is referred to as the URL field and the current value is about_us.html. Directly to the left of the URL field are two buttons: a Create link button (⊖) and a Remove link button (⊙). Currently both of these are inactive because there is no text selected.

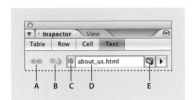

A. *Create Link.* B. *Remove Link.*
C. *Fetch URL.* D. *URL field.*
E. *Browse button.*

2 Click three times quickly on the About Us text to select it. Selecting the entire text now activates the Remove link button in the Inspector palette. The Create link button is inactive because there is already a link in place.

3 Click the Remove link button and the link is removed from the URL field and the About Us text is now just text. You can use the Remove link button to clear the value if needed.

4 Click the Create link button and GoLive displays (EmptyReference!) in the URL text field. The About Us text appears to be a hyperlink, and changes to the color blue with an underline; however, it is a broken link because a user clicking on it would go nowhere. You will now reconnect the About Us text to the about_us.html file using the Fetch URL button in the Inspector palette.

The keyboard shortcut to create a link is Ctrl+L (Windows) or Command+L (Mac OS).

5 Notice the Fetch URL button (⊚) located in the left side of the URL field. Click and drag the Fetch URL button to the site window, the site window comes forward. Dragging to any part of the site window will bring it forward, even if just a small section is visible.

If the site window is completely hidden by the open document, you have two options: you can release the Fetch URL button and move the site window to a better location, or you can click and drag the Fetch URL button to the Select window button in the Main toolbar.

6 Drag the Fetch URL button, and select the about_us.html file in the site window. The text is relinked to the about_us.html file.

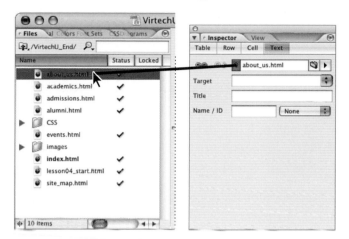

Now you'll create a hypertext link to another file within the site by using the Inspector's Browse button to locate a file.

7 Select the text "Alumni." In the URL field of the Inspector palette, click on the Browse button (📁) and the Open window appears. Navigate through your hard drive and locate the alumni.html file in Lesson04/lesson04start/web-content/ and click Open. This method is useful if you are more comfortable with the standard navigation of your computer's operating system.

Another way to create a link is to enter the file's pathname in the URL field of the inspector.

8 Select the "Site Map" text. In the URL field, type **site_map.html** and press Enter or Return to commit the change.

Note: If typing a URL, use ".../" to instruct a browser to go up one folder level, or "/" following a folder name to look into named folder for a reference, for example images/ events_sidebar.

All three methods of entering the link destination are valid. All three create links with a relative path, which means that the site folder name is implied. GoLive is aware of the site folder when it creates links. An absolute URL includes the complete pathname of a file, including the site folder name.

9 Choose File > Save to save the events.html file.

10 To preview the links that you just created, click the Preview in Browser button (⬛ ▾) on the Main toolbar, and then click a link to test it. If you've correctly connected each link, the page it's linked to will appear. If not, the browser will display an error message. Use the Back button in your browser to return to the events.html page. When you are finished testing the links, exit or quit your browser.

Note: If you haven't set up a preview browser, you will see a warning message. Choose Edit to add a browser. See Lesson 1, "Getting to Know the Work Area" for more information about previewing Web pages.

About absolute link paths

Site pages contain paths to a variety of linked files: other pages in the site, images displayed on the page, media items embedded in the page, and so on. GoLive automatically uses relative paths—paths that point to the location of a file in relation to the current file—for the destinations of links. In most cases, relative paths are appropriate to use. But, if necessary for special cases, you can selectively change the paths to make them absolute, or set a preference to have GoLive make all new paths you create absolute by default. When you make a path absolute, the entire path from the root folder to the linked file is provided. Otherwise only a relative path is provided.

For example, the page /root/pages/info/page.html (where root is the name of the root folder) references the image /root/images/image.gif. The absolute path to the image file is /images/image.gif. The relative path is ../../images/image.gif.

Absolute paths are useful in the following cases:

If a form references a CGI script at the root level of the site directory (or any other subdirectory), any references to that file are usually written as absolute.

If a common navigation bar is used on many pages that reside in folders at various hierarchical levels, you can use an absolute path specification throughout to reference its image files, allowing you to copy and paste the same code snippet onto all the pages.

However, absolute paths work only at sites where there is a Web server providing information about the location of the site's root folder. For the same reason, using absolute paths prevents you from previewing pages in a Web browser on your local computer—that is, a previewing browser has no way of locating this root folder.

Note: An absolute path in GoLive is not a full path from the file system root or a fully qualified URL.

—From GoLive Help

To create a null link, one that appears as a link, but does not link the viewer to any particular page, or produce an error message, replace EmptyReference! with the # sign. This can be helpful when setting up a page whose links have yet to be determined.

Adding links to a graphic

You can add a link to an image fairly easily using the Inspector palette. Users who click on the image will be sent to the link destination. You'll now link the VirtechU logo to the home page.

1   Open the events.html file if necessary. Click on the VirtechU logo in the upper left corner to select it.

2   In the Inspector palette, click on the Link tab to switch to the Link section of the Image Inspector.

3   Click on the Fetch URL button and drag it to the site window. Choose the index.html file and release the mouse. Users clicking on the logo will now be sent to the home page.

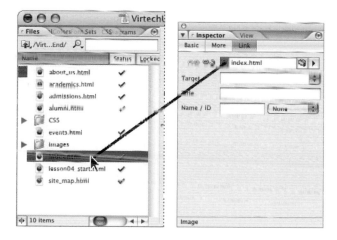

Note: Be sure not to set the source link in the Basic tab of the Inspector. The Basic tab looks similar to the Link tab; however, changing the source link tells GoLive to link the graphic to the index.html page, which will replace the image with a broken link. You can choose Edit > Undo to fix the broken link and try again.

4   If desired, click on the Preview in Browser button to open the events.html page in a browser. Clicking on the logo will send you to the home page. Close your browser and return to GoLive.

5   Choose File > Save and then File > Close to close the events.html file.

Using components

Using one of the hyperlink methods from the last exercise is the easiest way to create hyperlinks in your document. However, one consequence is that if you have multiple pages in your site, you would have to link the text navigation bar on every page. For example, if you had only ten pages in your site and each page had a navigation bar with 6 hyperlinks you would be creating 60 hyperlinks! This isn't particularly difficult, but it is time-consuming. Luckily, GoLive has a feature called "components" which can make this process much easier. You are introduced to components in this lesson, but you can learn more in Lesson 10, "Using Stationeries, Components, Page Templates, and Snippets."

A component is an element in your Web site which is shared between two or more pages. Once a component is added to your site, making a change to the single component will "ripple" through your site and the change will take effect on every page where the component has been added. In this exercise you will open a page which has a component added, and then you will add the component to other pages in the site.

1   Click on the site window to bring it to the front. Double-click on the about_us.html page in the site window to open it. Note that this file has the same navigation as the events page; the last two navigation elements, Alumni and Site Map, are not linked.

2   Try to click on one of the hyperlinks in the navigation bar and note that you cannot; this is because the navigation bar is part of a component.

You can determine that an object on a page is based on a component in two ways: The component will have a small green symbol in the top-left corner (⊘), and the elements within the component cannot be selected directly; they must be modified from within the source component file.

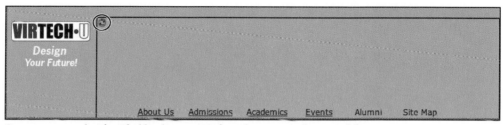

Components can be identified by the green circle with arrows in the upper left corner.

3   Double-click anywhere within the navigation bar and a separate file will open, called navbar.html. This file is the component and is nothing more than a single HTML page which includes a table with the navigation. The first four links in the component have been linked. You will now link the remaining text to their respective pages in order to see how a component works.

4   Highlight the Alumni text and then click and drag the Fetch URL button from the URL field of the Inspector palette to the site window. Choose the alumni.html file and release the mouse to create the link.

5   Repeat the last step again but select the site map text and link it to the site_map.html file.

6   When you are done, choose File > Save and an Updating Component window appears, click OK. Click OK to the second Updating Component window. Close navbar.html.

7   Click on the about_us.html page to make sure it is forward, then choose File > Save and File > Close.

8   Click on the about_us.html file in the site window. The navigation has been updated based on the changes you made to the component. You will now see what happens when you add more components to your site.

Adding components to a page

As you have seen, this component is nothing more than an HTML file with a table (although it could be any element you choose, such as a graphic). Components are created by placing a file into the components section of your Site. You will create a component from scratch, but first you will add the existing component navbar.html to other pages.

1   Open your site window by clicking on the Select window button (🗒.) in your Main toolbar. On the right-hand side of your site window, click on the Extras tab to display the various folders of extras on your site.

2   If necessary, click on the plus sign (Windows) or arrow (Mac OS) to the left of the Components folder to reveal the navbar.html file within.

The navbar.html file is stored in the Component folder.

3   In the left side of the lesson04.site window, double-click the admissions.html page to open it. This page has a blank header to which you'll be adding the navbar component.

4   Click on the site window and drag it down toward the bottom of the screen so you can see the admissions.html page behind it. Then click and drag the navbar.html document from the Components folder into the top header, next to the VirtechU logo and release. This adds the component to the admissions page.

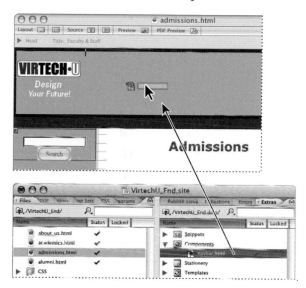

5   Double-click on the navigation bar in the admissions.html page and the navbar.html file will open. Click in front of the Events text and type **News &** so the text reads "News & Events."

6   Choose File > Save and you are now asked to update the components on the about_us and site_map pages. When you make changes to, and save, a component, if one or more of the pages with the component is not currently open, you will be asked if you want to update them. You can choose not to update specific pages if desired, but in this lesson choose to update the files. Click OK.

7   When the update is complete, click OK again. The changes you made to the text have been automatically saved. Using components in this manner can save much of your time.

8   Choose File > Save and File > Close for both the navbar.html and the admissions.html files.

Creating a component

Creating a component from scratch is very easy. It's a matter of making a new page with the element you would like to reuse throughout your site and then placing it into your Components folder.

In this exercise you will be making a copyright footer to be placed at the bottom of your pages.

1   Choose File > New > Web > Pages > HTML Page and click OK, to create a blank page. Click and drag a Table object (▦) from the Basic set in your Objects palette to the page.

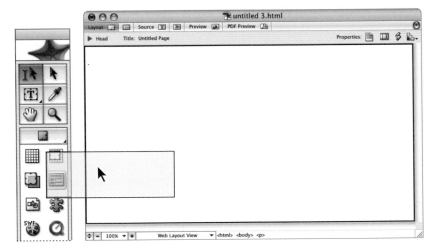

2   In the Table Inspector palette, change both the Rows and Columns to **1** and the width to **450 pixels**. Set the border to **0**. Press Enter.

3   Click inside the table and type **Copyright 2005 – VirtechU – All rights reserved**.

4   Choose File > Save. Click on Site Folder button (▢,) at the bottom of the Save As window and select Components. This part is crucial to making the component. If a file is not saved into the Components folder then it will not work as a component. Change the file name to **copyright2005.html** and click Save.

A Set Title window appears. Because you did not change the default title, GoLive offers to change it. Click on the checkbox Set title to document name and click Set. You now have an HTML file named copyright2005.html in your components folder.

5   Close the copyright2005.html file and return to your site window by clicking on it. You should see the copyright2005 file in the right side of your site window. You will now add this component to a page.

6   Double-click on the alumni.html page in your site window to open it. Scroll down to the bottom of the page. You will be placing the copyright component into the footer.

7   Click on the site window and rearrange the window, if necessary, so that you can see the alumni.html page. Click and drag the copyright2005.html component from the Extras tab into the footer to add it.

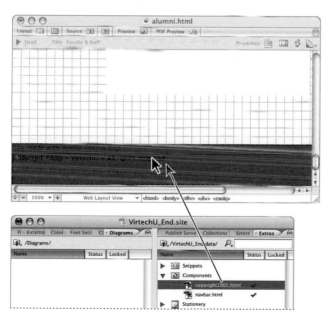

Adding this component to each page in your site would allow you to control the date of the copyright from one single file.

8   Click on the alumni.html page to make sure it is forward, then choose File > Save and File > Close.

Creating anchors

In this section, you'll create a link from an item in a list of events to a paragraph on the same page. Anchors allow you to place a "target" on a section of a page and to link directly to this target even if it's at the bottom of the page. A user who clicks on a link which points to an anchor will "jump" directly to the anchor. Anchors are especially useful for long pages of text which would normally cause a user to have to scroll down to locate the text. In this exercise you will create anchors to various university events. First you will create the anchors solely within the events page, then you will create a link on the home page, which links to an anchor on the events page.

You'll start by adding a link to the list of events to the paragraphs below.

1   Open the site window, if not currently open, and double-click on the events.html file to open it. This file features a list of upcoming events in a table. Below the table are the extended descriptions of the events. Scroll down the page to see the entire text, and then scroll back to the top.

2   Scroll down to the first event description on June 11. In the Objects palette menu, choose Basic Objects if not currently selected. Drag the anchor object (⚓) from the Objects palette to the first line of the paragraph; as you move your cursor over the line you'll see a short, vertical, black line appear. Place your cursor right before the June 11 text and release to add an anchor.

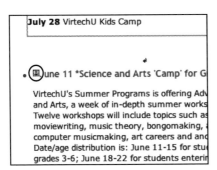

3   In the Anchor Inspector palette, rename the default name of the anchor to **June11** and then press Enter or Return to commit the change. Adding descriptive names to anchors helps you to update and identify broken links.

4 Scroll back to the top of the page and highlight the text "Science and Arts 'Camp' for Grades 3-12" in the first cell. Scroll back down the page until you can see the anchor icon.

5 In the Inspector palette, click and drag the Fetch URL button from the link tab to the anchor you added in step 2. This creates a link between the first event in the list and the first paragraph.

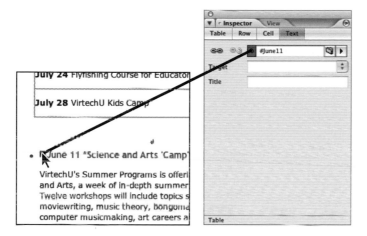

Note: In the URL field of the Inspector palette, the name of the anchor (June11) is now visible as "#June11." Anchors are always preceded by the # sign to distinguish them from standard links.

It is helpful to the viewer if you provide a link back to the top of a page. You will now add some text, and then create a link and an anchor to allow the user to return to the events list.

6 Click at the end of the paragraph of the June 11 event and type **Back to top**. Click and drag over this text to select it.

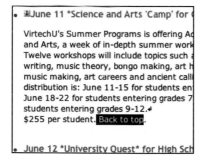

7 With the Back to top text selected, hold down Alt (Windows) or Command (Mac OS) and drag from the selected text up to the top of the screen. This keyboard shortcut creates a temporary Fetch URL button with a line extending from your start point. Move your cursor to the top of your document window to scroll through your document. Place your cursor to the left of the June 11 event at the top of the screen and release your mouse button to add an anchor.

Upcoming Events

June 11	Science and Arts 'Camp' for Grades 3-12
June 12	University Quest* for High School Seniors
June 18	Computer Camps Offered for Youth
June 19	Blood Drive
June 21	Unpluggable comedy troupe

Your document window will jump back to the start point and the Back to Top text is now linked. The Inspector palette will display a unique anchor ID generated by GoLive.

Note: You can use the Inspector to change GoLive-generated ID names to something more appropriate.

8 Choose File > Save to save your document. You will now test your anchors to make sure they work.

Testing anchors

You can test links in general, and anchors in particular, by using GoLive's Layout Preview or in a browser. The first time you add an anchor to a page, it's generally a good idea to test both.

1 Click on the Preview tab at the top of your document window to enter the Layout Preview mode.

2 Click on the June 11 link to jump down the page to the event description. Clicking on the Back to Top link jumps you to the top of the page.

3   Click on the Preview in Browser button (⊡.) in the upper right corner of the Main toolbar. Click on the same text to test the anchors. Anchors may function slightly different in a browser than in the Layout mode.

4   When you have finished previewing, exit or quit your browser. Then click the Layout tab in your document window to return to the Layout view.

5   Choose File > Close for the events.html file.

Using anchors within a site

Anchors are often used on a single page to make navigation easier; however, they are also very useful to direct users to a specific part of a page from another section of a site. You will now link text from the home page of your site to the June 11 anchor you created earlier.

1   In the lesson04.site window, and double-click on the index.html file.
In the left-hand column is text advertising the upcoming June 11th event.

2   Highlight the text "Click for more" to select it. You will now link this text to the events page.

3   In the URL field of the Inspector palette, click on the black arrow to open a menu of recently used hyperlinks and other categories of links used within the current site.

4   Click on the Anchor section of the menu and choose events.html#June11. This tells GoLive to link to the anchor named June11 on the events.html page.

5   Save your document and click on the Preview in Browser button in the upper right corner of your Main toolbar to open your Web browser. Click on the Click for More link to jump to the anchor on the events page. Close your Web browser and return to GoLive.

6   Choose File > Close to close the index.html file.

Note: Keep in mind that the size of your monitor determines how much of the page is shown at one time. Users with a large monitor may not see the jump to the anchor because the entire page is located within the browser window.

Using anchors for links

Don't place anchors directly on a layout grid. Instead, place anchors in the flow of HTML text, a layout text box, or a table cell. When you add an anchor to a layout text box or table cell, make sure that the box or cell has other contents. Otherwise, the anchor will not be recognized by Netscape Navigator. To work around this problem, you can add a nonbreaking space to the empty box or cell. To add a nonbreaking space, click inside the box or cell, and press Shift+spacebar (Windows) or Option+spacebar (Mac OS).

Place anchors near the left margin of the page, so that the anchors work more consistently across browsers.

Test links to anchors extensively in browsers before publishing your Web site. Anchors don't always work the same way in all browsers.

Note: You won't be able to preview certain link and anchor combinations in Layout Preview.

—From GoLive Help

Once you create an anchor on a page, a plus sign (Windows) or arrow (Mac OS) appears to the left of the page name in the Files tab of the site window. Click to reveal anchors created on the page. Some users find it easier to select an object and Alt+drag (Windows) or Command+drag (Mac OS) the Fetch URL button to the named anchor in the site window.

Creating external links

You have been creating links that refer to your site, but what if you want to link to another Web site? These are called external links or an external URL. An external URL references a page outside your file system—that is, a page with an address that begins with http://, ftp://, or so on, and must include a colon, for example, http://www.adobe. com. External links can easily be added into the URL field of the Inspector palette, but GoLive has a separate method which offers more power and flexibility if an external file is used many times within a site. In this exercise you will use both methods.

1   Double-click on the events.html page in the lesson04.site window to open it. Scroll down to the bottom of the page until you see the footer which reads "Site made with Adobe GoLive CS2."

2   Highlight the text "Adobe GoLive CS2" to select it. In the URL field of the Inspector palette, type **www.adobe.com** and then press Enter. GoLive recognizes this as a Web address and automatically enters the complete address.

3   Select the Preview tab. Scroll to the bottom of the screen and click on the Adobe GoLive CS2 link. If you are connected to the Internet and you typed the address correctly, you will go to the home page of the Adobe site.

4   Click on the Layout tab.

5   Choose File > Save, then File > Close to close the events.html file.

Creating external links with the External tab

Entering external links on a one-off basis into the Inspector palette is perfectly acceptable; however, oftentimes you will be using the same URL many times throughout a site. Storing your external URLs in the External tab of your site window allows you reuse your links and removes the possibility of error when typing long URLs into the Inspector. Additionally, if you need to update an external URL, you can do so automatically in the External tab.

1   Click on the External tab of the lesson04.site window. You will now scan your site for external URLs.

2 Choose Site > Update > Add Used > External Links and GoLive scans the current site for external URLs. Because you added http://www.adobe.com in the last exercise, it is collected in the External tab.

💡 *You can also right-click or Ctrl+click (Mac OS) inside the External tab of the site window to open a context menu that will allow you to scan your site.*

3 If necessary, click on the site window to bring it forward. Click on the Files tab and double-click on the index.html page to open it.

4 Scroll to the bottom of the page and highlight the Adobe GoLive CS2 text to select it. In the Text Inspector, click on the Fetch URL button. Click and drag the Fetch URL button to the External tab in the site window.

Note: *If the site window is not visible, click and drag to the Select window button (🖼️) at the top of the Main toolbar. When the site window comes forward, continue dragging to the External tab.*

5 Drag your cursor over the "adobe" URL and release to link it to the text.

Adding links in this fashion allows you to quickly add external URLs to your site. Now you will update the link to see how GoLive automatically refreshes the URLs.

6   In the External tab of the site window, click on the adobe URL and then click on the Edit button in the External Inspector. The Edit URL window opens. In the path field, change the text to the following URL: **http://www.adobe.com/golive** and then press OK. A Change Link window appears to inform you that the URL you are changing will be updated on the following pages: index.html and events.html. Click OK to commit the change.

Adding external links in this fashion can simplify much of the work that would otherwise have to be done by hand.

7   Make sure the index.html window is forward. Choose File > Save, and File > Close to close the index.html file.

Scan your Web site to make sure all external links are accurate by selecting the External tab of your site window and selecting Site > Check External Links.

Creating e-mail links

Now you'll add a link to the Events page that will allow users to click on a link and automatically open a mail program with the recipient's e-mail address. Similar to the way external links are stored, it is a good idea to keep e-mail addresses in the External tab.

In this exercise you will add e-mail addresses using the Address object from the Site set.

1   If necessary, select the External tab in the site window.

2   Choose Site from the Objects palette menu. Drag the Address button (▨) to the External tab of the lesson04.site window. The name field is active, allowing you to enter a name. Type **Events E-mail** and press Enter to commit the change.

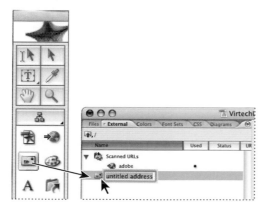

You can also right-click (Windows) or Ctrl+click (Mac OS) in the External tab and select New Address from the contextual menu.

3   In the External Inspector, the new name is reflected in the Name field. Change the default URL from mailto:untitled@1 to another e-mail address. If you wish, you can use your own e-mail—or type **info@virtechu.com**. When you press Enter or Return to confirm the address, mailto: is automatically added, making this a valid link to an e-mail address.

4   Choose the Files tab of the lesson04.site window and double-click on the Events page to open it.

5   Click on the External tab of the lesson04.site window to make your external links visible.

6   Return to the events.html page and select the text "Mailing List" in the left-hand column.

7   In the Text Inspector, click and drag the Fetch URL button from the URL field to the site window. If the site window is not visible, drag the Fetch URL button to the Select window button at the top of the Main toolbar to bring the site window forward choose the Events Mailing List link. The text is now linked.

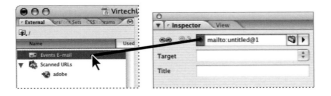

8   If you wish, click the Preview in Browser button on the Main toolbar to view your page in a browser. Click the e-mail link to launch an e-mail application. Based on your computer's system configuration, you may need to change the helper application to determine which e-mail program is used.

It is not necessary to add an address to the External tab first. You can also select text, or an object, and type an e-mail address directly into the Link tab of the Inspector. When you press Enter or Return "mailto:" is automatically added.

Changing a link's color

The traditional colors for links on the Web have long been blue for unvisited links and purple for links which the user has already visited. These are the default colors for hyperlinks in GoLive CS2, but they can be changed if needed. You may want to consider leaving the defaults in place unless there is a compelling reason to change the color; most users are used to the default blue and purple. You may want to change the hyperlink colors if they conflict with the color scheme of your site.

1 Open the events.html page if necessary, make sure the Layout tab is selected and click the Show page properties button (📄) in the upper right corner of the document window. The Page Inspector reflects the Page properties.

2 Double-click on the color swatch next to the Link section of the Inspector palette to open the Color Picker. You will be learning more about the Color Picker in Chapter 6, "Working with Color." For now, place your cursor in the horizontal color section at the top of the window and click in a bright yellow section. Click the Tab key and then OK to commit the change.

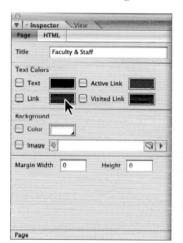
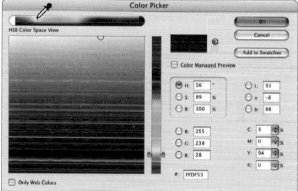

3 Repeat step 2 but double-click on the visited link color swatch instead, and choose a dark green color.

💡 *Make the link color and the visited color the same color if you would like to remove the effect of visited links. Keep in mind, however, that users may be expecting to see a different color for their visited links.*

4   To preview the link colors and how it changes when the link is clicked, click the Preview in Browser button in the Main toolbar. The document appears in your Web browser. Click on a link at the top and then click your browser's Back button. The link you clicked is a different color than the non-visited links.

5   When you've finished testing the links, quit your browser and return to GoLive.

Note: You may have noticed that the colors in the other pages did not change. This is because the styles for the links were determined for the events page only. To change the color of links site-wide would ideally require the use of an External Style Sheet. By changing the element style named "a" to a different color you can effect all links that are on pages linked to the External Style Sheet." Read more about CSS in Lesson 5, "Adding and Formatting Text."

6   In the Inspector palette, deselect the check boxes to the left of the Link and Visited Link text colors. Even though your color selections remain in the color box, the link colors return to their default blue and purple.

7   Choose File > Save and File > Close to close the events.html file.

Changing preferences for link warnings

GoLive signals broken links on pages within your site with link warnings. You can control the appearance of link warnings. The default color for broken links is red. You will now intentionally "break" a link to see how link warnings can be modified.

1   Double-click on the academics.html file in the File tab of the site window. The text About Us is linked to an empty reference at this time. This returns a warning when the Show link warnings button is active.

2   Click on the Show link warnings button (✿) at the top of your Main toolbar and the About Us text is highlighted in red. GoLive identifies links which are broken and allow you to make changes. In this case, the red of the background and the red of the highlight are very similar. You will now change the highlight color to green to make it stand out against the background.

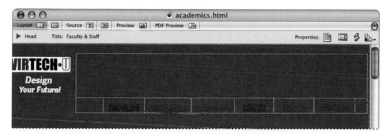

3   Click on the View palette located in the same window as the Inspector palette. Then click on the Highlight tab. This palette allows you to customize the way elements in GoLive appear on screen.

4   Click on the arrow next to the Highlight Colors to open the controls for the Link Warnings. Double-click on the red color swatch next to the Link warnings and the color picker appears. Click in the bright green section of the horizontal color spectrum at the top of the window and click OK. The red link warning is now green.

Link warnings disappear when the text is linked to a valid URL. You will now link the About Us text to its correct file.

5   Click on the Inspector palette to bring it to the front. Highlight the About Us text to select it. Click and drag the Fetch URL button from the URL field in the Inspector palette to the site window. If the site window is not visible, drag the Fetch URL button to the Select window button (▣.) at the top of the Main toolbar.

6   Choose the about us html to link the text to the file. Click again on the academics.html document and note that the link warning is gone.

7   Choose File > Save and File > Close for the academics.html file.

Using the In & Out Links palette

A useful tool in GoLive CS2 is the In & Out Links palette. This feature allows you to identify all the files which are linked to a particular page. You can use the In & Out Links palette with any file or non-file item in the web-content folder—that is, with any file or item listed in the Files, External, Colors, Font Sets, CSS, Extras, Collections, or Errors tabs in the site window.

1   Open the events.html file by double-clicking it in the site window. Choose Window > Site > In & Out Links to open the In & Out Links window.

2   If necessary, click and drag the lower right-hand corner of the In & Out Links window to expand it. You want to be able to see all the documents on the left-hand side of the events.html page (these represent the incoming links, i.e., pages which link to events.html) and all the documents on the right-hand side (these represent the outgoing links, i.e., the pages to which events.html links).

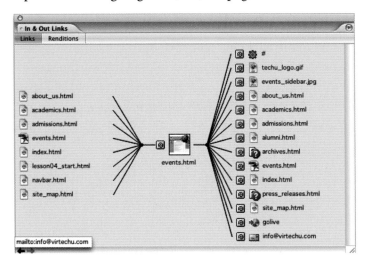

In the outgoing links, the two files, archives.html and press_releases.html are missing, as noted by the question mark symbol. After importing these files into the site window, you will link them.

3   Click on the Files tab of the site window and choose File > Import > Files to Site.

4   Navigate to the Lesson04 folder and open the events_pages folder.

5   Select both files, archives.html and press_releases.html and click Open (Windows) or Choose (Mac OS). The files are added to the Files tab and the errors icons are removed.

Note: If you add files to your site and they are not recognized, click and drag the Fetch URL button next to unreferenced file, in the In & Out Links palette, to the site window . Then point to the file you wish to reference.

6   Test the site by clicking on Preview tab. When finished, close the document. Congratulations! You have finished the lesson.

Note: You can also access all link errors in the site by selecting the Errors tab on the right side of the site window.

Exploring on your own

1   Open the events.html page and add anchors to the remaining events. Make sure you add a "Back to top" link after each event to allow users to jump to the top of the page.

2   Create an anchor anywhere on the events.html page. Open the index.html and add another link in the left-hand column to the new anchor on the events html page.

3   Add a new external and e-mail link to the page of your choice. Be sure you use the External tab.

Review

▶ **Review questions**

1   What is an anchor?

2   Why would you create a link from one page in your site to an anchor on another?

3   What is the difference between a relative and absolute pathname? Why is this difference significant for links?

4   What is a link warning and what can you do when you receive one?

▶ **Review answers**

1   Anchors act as a target for links within the same page. You can create a single link that connects to a single anchor. You can also create several links that point to a single anchor.

2   Anchors allow you to break your page into discrete segments. For example, you may want to link to an item which is located in the middle of a page. Linking to this anchor would make the process of navigation easier for a user.

3   Absolute URLs include the complete pathname of a file, including the site folder name. Relative URLs don't include the full pathname and can refer to a file in a subdirectory from which the file is linked. When you browse for the link destination or enter the URL, you can enter just the relative path (with the site folder name implied). By default, GoLive is aware of the site folder, so you don't need to enter it into the URL.

4   Link warnings alert you to files with broken or invalid links should be correctly referenced before uploading files to a Web server. You can use any of these methods to fix a link warning:

- Use the In & Out Links palette to track and reconnect broken links.

- Click on the Errors tab of the site window. Then use the Fetch URL to link to the file.

- With a page open, select the Show link warnings button on the Main toolbar to highlight errors on a page. Then select the highlighted errors on the page and type a new location in the URL text field of the Inspector or browse to locate the correct file.

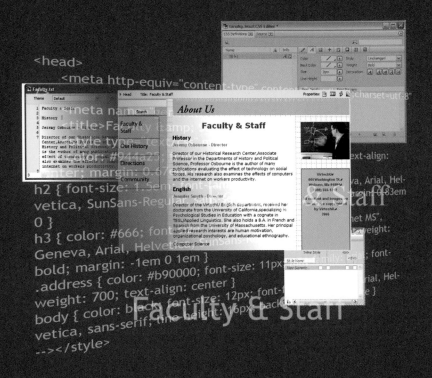

You can use GoLive CS2 to add and edit text in your documents in a variety of methods. Text can also be formatted and colored. Using Cascading Style Sheets allows you to modify text appearance easily and gives you the flexibility needed to experiment with the look of your Web pages.

5 | Adding and Formatting Text

In this overview of using text in GoLive CS2, you'll learn how to do the following:

- Import and enter text into your document.
- Change the color of text.
- Format and stylize text.
- Create numbered and unnumbered lists.
- Style text using CSS.
- Create an Internal Style Sheet.
- Convert an Internal Style Sheet to an External Style Sheet.

Getting started

In this lesson, you will be working on a single HTML file which has already been created for you, and learn how to use the various tools, palettes and windows.

1   To ensure that the tools and palettes function as described in this lesson, delete or deactivate the Adobe GoLive CS2 preferences file. See "Restoring default preferences" on page 3.

2   Launch Adobe GoLive CS2. Close the Welcome Screen if it appears.

3   Choose File > Open. Navigate to the Lesson_05 folder inside the Lesson_05 folder on your hard drive, and open the file named Lesson05.site. Click Open and the site window appears.

4   In the site window, double-click on the file named lesson05_end.html. The document window containing the HTML file "lesson05_end.html" opens on your screen. This document represents the final version of your file; you may keep it open for reference during this lesson, or choose File > Close.

5   In the site window, double-click on the file named lesson05_start.html to open the file.

6   With the lesson05_start.html page forward, choose File > Save As and name the file **faculty.html**. Click on the Site Folder button (🗀,) at the bottom of the Save As window and select Root (Windows) or Root folder (Mac OS). This directs you to the Lesson_05 web-content folder. Click Save.

Importing and working with text

You can type text directly into a text box in GoLive CS2 or you can import a .txt file from a word processor, and copy and paste the text. Once the text is in your document, GoLive provides several ways to format it.

1   Choose File > Open and navigate to the Lesson_05 folder. Select the file faculty.txt and click Open.

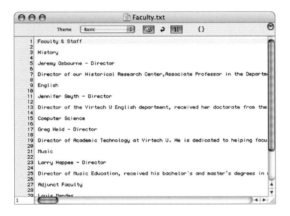

2   Choose Edit > Select All to select the text. Then choose Edit > Copy. You could have also used the keyboard shortcuts Ctrl+A (Windows) or Command+A (Mac OS) to select the text and Ctrl+C (Windows) or Command+C (Mac OS) to copy it. Choose File > Close to close the faculty.txt file.

3   Choose the Standard Editing tool (ᛁᛉ), and click once in the currently empty center layout text box. Choose Edit > Paste or use the keyboard shortcut Ctrl+V (Windows) or Command+V (Mac OS) to paste the text.

Basic formatting in HTML

In this exercise you will learn the fundamentals of formatting your text in HTML. Basics, such as justifying and bolding text, are often easily accomplished in GoLive CS2. Controlling paragraph attributes, such as alignment, are often referred to as paragraph styles, whereas controlling text attributes, such as color or bolding, are referred to as physical styles.

1   Place your cursor anywhere in the first paragraph, Faculty & Staff, and then click on the Align center button (≡) in the Main toolbar. This centers the text within the layout text box. Click on the Align right button (≡) to align it to the far right of the text box. Finally, click on the Align left button (≡) to align the paragraph to its original location.

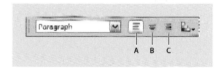

Alignment Controls:
*A. Align left. **B.** Align Center. **C.** Align Right.*

2   Click and drag over the Faculty & Staff paragraph to highlight the text. Then click on the Set Font Size drop-down menu, which is located to the right of the alignment controls. Choose the number 6 from the list and the selected text gets bigger. Font size works on relative scale; a font size of 3 is the default font size. Choosing numbers larger than 3 results in a larger font size, and choosing numbers smaller than 3 results in a smaller font size.

3   Click on the Set Font Size drop-down menu again and choose None from the list to remove the size.

Immediately to the right of the Set Font Size drop-down menu are the Strong, Emphasize, and Teletype buttons.

4   Click on the Strong button (**T**) in the Main toolbar; this renders your text in a bolder style. Click on the Strong button again to remove the formatting.

5 Click on the Emphasis button (_T_) in the Main toolbar; this is the equivalent of italicizing your text. Click on the Emphasis button again to remove the formatting.

6 Choose Type > Style to view the other style options available to you. Experiment with the other styles if you wish, make sure you select the style again to deselect it.

Creating lists from text

GoLive CS2 allows you to create bulleted and numbered lists, which can be useful when you need to visually organize information.

1 Scroll to the bottom of your document and locate the four names at the bottom. Each name is in its own paragraph. Select the four names by clicking and dragging over the names.

2 In the Main toolbar, click the Numbered List button (1) to format the selected names as a numbered list.

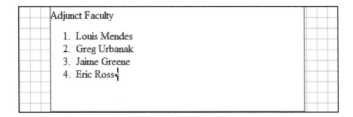

3 Click the Unnumbered List button (•) to convert the names to an unnumbered or bulleted list.

4 Click once after the second name in the list and then click on the Increase List Level button (▸) to increase the indentation of the bullet and the name.

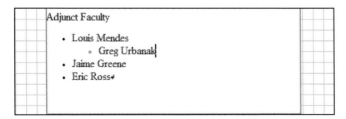

5 Select the entire list and click on the Unnumbered List button again to remove the list formatting.

Setting text color

Easily change your text color in GoLive CS2.

1   Select the headline Adjunct Faculty by clicking and dragging over the text.

2   In the Main toolbar, double-click the Set text color button to open the Color Picker.

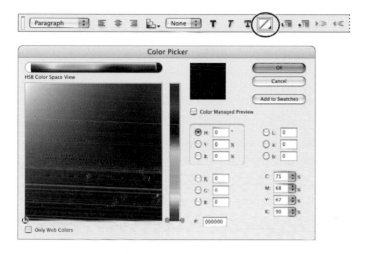

3   Click on a red shade, click the Tab key and then OK to apply the color.

4   Click and hold on the black triangle in the lower right corner of the Set text color button to access the color menu. Choose the first option, Remove Color, to remove the color formatting.

Note: You will be working more with color and the color controls in Chapter 6, "Working with Color."

Using the CSS palette and editor

The paragraph formatting in the last section is useful for quickly styling your text, but there are disadvantages as well. Each time you add a style, such as coloring your text or bolding a word, you are adding tags around the elements that you manually add to each selection. For example, if you wanted to bold a product name on every page in your Web site, you would have to locate it and apply the strong formatting. However, if at some point you choose to remove the bolding, you would have to locate every instance of the formatting and manually remove it, a process which could be quite cumbersome on a large site.

A useful alternative to this process is to use GoLive CS2's CSS Editor to stylize your text. Cascading Style Sheets (CSS) make it easy to update text properties and other attributes throughout a Web site. If a CSS style needs to be updated, you simply edit the style, and all content that uses the style automatically reflects the new properties. With style sheets, you can set text size to display more consistently across different platforms, and control the position of content on a page with pixel-level precision. An External Style Sheet can be shared by an entire site, giving your pages a consistent presence, and enabling you to update the site's styles with a single file.

The GoLive CSS Editor allows you to create CSS styles, edit style properties, and reference or create External Style Sheets. It can also preview how many of the style properties will appear. Sample style sheets are available in the New dialog box.

The CSS palette displays the existing CSS attributes in your document. You will now make sure you can adequately view your CSS palette for this exercise.

Paragraph formatting

You can use CSS to redefine existing HTML tags. In this exercise you will change the Head tags of your paragraphs in order to prepare them for formatting with the CSS Editor.

1 Choose Window > Workspace > Default Workspace to restore your workspace to GoLive's original settings.

2 Click on the arrow to the left of the Color tab to collapse the Color palette. Then click on the arrow to the left of the CSS tab to expand the CSS palette. The Style Apply tab is in the forefront. The Style name lists New Generic. As you add more styles, this window will list the various styles.

Click on the arrows to collapse and expand the palettes.

3 Select the Standard Editing tool and click once at the end of the first line, Faculty & Staff. You will now change the formatting of this paragraph to a Header using the paragraph format menu. Headers are used in HTML to define the level of importance in a heading hierarchy. Browsers display the header text in bold formatting with a default point size. Header 1 is the largest size, and Header 6 is the smallest.

4 In the Main toolbar, click on the Set paragraph format drop-down menu on the far left and choose Heading 1 from the list. Because the Faculty & Staff text is in its own paragraph, it increases to the default Heading 1 format and size.

5 Click once after the word History and change the paragraph format to Heading 2. This makes the paragraph formatting of the second line bold but slightly smaller than the Heading 1.

6 For the paragraph "Jeremy Osbourne—Director," repeat the last step, formatting the paragraph as Heading 3. In the next exercise you will apply CSS styles to the headings.

Using the CSS Editor to redefine markup elements

Markup Elements can be thought of as the tags used in HTML. For example, formatting the first paragraph as a Heading 1 assigned the <h1> tag to the paragraph. The actual source code looks like this: <h1> Faculty & Staff </h1>, where everything inside the opening and closing <h1> tags are assigned this attribute. However, these Heading tags are given default properties when rendered in a browser. CSS allows you to assign different properties to the tags, such as font family, color, point size, line height, and more. This provides designers with more control and flexibility over the appearance of text in their documents.

1 Click once on the CSS Editor button (🖺), located in the bottom left corner of the CSS palette. The CSS Editor window opens.

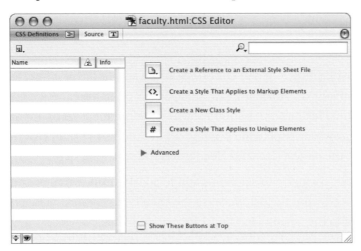

2 If necessary, reposition your CSS Editor window so that the Faculty and Staff heading in your document window is visible. Changes you make in the CSS Editor will be automatically applied to your document. In the CSS Editor, click and hold the button marked Create a Style That Applies to Markup Elements (⌐) to open a list of tags.

3 Select the h1 tag, and the h1 tag appears in the CSS Definitions tab. If the Font
Properties tab (*A*) is not visible, select it now.

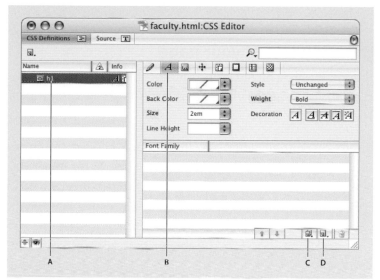

*A. h1 style. **B**. Font Properties. **C**. Create New Font Family. **D**. Create New Font.*

You will now assign a font family to your Heading 1 tag.

4 At the bottom right of the Font Properties tab, click on the Create new font family
button (⬛) to access a list of various font sets. A font set is a list of fonts that the browser
will use to display your Heading 1 text.

5 Choose the Trebuchet set from the menu and a list of fonts appears in the Font
Family window. Click on your document window and, if necessary, scroll through your
page to see the heading with the Trebuchet style applied to it.

Faculty & Staff	**Faculty & Staff**

Heading 1 with no CSS styling. *Heading 1 with CSS styling.*

Note: *The list of fonts in a font set refers to the font order to be used when a user opens the
HTML page in their Web browser. In this example, Trebuchet will be used first to display
the Heading 1; if the user does not have Trebuchet on their machine, then the next font on
the list (Geneva) will be used, then Arial, Helvetica, etc.*

6   Click on the Preview tab to view your page in your default browser. The heading Faculty & Staff is now being rendered in the Trebuchet MS font in your Web browser. Click back on the Layout tab to enter the Layout Editor.

Formatting the body text of your page

Headings are used to emphasize a hierarchy in your documents. However, all of your visible text is also contained within the <body> tag of the html page. You will now format the properties of your body text.

1   If the faculty.html CSS Editor window is no longer open, click on the Open CSS Editor button ( ) in the upper right of the document window. In the upper left corner of the CSS Editor, click and hold the small page icon ( ) located directly below the CSS Definitions tab to open a menu. This menu offers an alternative way to redefine a markup element, as you did in the last exercise.

2   Choose New Style from the menu and select the first option: body.

3   Click on the Create new font family button ( ) at the bottom of the CSS Editor and choose Verdana Set.

4   In the Font Properties tab ( ) in the CSS Editor window, click on the arrow to the right of the Size property. In the menu that appears, choose pixel from the list.

The Size property allows you to define what unit of measurement you would like to use for your fonts.

5 In the size field, type **12**. Press the Tab key to enter the Line Height field; type **16**. Press the Tab key. Line height is defined as the amount of spacing between the baselines of your text; greater values result in more space between lines. This is similar to leading if you are familiar with typesetting terms

Using CSS styles to format your text

In addition to changing the font style and line height of your text, CSS allows you to do much more. Color, margins, and background are all properties of text that can be modified. In this exercise you will first modify the h1 style that you created in a previous exercise, then you will create new styles on the remaining headers.

1 Make sure that the faculty.html: CSS Editor is forward. If it is not, click on the CSS Editor button in the bottom left corner of the CSS palette or in the upper right of your document window. Once open, position the CSS Editor window toward the bottom of the screen; you want to be able to see your Heading 1 and the CSS Editor at the same time. Click on the h1 name in your CSS Editor.

2 Double-click the color swatch in the Font Properties window to open the color picker. By default, there is no color associated with text. The color picker allows you to choose your own colors by locating a range in the color spectrum or by entering specific numbers in the fields.

3   In the Color Picker, locate the field next to the # sign and type **944A25**. This is a hexadecimal number and corresponds to a dark brown color. Press Tab, then click OK to commit the change. The Heading 1 is now dark brown.

Note: *Hexadecimal numbers are commonly used in HTML pages to designate colors. You will be working with color and the color picker in Lesson 6, "Working with Color."*

4   Click on the Text Properties tab (▣) located immediately to the right of the Font Properties tab in the CSS Editor. Each tab allows you access to different CSS Properties.

A. *Selector and Properties.* B. *Font Properties.*
C. *Text Properties.* D. *Block Properties.*
E. *Margin and Padding Properties.* F. *Border and Outline Properties.*
G. *List Item and Other Properties.* H. *Background Properties.*

5   In the Text Alignment menu, choose Center. Although alignment can also be done in the Layout view, formatting alignment in CSS can often be more efficient. For example, changing alignment in the Layout view must be done on an individual basis. If you have six headings, each one would have to be reformatted in the Layout view. CSS allows you to apply global changes with a single command.

6   In your GoLive document window, locate the second paragraph, History, and click once at the end of the paragraph. Click on your CSS Editor window to bring it into the forefront. If your CSS Editor is obscured by your document window, you could also choose the Window menu and select the CSS Editor option at the bottom.

7   In the upper left-hand corner of the CSS Editor, click and hold the small page icon (▣.) located directly below the CSS Definitions tab to open the menu. Choose New Style from the menu and then choose h2 from the submenu that opens.

8   Make sure you are still in the Font Properties tab (*A*). Click the Create new font family button (▣.) and choose Trebuchet Set from the list.

9   Repeat steps 7 and 8, but modify the h3 tag, selecting the same Trebuchet Set, but also double-click on the box to the right of "Color" and assign the color **944A25** to the h3 tag. Don't forget to press the Tab key after typing a hexadecimal value in the Color Picker, before pressing OK.

10 Close the CSS Editor when done.

Applying CSS to the body of your text

After you have defined the CSS properties, you can apply them easily to your text by simply changing the formatting of your text. In this exercise, you will apply your CSS styles to the second section of your document.

1 Scroll down your document and locate the second heading ENGLISH and click once anywhere inside the paragraph.

2 In the Main toolbar, click on the Set paragraph format drop-down menu and choose Heading 2 from the list. Because that heading has a CSS style associated with it, it automatically assumes those properties.

3 Click once inside the paragraph Jennifer Smyth—Director, and choose Heading 3 from the Set paragraph format drop-down menu. The heading automatically updates to the style you set in the earlier exercise.

Now you will change the color and adjust the margins between your Heading 2 and Heading 3 paragraphs using the Margins and Padding Properties.

4 Click on the CSS Editor button in the bottom left corner of your CSS palette to open the CSS Editor.

5 Click on the h3 element in the CSS Editor and then double-click on the color swatch to open the Color Picker. In the hexadecimal field, type in **666666**, press the Tab key and then click OK to update the color of your h3 headings to dark grey. Notice that both of your Headings were instantly updated. The ability to make global changes across a page (and even a whole site) allows you to experiment creatively with colors and styles.

6   With the h3 element still selected, click on the Margin and Padding Properties tab (▦) in the CSS Editor.

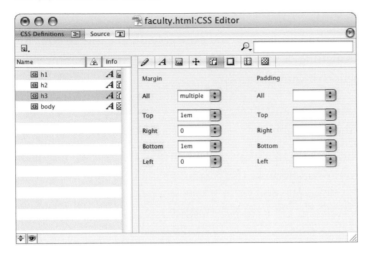

7   In the Top field of the Margin section, type **-0.2em** and then press the Tab key, and the change will be applied. CSS allows you to modify the top, bottom, right, and left margins of any given element.

8   Choose File > Save to save the changes made to your document.

Adding a CSS class style

Adobe GoLive CS2 lets you create and apply class styles to text in your documents. A class is not specific to a given tag, so you have more formatting flexibility than with tags alone. For example, if you wanted the first word of each paragraph to be a different color, you could create a class for that color; but, the style for the entire paragraph would remain the same. In this exercise you will create and then apply a class style to the school address information in the right-hand sidebar.

1   With the faculty.html page forward, select the Standard Editing tool (⇖)—if not already selected—and highlight the address information in the sidebar on the lower right or your page.

💡 *If you click inside a paragraph four times rapidly, you can select the entire paragraph.*

2   If your CSS window is not currently open, open it by choosing Window > CSS. In the Style Apply tab you will see four checkboxes: Inline Style, Block Style, <p>, and <div>. These represent the CSS formatting options currently available to you.

Class style format options

You can choose from the following formatting options in the CSS palette or the inline CSS Style preview:

Inline Style formats an item inline.

Block Style creates a division that is disconnected from the normal flow of HTML.

<p> formats an entire paragraph with a style. You don't need to select the entire paragraph; either place an insertion point in the paragraph or select a portion of it.

<body> applies a style to the entire body of a page. If this option isn't listed, select the <body> tag in the markup tree at the bottom of the page, or place an insertion point anywhere in the Layout Editor, except inside a table or layer.

Specific HTML tags apply the style to a selected object, such as a table cell, image, or layer. For example, the <td> tag for a table cell, the <img> tag for an image object, and the <div> tag for a layer.

—From GoLive Help

3   Click on the checkbox below the <p> and the New CSS Style window appears. Type **address** and click OK.

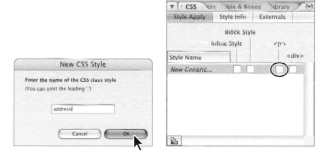

The CSS Editor window will appear and the .address class appears in the CSS palette. You will now format the address text.

4   In the CSS Editor, be sure you are in the Font Properties tab (**A**). Click on the Create new font button (▣.) on the bottom right side of the CSS Editor window. From the menu that appears, choose arial.

5   Click in the box to the right of Size and type **11px**, then press Enter. If necessary, reposition the CSS Editor window to see the text change in your sidebar.

6   Double-click the Color swatch to open the Color Picker. In the hexadecimal field, type **B90000** to select a dark red color. Press Tab and then click OK to apply the change.

7   Click on the arrow next to the Weight field and choose 700 (Bold) from the list.

8   Click on the Text Properties tab (▣), click on the Text Alignment menu, and choose the Center option. Close the CSS Editor window.

Applying a CSS class style to a div

Understanding the difference between a paragraph and a div can be tricky if you're not accustomed to tags. In the last exercise you selected a paragraph and applied a class style named ".address" to the selection. However, the paragraph is also contained within the entire sidebar. In the source code this sidebar begins with an opening <div> tag and ends with a closing div tag, </div>. Class styles can be applied to an entire div if needed.

1   In the CSS palette, place your cursor over the checkbox for the <p> tag (in the address style), but do not click it. A preview window will appear to the left of the CSS palette. Although this window can be helpful when previewing changes, you will disable it in order to see your document window more clearly.

2   Click on the arrow located on the top right of the CSS palette to open the menu. Deselect the option Show Apply Information. Repeat this step twice to deselect the Show Cascaded Preview and Show Cascaded Properties.

Deselect these three options.

3   In the CSS palette, click on the checkbox for the <p> tag to deselect it. The style is removed from the paragraph.

4   In the CSS palette, click on the checkbox for the <div> tag. All text in the sidebar is formatted with the .address style.

5   Click the checkbox for the <p> tag to select it. This centers the paragraph.

Div with .address class applied.

Exporting an Internal Style Sheet

The code that GoLive has been generating for the styles you have created in the last few exercises has been written into the document itself and is referred to as an Internal Style Sheet. In fact, the code for cascading style sheets can be placed in different locations. One of the most useful techniques is to create an External Style Sheet, which is a separate document with the extension .css. This document can be linked to multiple Web pages or an entire Web site. The benefits of this are that it becomes a simple matter to make one change to the External Style Sheet and automatically have the changes reflected in the linked pages.

You can create an External Style Sheet from scratch, but you can also take a page with existing CSS and convert the CSS to an External Style Sheet.

You will quickly identify the CSS code in your current document to help you understand the structure of CSS in relation to HTML documents.

1   Click on the Source tab at the top of your document window to view your page as source code. Scroll to the top of your document and locate lines 9-15. These lines represent the CSS code you created using the CSS Editor.

```
 9        <style type="text/css" media="screen"><!--
10  h1 { color: #944a25; font-size: 2em; font-weight: bold; text-align: center; margin
11  h2 { font-size: 1.5em; font-family: "Trebuchet MS", Geneva, Arial, Helvetica, SunSe
12  h3 { color: #666; font-size: 1.17em; font-family: "Trebuchet MS", Geneva, Arial, He
13  .address { color: #b90000; font-size: 11px; font-family: arial; font-weight: 700; t
14  body { color: black; font-size: 12px; font-family: Verdana, Arial, Helvetica, sans-
15  --></style>
```

2   Click on the Layout tab to return to the Layout view. Open the CSS Editor by clicking the CSS Editor button. You could also choose Special > CSS > Open Editor.

3   In the CSS Editor window, click on the button on the top right corner to open the menu. Choose the Export Internal CSS option.

4   You will be prompted to name and save the file. If necessary, browse to your Lesson_05 folder to ensure that your CSS file is saved there. Name the file **virtechu_ styles.css** and click the Save button. This creates the standalone CSS file to which you can link other documents in your site.

5   Chose File > Close to close the virtechu_styles.css file.

Importing an External Style Sheet

Now that you have created an External Style Sheet, you need to link it to another page in your site.

1   Choose File > Open and select the file our_history.html located in your Lesson_05 folder. This file has a similar layout and the paragraphs have already been formatted with their respective headings.

2   Open the CSS Editor by clicking on the CSS Editor button (🖺). Click on the arrow in the top right corner to open the menu, and choose the Import External CSS command.

3   Locate the virtechu_styles.css file in your Lesson_05 folder and select it. Click the Open button to apply it. The changes are updated automatically.

> 💡 *You can also apply an external style by selecting the virtechu_styles.css file from the Files tab of the site window and dragging it on top of the Show page properties button on the our_history.html page.*

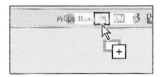

Congratulations! You have finished the lesson.

Exploring on your own

1   Apply the Heading 2 and Heading 3 paragraph formatting to other text in the events.html page. Then experiment with changing the colors, font family, and font size in the CSS Editor.

2   Add a bottom margin to the h1 heading to add more space between the Faculty & Staff paragraph and the History paragraph.

3   Create a new class style for the text Home > About Us > Faculty & Staff located above the search box.

Review

▶ **Review questions**

1   Name two ways of adding text to a document.

2   What are paragraph and physical styles and how are they applied to text?

3   When using CSS, what is the difference between changing markup elements and creating a class style?

▶ **Review answers**

1   You can type text directly into a text layout box, or you can open a file created in a word processing program and copy and paste the text directly into GoLive.

2   Paragraph and physical styles are formatting that you apply to text using the controls in the Main toolbar or in the Type menu. An example of a paragraph style would be applying a header; an example of a physical style would be bolding text using the strong control.

3   When using CSS, a user can redefine the markup elements, such as a paragraph or heading tag, in order to change the default appearance based on the CSS properties. Additionally, users can create a class style which is a CSS styling that can be applied to a single word, a single tag, or a div.

Color adds life and depth to your Web sites and GoLive CS2 gives you the power and flexibility to experiment with different looks. You will learn how to use the Color palette, work with swatches, site colors, and more.

6 | Working with Color

In this overview of using color GoLive CS2, you'll learn about the following:

- How to use the Color palette.
- How to use the Swatches palette.
- Take advantage of site colors.
- Change link colors.
- Learn about color management.

Getting started

In this lesson, you will be working on a single HTML file which has already been created for you, and learn how to use the various tools, palettes, and windows to make working with GoLive easier.

1 To ensure that the tools and palettes function as described in this lesson, delete or deactivate the Adobe GoLive CS2 preferences file. See "Restoring default preferences" on page 3.

2 Launch Adobe GoLive CS2. Close the Welcome Screen if it appears.

3 Choose File > Open and locate the file lesson06.site in the Lesson06 folder on your hard drive. Click Open and the Lesson06. site window appears.

4 In the lesson06.site window, double-click on the file named lesson06_end.html to open it. This document represents the final version of your file, and you may keep it open for reference during this lesson or close it now.

5 In the lesson06.site window, double-click on the file named lesson06_start.html. You will complete this Web page.

6 If you have two documents open, select lesson06_start.html from the bottom of the Window menu. Choose File > Save As and name the file **academics.html**. Click on Site Folder (📁,) at the bottom of the Save As window and select Root (Windows) or Root folder (Mac OS). Then click Save.

Setting page background color

By default, the background color of a Web page in GoLive CS2 is white. You might choose an alternative color with the knowledge that you will add layers, tables, or CSS layouts on top of the background.

The following describes how to work with color on a page which has no external CSS (cascading style sheet) file associated with it. This distinction is important to note because when you create a new site in GoLive, an index file with a link to an external stylesheet is automatically generated. One of the properties this CSS file uses is the background color of white, which may not be overridden with your color selection. You will learn how to change the background color using CSS in a later exercise.

1   In the Lesson06.site window, double-click on the index.html file in the Files tab of the site window to open it. This document has only a layout grid added to the page.

2   Choose Special > Page Properties. The Inspector becomes a Page Inspector.

3   In the Background section of the Page tab, locate the white color field next to the Color checkbox. Click and hold down on the black triangle in the lower right corner of the color box to view a list of color libraries. A color library consists of a specific set of colors that you can access and use in your document. GoLive CS2 includes many libraries for your use. Choose the Web Named Colors library from the list.

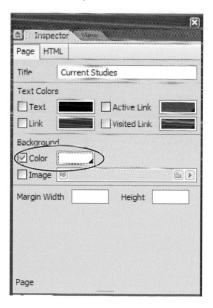

4   Click and hold the mouse down on the black triangle of the color field again. Upon choosing a color library, the Web Named Color swatches appear at the top of the menu. Do not release the mouse but pass your cursor over the color swatches. Each swatch has a name associated with it. Choose the SteelBlue color located in the bottom left corner of the library. The SteelBlue color is applied to your background.

Note: Web Named Colors are a special library which associates common color names with the hexadecimal values used for the Web.

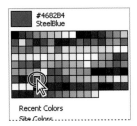

5   Click on the Source tab in the document window. On line 11 the code <body bgcolor="4682b4"> signifies that the background color of this page is being specified within the HTML document.

6   Choose File > Save and File > Close for the index.html file.

Setting page background color with CSS

If you create a site in GoLive CS2 first, and then create a new page, the new page, by default, has an external CSS file associated with it. In contrast to the last exercise, the background color is controlled by the CSS file, not the Page Properties. In this exercise, you will open the index page from a site and then modify the CSS background page color. It is important to learn both techniques.

1   In the Files tab of the Lesson06.site window, open the css folder to reveal two styles sheets, basic.css, and basic_end.css. This basic.css file was created by default when the site was created. It controls the background color as well as the default colors of hyperlinks.

2   If the academics.html document is not open, double-click on it in the site window to open it now. Click on the Open CSS Editor button (📄.) in the upper right of the document window to open the CSS Editor window.

3   In the CSS Definitions tab, double-click basic.css to open the basic.css window. This window allows you to control all the properties associated with the external stylesheet.

4   In the CSS Definitions tab, click on the body name to access the properties of the body tag. Click on the Background Properties tab to access the controls for the background. The color property is highlighted blue which tells you that this property currently has a defined value. The default value GoLive assigns for the background color is white.

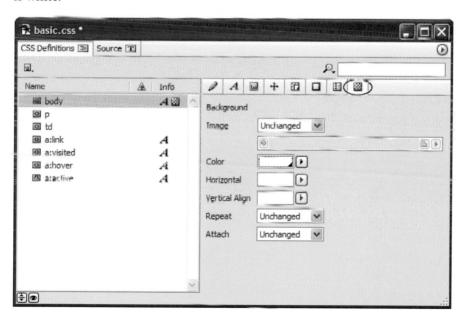

5   In the Color section of the CSS definitions tab, click and hold down on the black triangle located on the bottom right-hand side of the color swatch. This opens the menu of color libraries. If it is not still selected, choose the Web Named Colors library. Click on the color swatch again to access the color swatches at the top. Roll over the colors at the top and choose the DarkSlateBlue color.

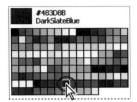

6   Close the basic.css window by clicking the Close button. You will be prompted to save your .css file. Click Yes (Windows) or Save (Mac OS). Click the Close button in the CSS Editor. Because the basic.css document is an external stylesheet, changes need to be saved in order to be applied. Your background color is now applied. Note that although the result of this exercise is the same as the first exercise, the methods are very different.

7   Choose File > Close to close the academics.html page.

Using the Color palette

The Color palette contains color models for Grayscale, RGB, CMYK, HSV, and HSB. You can use the Color palette to control the color for many objects in GoLive, such as layout grids, text boxes, tables, cells, and more. You can mix your own colors or GoLive can locate a pre-existing hexadecimal color for you.

1   If your Color palette is not currently visible, choose Window > Color to open it.

2   Click on the academic.html page to activate the tools, then using the Object
Selection tool (↖), click on the dark gray text box directly below the logo. This box
contains some of the site navigation and already has color applied to it. In the Inspector
palette, click on the color field next to the Color property. A dotted border appears
around the color swatch indicating that it is selected and ready to be modified.

*Clicking on the color field activates the
Color palette.*

The Color palette has five color models which you can select colors from.

A. Grayscale Slider.
B. RGB Sliders.
C. CMYK Sliders.
D. HSV Picker.
E. HSB Wheel.

3   Click on the first button in the Color palette to select the gray slider. The gray
slider allows you to change your colors only in shades of gray. Currently the value of
the selected text box is 136 which is approximately halfway between the extremes of
grayscale. The value of 0 would be black and 255 would be white.

4 Click on the RGB sliders button. Notice that the value of each color is 136. Equal values of red, green, and blue will always result in a shade of gray. Below the RGB sliders is a field for the Hex value. Hex refers to hexadecimal, a standard for displaying color on the Web.

What are hexadecimal colors?

Hexadecimal colors are always 6 digits with the first two digits representing the red component in the color, the third and fourth digits representing the green component, and the fifth and sixth digits representing the blue component. The digits range from numbers 0-9 and letters A-F.

Additionally, certain hexadecimal colors are referred to as web-safe colors. Web-safe colors are a color palette based on the fact that older computer systems are capable of displaying only 256 colors. To prevent dithering, a specific set of colors was chosen which would display the same across platforms (although this number actually is reduced to 216 colors when using both Mac and PC platforms). Using web-safe colors in a layout is not as important as it once was; most modern computer monitors are capable of displaying millions of colors. However, you may find the need to use web-safe colors from time to time.

You can force the Color palette to display only web-safe colors by clicking on the arrow on the right of the palette and choosing Only Web Colors from the menu. Every color that you choose in the Color palette will automatically snap to a web-safe color.

5 Click and drag the red slider all the way to the right to the value of 255. Dragging the slider adds red to the color in the text layout box. As you drag, notice the Hex Value changes accordingly to a value of FF8888.

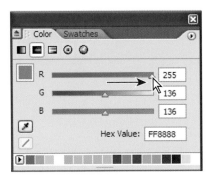

6 Highlight the current value in the Hex Value field of the Color palette and type **DA2323** (a bright red) and then press Return. You can apply specific hex values to an object using this technique.

7   Click on the Eyedropper button located at the left side of the Color palette, then move your cursor over different elements on the page, including the image at the top of the page. GoLive can sample colors used on your page, and even in images. Click on any color in the image of the students. The selected color is applied to the text box.

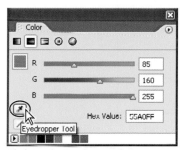

Click on the Eyedropper button.   Then click to select a color in the image.

The Eyedropper button allows you to sample any color viewable on your monitor and apply it to a selected object. You can even sample colors in documents that are not open in GoLive CS2, as long as the document is visible in the monitor.

Located at the bottom of your Color palette is a recent color list. The colors you have been choosing in this exercise have all been added to this list. This makes it easier to reuse and re-apply the same colors in your pages.

8   Click on a Gray color to apply it to the layout text box.

Choosing CMYK and Spot colors using the Swatches palette

CMYK and spot colors are color models used primarily for print. A CMYK color is also referred to as a process color and is a mix of the Cyan, Magenta, Yellow, and Black inks. A spot color is a specific color (which may look identical to a process color on the monitor) that correlates to a specific ink that a printer will use in a project. CMYK and spot colors obviously have little relevance to the Web, except for those cases when a designer needs to translate a color that may have been used in a print project and wishes to make it consistent on the screen. An example of this would be the distinctive color of a particular brand, product, or logo.

1   If your Swatches palette is not separated from the Colors palette, click and drag the tab of the Swatches palette to another location to separate it now. Having both palettes visible at the same time will be helpful throughout this lesson.

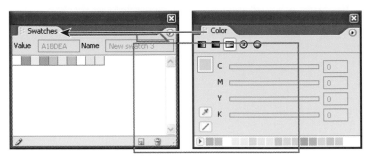

Separate the Swatches palette from the Color palette for better visibility.

2   Using the Object Selection tool (↖), select the vertical layout text box on the left side of the page.

3   Click on the box to the right of Color in the Layout Text Box Inspector.

4   In the Color palette, click on the CMYK sliders button (⊟). Move the CMYK sliders, or type in the values **65**, **50**, **0**, and **15** respectively and press Tab. This gives you a light blue color.

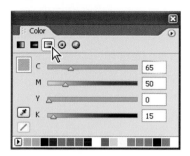

5   If you do not see the Swatches palette, choose Window > Swatches or click on the Swatches palette to bring it forward. The Swatches palette allows you to access pre-defined libraries of color. It also allows you to create libraries of your own.

6   Click and hold on the Swatches palette menu arrow (◉) to choose Open Swatch Library. Then choose Pantone Solid Coated from the list of libraries. This opens the Pantone solid Coated palette in a separate window.

Each swatch in this window corresponds to a named color in the Pantone Solid Coated library.

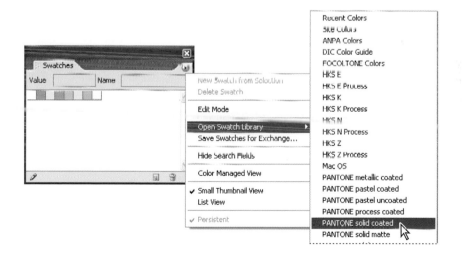

7   Click on the palette menu of the Pantone Solid Coated window (not the Swatches palette) and choose List View to view the Pantone colors by name. This view can help you find a PMS, Pantone Matching System, number if you already have one in mind.

8   If the list of numbers is grayed out, click on the Color box in the Layout Text Box Inspector to make them active. Scroll down, about one third of the way through the list of Pantone colors, to locate Pantone 2717 C. This is a light blue color, click on it to apply the color to the layout text box. If you do not wish to scroll, you can type the hexadecimal value **a1bdea** into the Value text field and press Enter. Then click on the highlighted color swatch to apply the color

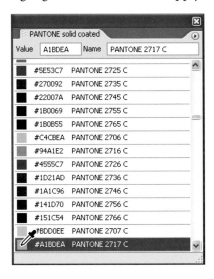

9   Close the Pantone Solid Coated window.

Adding colors to your Swatches palette

Designers often reuse the same colors throughout a site. The Swatches palette is designed to let you access these shared colors easily. In this exercise you will save the blue Pantone color you selected in the last exercise and then create a new color to save into your Swatches palette.

1   If it is no longer selected click on the blue text box with your Object Selection tool (▸). In the Layout Text Inspector, click on the blue color field to the right of the word Color. Click on the Swatches tab to access the Swatches palette.

2   Click on the Create new swatch button, in the lower right of the Swatches palette. The blue color in the color field of the Inspector is added to your Swatches palette.

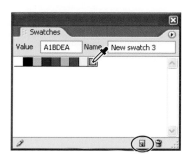

3   Click on the blue color swatch you just added. In the Name field of the Swatches palette, type **Pantone 2717 C** to help you identify it later. Press Enter.

4   Click on the Create New Swatch button at the bottom of the Swatches palette to create a duplicate of the last swatch. You will now edit this swatch in order to add a different color to your Swatches palette.

5   Click on the Toggle edit mode button (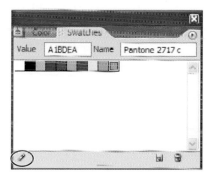) in the lower left corner of the Swatches palette. This switches you into the edit mode, allowing you to modify existing color swatches.

6   Double-click on the last color swatch in the Swatches palette, the duplicate blue swatch. The Color Picker Appears.

Note: If the Color Picker does not appear, click on the Toggle edit mode button again, then double-click on the swatch.

7   In the Hexadecimal field (marked with a # sign), type **DDE6FE** to choose a light blue color. Click OK. Press Enter.

How do you use the Color Picker?

In the Color Picker, you can select colors based on the HSB (hue, saturation, brightness), RGB (red, green, blue), CMYK (cyan, magenta, yellow, black), or Lab color models. The Color Preview field displays the currently selected color above the previously selected color. You can also specify a color based on hexadecimal values, and add colors from the Color Picker to the Swatches palette. The Color Picker can be set so you choose from only web-safe colors.

Click the H option to display all hues in the color slider.

Click the S option to display all hues in the color field, with their maximum saturation at the top of the color field and their minimum saturation at the bottom.

Click the B option to display all hues in the color field, with their maximum brightness at the top of the color field and their minimum at the bottom.

Select a color with a specific hue, saturation, and brightness by using a combination of the color slider and the color field, or by entering numeric values in the H, S, and B text boxes.

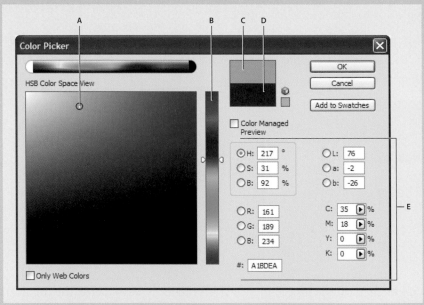

A. Picked color. *B. Color slider.* *C. Adjusted color.* *D. Original color.* *E. Color values.*

Extracting color from an image

You can sample colors from images in your document and save them as swatches in your Swatches palette. This can be useful when you need to blend a background of a photograph into a table or a CSS div.

1   Use the Object Selection tool (➤) to select the layout text box containing the book image and the contact information for VirtechU.

2   Select the box to the right of the word Color in the Layout Text Inspector to activate it.

3   If the Color palette is not currently open, choose Window > Color. Click on the Eyedropper tool (✐) in the Color palette.

4   Move the eyedropper around the image and notice that the color swatch in the Color palette picks up the slightest variation in color. Click outside the books where the green color is solid. The green color is applied to the text box.

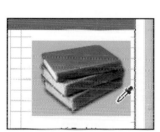

Click on the green background   Result.
with the Eyedropper tool.

Note: *If you want to experiment with different colors you will have to click on the Eyedropper tool before each new color selection.*

5   If the Swatches palette is not forward choose Window > Swatches. Then click on the box to the right of Color in the Layout Text Inspector. Select New Swatch from Selection from the Swatches palette menu (◉). The sampled color is added to your swatch library.

Saving the custom colors in your Swatches palette

GoLive CS2 allows you to save the colors you have added to your Swatches palette in the Adobe Swatch Exchange format (.ase) and reuse them in other CS2 applications. The colors appear the same in all Adobe CS2 applications, assuming your color settings are synchronized.

1   In the Swatches palette, click on the palette menu and choose the Save Swatches for Exchange.

2   In the Save swatch library window, rename the file to **VirtechU.ase**. The file is saved by default into the Color Swatches subfolder of your GoLive CS2 subfolder. Click Save.

Loading Adobe Swatch Exchange files

You can load swatch libraries from other CS2 applications, such as Photoshop CS2 and Illustrator CS2. This is useful when you want to keep color themes consistent across media.

1   In the Swatches palette, click on the palette menu and choose Open Swatch Library. From the list of options, choose Other Library. This opens the Select a Swatch Library window.

2   The VirtechU swatch library is visible. Select the library and click Open.

Note: If you do not see the VirtechU swatch library, for Windows, navigate to your Document and Settings folder > username > Application Data > Adobe > Adobe GoLive > Settings8 > Color Swatches > VirtechU, and open the file; for Mac OS, navigate to Users > Username > Library > Preferences > Adobe > GoLive > Settings8 > Color Swatches > VirtechU, and open the file.

3   Click the Close button to close the VirtechU swatches window. Then choose
File > Close to close the academics.html file. If you are asked to Save the file, click Yes
(Windows) or Save (Mac OS).

Working with site colors

GoLive CS2 allows you to scan a document for the colors used and then organizes them
in the Color tab of the site window. Once the colors have been added to the site window,
they can be used in other documents within the site. Additionally, using the colors from
the site window allows you to link the colors to the site documents. Changing a site
color automatically updates that color wherever it is used.

1   Click on the Colors tab of the lesson06.site window.

2   Choose Site > Update > Add Used > Colors. This scans your currently opened
document for colors used and organizes them into the scanned colors folder.

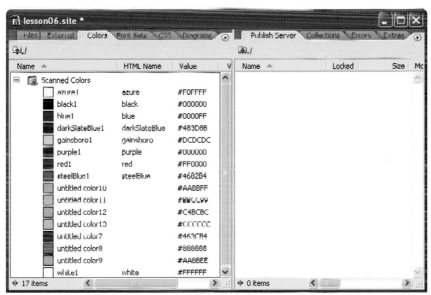

*Scanned Colors. Depending upon how much experimenting you have done with colors,
your site colors can appear different than what is shown.*

3   Click on the Files tab of the Lesson06.site window and double-click on the college_
of_arts.html file to open it.

4   Click on the Colors tab of the Lesson06.site window. Position the college_of_arts. html page so that you can see the Colors tab of the Lesson06.site window at the same time.

5   Select the SteelBlue color in the Scanned Colors folder. The Color palette becomes active.

6   If you do not see the Color palette, choose Window Color. Click on the RGB button.

7   In the Hex Value field of the Color palette, type **46826B** and press Return. A Change Link window appears informing you that the college_of_arts.html file needs to be updated. Click OK to accept the changes.

Note: The index.html file may appear as well.

Congratulations! You have finished the lesson.

Exploring on your own

1   Experiment with color by applying a background color to a page.

   a   Have the Lesson06.site window forward and click on the Create new page button in the Main toolbar.

   b   Change the background color to make sure you understand the process that you need to follow when an external cascading style sheet is automatically applied.

   c   With your new page still open, reveal the head section of the page by clicking on the arrow to the left of the word Head at the top of the document window.

    d   Select the External Style Sheet button and press delete. Your background color, if assigned using the <body> tag of the external style sheet, is now removed.

    e   Using Page Properties, assign a background color.

2   Add the following color to your Swatches palette: Pantone 204 M, located in the Pantone Solid Matte color library. Refer to the section, "Choosing CMYK and Spot colors using the Swatches palette," if you need a refresher on how to accomplish this task.

3   Open the academics.html page you created. Using the Eyedropper tool on the Color palette extract three colors from the image of the students and add them to your Swatches palette. Refer back to the section "Extracting color from an image," if you need a refresher on how to accomplish this task.

Review

▶ ## Review questions

1 What is the difference between changing the background of a default site page, referencing the default External Style Sheet, and a page that is not referencing the default External Style Sheet?

2 What are web-safe colors and when would you want to use them?

3 What is an Adobe Swatch Exchange file and when would you use one?

▶ ## Review answers

1 If a new site page is generated, using the GoLive site defaults, the background color is controlled by an External Style Sheet named basic.css. If a page is not using style sheets to define the background color, then it is controlled by the Page Properties button in the upper right of the document window.

You can check to see if a page is referencing an External Style Sheet by clicking on the arrow to the left of Head in the upper left of the document window. If an External Style Sheet is referenced, a stair icon with a chain is visible in the head section.

2 Web-safe colors are a small subset of available colors which display the same on all browsers. Developed in the early days of the Web to ensure consistency across 256-color monitors, web-safe colors are not as important as they once were, but occasionally still come into use.

3 An Adobe Swatch Exchange file is a collection of color swatches which are created in one program (such as Adobe Illustrator CS2) and can be imported into GoLive CS2. They are useful when trying to maintain color consistency from one project to another.

GoLive's seamless integration with other Adobe applications makes placing properly sized and optimized images on Web pages easy. Find out which file formats work best for your graphics and how to build them into your pages.

7 | Using Graphics in GoLive

In this lesson about using images in GoLive CS2, you'll learn how to do the following:

- Format images for the Web.
- Place optimized images.
- Create an image map.
- Add alt text.
- Use Smart Objects.
- Crop a Smart Object.
- Use Variables.
- Use Text to Banner.
- Align text.

Getting started

Make your pages more interesting and interactive by adding graphics. Graphics can include logos, photographs, maps, and navigational tools, such as images with clickable regions and buttons. Images add impact and generate more viewer activity.

Images on the Web are optimized; this means that they have been saved in a format that a browser recognizes. The size of the image file needs to be as small as possible, allowing for minimum download time. Optimizing involves a lot of "give and take." You can't always have the smallest file at the best quality, but you can learn to use the tools available to get a suitable median.

You can optimize an image prior to placing it on the page, using Photoshop, ImageReady, and Illustrator, for example, or during the placement in GoLive, using Save for Web.

Understanding Web file formats

Generally, graphics that have been optimized for the Web fall into two categories: bitmap and vector. A bitmap image is created from a series of pixels. Each pixel in a bitmap image has a fixed size and is therefore resolution-dependent, meaning that dimensions of the image depend on the resolution of the monitor on which it is viewed. The vector format describes artwork mathematically. Because of this, vector graphics are resolution-independent and can be scaled up or down without losing image quality.

Bitmap Image.   *Vector Image.*

The following formats are bitmapped:

GIF—GIF is the standard format for compressing images with large spans of solid color and crisp detail, such as line art, logos, or illustrations with type. GIFs support animation and transparency.

PNG—There are two levels of PNG that you can choose to save in the Adobe Save for Web window: PNG-8 and PNG-24. PNG-8 is similar to the GIF file format, as it supports 8-bit color and up to 256 colors. PNG-8 is good for images with lots of solid spans of color. PNG-24 supports compression of continuous-tone images, as it can preserve up to 256 levels of transparency in an image.

JPEG—JPEG is the standard format for compressing continuous-tone images such as photographs. JPEGs do not support animation or transparency.

Image that would work well in the GIF or PNG-8 format.   *Image that would work well in the JPEG or PNG-24 format.*

WBMP—WBMP format is the standard format for optimizing images for mobile devices, such as cell phones. WBMP supports 1-bit color, which means that WBMP images contain only black and white pixels.

The following formats are vector and are resolution independent:

SWF—The Macromedia® Flash™ (SWF) file format is a vector-based graphics file format for the creation of scalable, compact graphics for the Web.

SVG—SVG is a vector format that describes images as shapes, paths, and text.

Creating the page

For this lesson, you will create a new blank site and add graphics to the index page.

In this section, you will learn how to place an optimized image into a GoLive page. You'll discover how to check scaling, add alt text, and set up text alignment around the image.

1   To ensure that the tools and palettes function exactly as described in this lesson, delete or deactivate (by renaming) the Adobe GoLive CS2 preferences file. See "Restoring default preferences" on page 3.

2   Start Adobe GoLive CS2. Close the Welcome Screen if it appears.

3   Choose File > Open. Navigate to the Lesson07 folder and select lesson07_complete. site, click Open.

You can keep the lesson07_complete.site window open for reference, or choose to File > Close it.

4   Choose File > New.

5   When the New options window appears, choose Site > Create Site, then select Blank Site. Press Next.

6   Name the site **image** and select the Browse button. Navigate to the Lesson07 folder on your hard drive. Click OK or Choose, then click Next.

7   In the next window, choose "Don't Use Version Control." Click Next.

8   In the next window, choose to "Specify Server Later." Click Finish. The image.site window appears.

You will now add some completed pages with images to your new site.

9   Once the site window is open, choose File > Import > Files to Site. Open the folder named add_to_site in the Lesson07 folder. Select all the files in the add_to_site folder using Shift+click, then select Open or Choose.

When the Copy Files dialog window appears, uncheck the checkbox under Update, click OK. The files are placed into the image.site window.

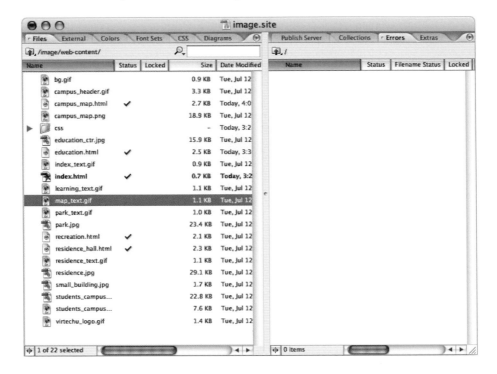

For this page you will use the Layout Grid object to format the page.

10   Double-click on the index.html page and make sure the Basic section of the Objects palette is visible.

11   Double-click the Layout Grid object. The grid is inserted on the index page.

12   With the grid still selected, choose Window > Inspector to show the Layout Grid Inspector, if it is not already showing. Type **700** into the Width text field and **450** into the Height text field. Press Tab.

13   Choose File > Save. When the Set Title alert window appears, type **See the campus** in the title text field and click Set.

Placing the top image

The first object you will place is an image that was optimized using the Save for Web feature in Photoshop. Understand that for best results, images that are already optimized should be saved at the size they appear on the Web page.

Scaling an optimized graphic file on the GoLive page is generally not wise, unless it is a Smart Object, which is discussed later in this lesson. If you must scale, you can hold down the Shift key, click the lower right corner and drag it in or out, to make it smaller or larger. If you inadvertently scale an image in GoLive, a warning icon (⊡) appears in the lower right corner of the image. To quickly return the image back to its actual size, click on the matching icon in the Basic tab of the Image Inspector.

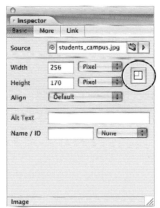

1   Select the Image object and drag it to the upper left corner of the layout grid.

2   Position the page so that you can see the Files tab of the site window. You can click and drag in the lower right corner of the page to reduce the size of the document window.

3   Click and drag from the Fetch URL button (⊚) on the Image Inspector to select the file named campus_header.gif in the Files tab of the image.site window.

If you cannot see your site window, click and drag the Fetch URL button directional line to the Select window button (⊞.) in the Main toolbar or to the site window itself. This brings the site window forward.

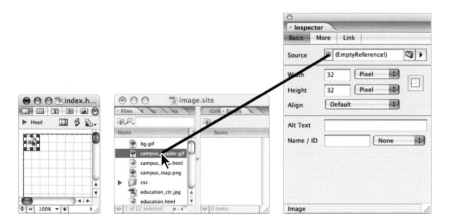

💡 *You can Alt+click and drag (Windows) or Command+click and drag (Mac OS) directly on a placed image object to access the Fetch URL without the Inspector.*

Creating an image map

The Image Map feature allows you to use an image and define clickable regions to it. Use this for maps, navigation bars, or any graphic you place in GoLive. In this part of the lesson you will add clickable areas to the campus_banner image just placed. You will use the pages you imported in the beginning of this lesson to link each heading to the appropriate page.

1   Using the Standard Editing tool (I↖), select the campus_banner image. If the Inspector is not visible, choose Window > Inspector.

2 Click on the More tab in the Image Inspector and check the box Use Map. A default name is assigned in the Name/ID text field. For this lesson you will leave this unchanged.

When Use Map is checked, the Main toolbar changes to reflect tools needed for creating image maps. The Inspector is also changed from an Image Inspector to a Clickable Image Map Inspector.

Check Use Map.

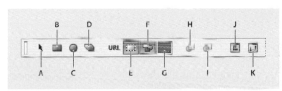

The Image Map tools become available.

A. Select Map-area tool. **B**. Rectangular Map-area tool. **C**. Circular Map-area tool. **D**. Polygonal Map area tool. **E**. Show map area edges. **F**. Colorize map areas. **G**. Select map area color. **H**. Send area to back **I**. Bring area to front. **J**. Open Align palette. **K**. Open Transform palette.

3 Select the Rectangular Map-area tool (■), then click and drag to surround the first button, Education Buildings. The Inspector becomes a Map Area Inspector.

Note: Be sure to click inside the boundary to get the + cursor, and then click and drag to surround the text button.

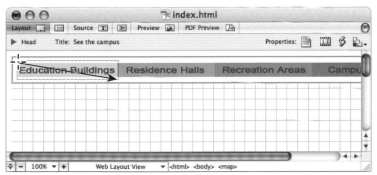

Click and drag to create a clickable region.

If it is difficult to see your image map area, click on the Select map area color button to assign a more appropriate color. Colors and area edges are assigned for your use in GoLive; they are not visible in the browser.

4 Return to the Inspector. Use the Browse button to the right of EmptyReference! to browse to the image folder located inside the Lesson07 folder. This is the folder automatically created when you created the new blank site, named image. Open the image folder and then the web-content folder. Select the page named education.html. Click Open. You have just created a clickable area from a region on the image to the education page.

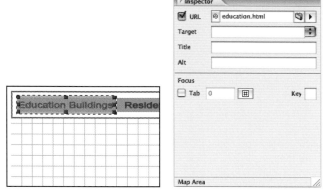

5 Now use the Rectangular Map-area tool to click and drag a map area surrounding the section of the banner for Residence Halls.

6 In the Map Area Inspector, use the Browse button to link this map area to the file named residence_hall.html, located in the image folder.

7 Create rectangular map areas for the last two sections: Recreation Areas and Campus Map. Use the Browse button on the Image Area Inspector link to recreation.html and campus_map, respectively.

8 Use the Select Map-area tool (⬦) to adjust the handles on the map areas to better line up with the text.

You can click on the Open Align palette button (▣) to take advantage of precise align and distribute features for your map areas. Simply Shift+click on the map areas that you wish to align, and choose the appropriate button on the Align palette.

Adding alt text

Alt text provides alternative text when non-textual elements, typically images, cannot be displayed.

• Alt text is important because it displays descriptive text when the viewer does not want or cannot see the images on a Web page.

• Alt text containing keywords can also improve the search engine ranking of the page for those keywords.

• Alt text assists in navigation when a graphics-intensive site is being viewed over a slow connection, enabling site visitors to make navigation choices before graphics are fully rendered.

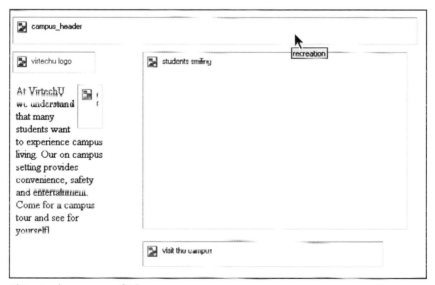

Alt text as it appears in the browser.

In this part of the lesson, you will add Alt text to the map areas in the campus banner image.

1   Use the Select Map-area tool ([⬚]) in the Main toolbar to select the Education Buildings map area.

2   Make sure the Map Area Inspector is visible. If it is not, choose Window > Inspector. Type **education** in the Alt text field. Press Enter.

The Alt text for this map area is now defined.

Use Queries to help you find images that do not have Alt text in your site. The Queries window lets you search for files using a wide range of criteria. You can search in open sites and collections, in a user-defined list of files, or in a result list; and you can view the results in the Query Results window. Find out more by reading "Generating queries" in GoLive Help.

3   Now, using the Select Map-area tool, select the second map area, Residence Halls. Type **Residence Halls** into the Alt text field in the Map Area Inspector.

4   Select, one at a time, the last two map areas, Recreation Areas and Campus Map and use the Map Area Inspector to give them alt text of **Recreation** and **Campus map**, respectively.

5   Click on the campus_banner image, outside a map area, but yet still within the image. Assign Alt text to the main image by typing **Campus Header** into the Alt text field in the Basic tab of the Image Inspector.

6   Test your image map by selecting the Preview tab of the document window. Click on the areas where you created the map regions. You are linked to the pages you loaded into the site at the beginning of the lesson.

7   Return to the Layout View and choose File > Save. Leave the page open.

Adding a background image

Next you will add a background image to the page. As a default, the browser will repeat an image defined as a background to fill the size of the browser window. This can work well if you have an appropriate image to use as a pattern. In this sample you will use an image that is very wide (2000 pixels). It will not repeat horizontally. It is only 15 pixels high, so it will repeat vertically.

1   Click once on the Show Page Properties button (📄) in the upper right of the document window.

The Inspector turns into a Page Inspector.

2 Check Image in the Background section. Either use the Fetch URL or Browse button to choose the image named bg.gif as the background for this page. The background repeats on the page. Select the Preview tab to see the result without viewing the grid.

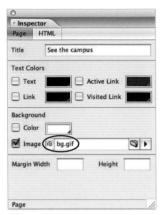

Choose an image.

💡 *You can drag and drop an image on top of the Page Properties button to quickly define it as the background image.*

Note: *Using the element <body> in cascading styles sheets, you can instruct a background image to repeat once, or just vertically or horizontally. Read more about CSS in Lesson 5, "Adding and Formatting Text."*

Smart Objects

Design with amazing flexibility by using Smart objects. Bring native Illustrator, Photoshop, and PDF files directly into GoLive. GoLive automatically launches Save for Web, from which you can choose a variety of optimization settings, including format, colors, and size. Because Smart objects keep a link to the original image, you can change the optimization settings and image size as many times as you need with no degradation to the image. You can also edit the native file and have the changes reflected automatically in the placed Smart object in your GoLive page.

In the Smart section of the Objects palette, GoLive has five Smart Objects from which to choose:

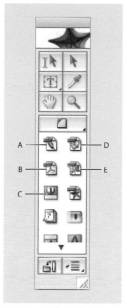

A. *Smart Photoshop.*
B. *Smart PDF.*
C. *Smart Favorite Icon.*
D. *Smart Illustrator.*
E. *Smart Generic.*

Smart Photoshop—For native Adobe Photoshop files. You can also use the Smart Photoshop object to re-optimize other bitmap formats typically recognized by Photoshop. In other words, you can re-optimize a .jpg file by using a Smart Object instead of an image object when placing it on the page.

Smart Illustrator—For native Adobe Illustrator files (.ai).

Smart PDF—Use the Smart PDF to place an image of a page, such as a cover to a publication, or even a data sheet, into your GoLive page. As you make changes to the PDF file, the Smart PDF object will automatically update the placed image of the PDF.

Smart Generic—Allows you to link to other image file types, such as TIFF and EPS.

Smart Favorite Icon—Favorite icons let you specify an image that appears with your page's title in the Favorites or Bookmarks menu of a Web browser.

In this lesson you will use the Smart Photoshop and Smart Illustrator objects.

As previously mentioned, when using a Smart object in GoLive, the native file that you select remains linked to your optimized image. The native file does not need to be uploaded to the server when you post your site. If you are planning to use images as a Smart object, it is wise to store them within the Smart Objects folder of the site. Since the Smart Objects folder is in the Extras tab of the site, not the Files, it will not be loaded to the FTP server.

1   Click on the Extras tab in the site window. Then double-click on the SmartObjects folder to open the folder.

2   Choose File > Import > Files to Site. Browse to the Lesson07 folder and select the images generic_text.psd, students_campus.psd, and virtechu_logo.ai. Click Open (Windows) or Choose (Mac OS). The files are added to the SmartObjects folder.

You will now place a Smart Object using two different methods, drag and drop, and placing a Smart Object.

3   Position the site window so that you can see the index.html and the image.site window.

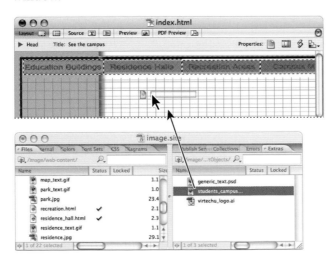

4   Select the students_campus.psd file in the SmartObjects tab and drag it to the center top of the layout grid. GoLive recognizes that this is a native Photoshop file and automatically opens the Save for Web window.

Since this image is a continuous tone image, with many variations and gradations of color, it is best saved as a JPEG image.

5   Select the 2-Up tab in the top left of the Save for Web window. This shows you the original image (left) and the optimized preview (right) based upon your selected settings.

You will now use the settings panel to the right of the Save for Web window to choose the optimization settings for this image.

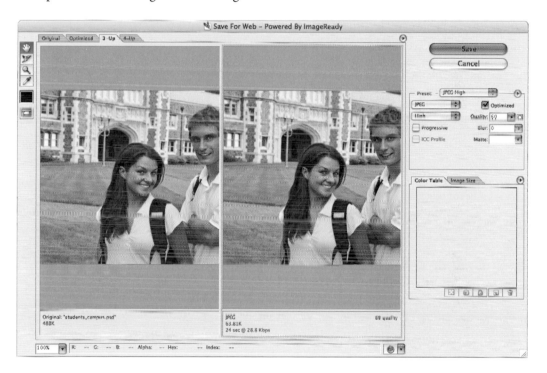

6   Choose JPEG High from the Preset drop-down menu. Standard settings for a high compressed JPEG file are selected, but you can use the controls under the Preset drop-down menu to customize the settings.

Optimization options for JPEG format

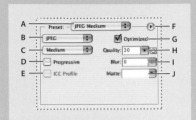

A. *Preset drop-down menu.*
B. *Optimized File Format drop-down menu.*
C. *Compression Quality drop-down menu.*
D. *Progressive checkbox.*
E. *ICC Profile checkbox.* F. *Palette menu.*
G. *Optimized checkbox.* H. *Quality slider.*
I. *Blur slider.* J. *Matte drop-down menu.*

Preset—These are saved optimization settings. If you choose a preset, you do not have to make changes to the other options. If you make changes to other options, the preset is changed to Unnamed. You can save your own settings by selecting Save Settings from the palette menu. Your saved preset then appears in the Preset drop-down menu.

Quality—Determines the level of compression. The higher the Quality setting, the more detail the compression algorithm preserves. View the optimized image at several quality settings to determine the best balance of quality and file size.

Optimized—Creates an enhanced JPEG with a slightly smaller file size. The Optimized JPEG format is recommended for maximum file compression; however, some older browsers do not support this feature.

Progressive—Creates an image that displays progressively in a Web browser. The image will display as a series of overlays, enabling viewers to see a low-resolution version of the image before it downloads completely. The Progressive option requires use of the Optimized JPEG format.

Note: Progressive JPEGs require more RAM for viewing, and are not supported by some browsers.

Blur—Specifies the amount of blur to apply to the image. This option applies an effect identical to that of the Gaussian Blur filter and allows the file to be compressed more, resulting in a smaller file size. A setting of 0.1 to 0.5 is recommended.

ICC Profile—Preserves the ICC profile of the artwork with the file. ICC profiles are used by some browsers for color correction. This option is only available if the source file contains an ICC profile.

Matte—Specifies a fill color for pixels that were transparent in the original image. Click the Matte color swatch to select a color in the color picker, or select an option from the Matte menu: Pixels that were fully transparent in the original image are filled with the selected color; pixels that were partially transparent in the original image are blended with the selected color.

—From GoLive Help

7 Choose the Image Size tab. Type **450** in for the width. Click Apply.

You will now preview your file in a default browser before saving the optimized image.

8 Click and hold on the Select Browser button at the bottom of the Save for Web window. Choose Edit List.

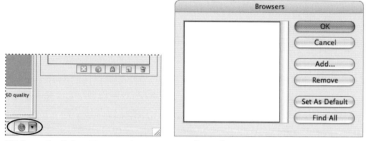

Click on the Select Browser button to configure browser previews.

9 When the Browsers window appears, click the Add button. Navigate to locate the browser in which you wish to preview your image. As an example, you can navigate in Windows to the C: Program folder > Internet Explorer folder and select iexplorer.exe, or on Macintosh you can navigate to Applications > Safari. Click Open and then OK. The Select Browser button is now Preview in default browser button.

10 Now click on the Preview in Default Browser button. The button's icon may change to reflect the default browser you just selected.

The image is opened in the browser. This preview can help you check settings and size. Choose File > Close Window in the browser and return to GoLive. The Save for Web window is still open.

11 Click the Save button at the top of the Save for Web window. When the Save the Smart Object target file window appears, leave the name unchanged and click on the Site Folder button (📁,) at the bottom of the window. Select Root (Windows) or Root folder (Mac OS); this directs you to the web-content folder of the image.site. Click Save. The image now appears on your page.

Testing the Smart object

Test the Smart object by making these changes to the placed file.

1   Hold down the Shift key and click and drag the handle in the lower right corner to make the image smaller. GoLive optimizes the file to accommodate the smaller file size.

2   Now select the lower right corner handle again, holding down the Shift key, and make the image larger. You can see the image adjust to accommodate the new size.

3   In the Main toolbar, type **161** in the Horizontal Position text field. Type **48** in the Vertical toolbar. Press Tab.

Note: If you were to edit and save the original Photoshop file, the changes would be reflected immediately in GoLive.

Using the Smart Illustrator object

Now you will import a native Adobe Illustrator logo.

1   Make sure the Smart section of the Objects toolbar is visible. If it is not, Choose Window > Objects and select Smart from the palette menu.

2   Select and drag the Smart Illustrator object (📷) to the left side of the layout grid.

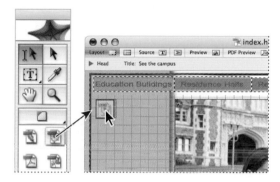

3   In the Inspector, click on the Browse button to the right of the Source text field. When the Open dialog window appears, browse to the Lesson07 folder. Open image > web-data > SmartObjects and select the virtechu_logo.ai. Click Open.

4   When the Conversion Setting dialog window appears, click OK to the default setting of Bitmap formats.

The Save for Web window appears.

Since this image has large spans of solid color, it will compress well in the GIF format.

5   Choose GIF 32 No Dither from the Preset drop-down menu.

Optimization options for GIF and PNG-8 formats

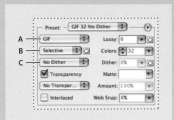

A. File format menu.
B. Color Reduction Algorithm menu.
C. Dithering Algorithm menu.

Lossy (GIF only)—Reduces file size by selectively discarding data. A higher Lossy setting results in more data being discarded. You can often apply a Lossy value of 5–10, and sometimes up to 50, without degrading the image. File size can often be reduced 5%–40% using the Lossy option.

Note: You can't use the Lossy option with the Interlaced option or with Noise or Pattern Dither algorithms.

Color Reduction Method and **Colors**—Specifies a method for generating the color lookup table and the number of colors you want in it. You can select one of the following color reduction methods:

Perceptual—Creates a custom color table by giving priority to colors for which the human eye has greater sensitivity.

Selective—Creates a color table similar to the Perceptual color table, but favoring broad areas of color and the preservation of Web colors. This color table usually produces images with the greatest color integrity. Selective is the default option.

Adaptive—Creates a custom color table by sampling colors from the spectrum appearing most commonly in the image. For example, an image with only the colors green and blue produces a color table made primarily of greens and blues. Most images concentrate colors in particular areas of the spectrum.

Restrictive (Web)—Uses the standard 216-color color table common to the Windows and Mac OS 8-bit (256-color) palettes. This option ensures that no browser dither is applied to colors when the image is displayed using 8-bit color. Using the Web palette can create larger files and is recommended only for audiences using older 256-color monitors.

Custom—Preserves the current perceptual, selective, or adaptive color table as a fixed palette that does not update with changes to the image.

Dithering Method and **Dither**—Determines the method and amount of application dithering. Dithering refers to the method of simulating colors not available in the color display system of your computer. A higher dithering percentage creates the appearance of more colors and more detail in an image, but can also increase the file size. For optimal compression, use the lowest percentage of dither that provides the color detail you require. Images with primarily solid colors may work well with no dither. Images with continuous-tone color (especially color gradients) may require dithering to prevent color banding.

Using the color table

Perhaps it is important that the red in the VirtechU logo always use the closest web-safe color. In this part of the lesson you will convert only the red in the logo to be web-safe.

1   Click once in the right window to activate the optimized preview in the Save for Web window. Then select the Eyedropper tool (✐) and click on any red area in the VirtechU logo in the optimized preview window.

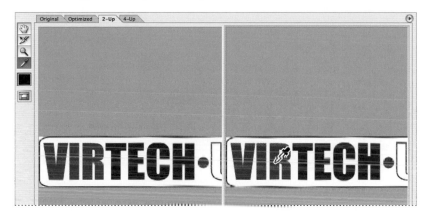

The sampled color appears in the Eyedropper Color box on the left side of the Save for Web window. The color is also highlighted with a border around it in the Color Table tab on the right.

2   Click once on the Shifts/unshifts selected colors to Web palette button. The color is locked and shifted to the closest web-safe color.

To customize the color table for GIF and PNG-8 images

You use the Color Table palette in the Save For Web dialog box to customize the colors in optimized GIF and PNG-8 images. With a maximum of 256 colors, you can add and delete colors in the color table, shift selected colors to web-safe colors, and lock selected colors to prevent them from being dropped from the palette.

To add new colors to the color table, select the Eyedropper tool, and click a color in the image. (Alternatively, click the color selection box, and use the color picker to select a color.) Then, click the New Color button in the Color Table palette. A small white square with a dark center appears in the lower right corner of the new color, indicating that the color is locked.

Note: If the color table already contains the maximum number of colors (256, or 255 with transparency), you cannot add a new color.

To change a color in the color table, double-click it. A small plus sign appears in the center of each edited color.

To delete a color from the color table, select the color and click the Delete button. When you delete a color, areas of the optimized image that previously included that color are re-rendered using the closest color remaining in the palette. Deleting a color changes the color palette type to Custom to prevent the color from being added back to the palette if you re-optimize the image.

To shift a color to a web-safe color, select the color and click the Web Shift button. A small white diamond appears in the center of selected colors that have been web-shifted (and in all web-safe colors). To restore a shifted color to its original value, click the Web Shift button again. Alternatively, select Shift/Unshift Selected Colors To/From Web Palette or Unshift All Colors from the Color Table palette menu. To specify a tolerance for shifting colors, specify a value for Web Snap in the Settings section of the Save For Web dialog box. A higher value shifts more colors.

To lock a color so that it won't be dropped from the color table if you reduce the number, select the color and click the Lock button. A white square with a red center appears in the lower right corner of each locked color. To unlock a color, click the Lock button again. To unlock all colors, select Unlock All Colors from the Color Table palette menu.

To select multiple colors in the color table, press Shift and click another color. All colors in the rows between the first and second selected colors are selected. To select a nonadjacent group of colors, press Ctrl (Windows) or Command (Mac OS) and click each color that you want to select. The Color Table palette menu also provides commands for selecting colors.

To sort the colors in the color table, select a sorting command from the Color Table palette menu. You can sort colors by hue (neutral colors are assigned a hue of 0 and located with the reds), luminance (the lightness or brightness of a color), or popularity, making it easier to see an image's color range and locate particular colors.

To save a color table, select Save Color Table from the Color Table palette menu. By default, the color table file is given the extension .act (for Adobe Color Table).

To load a color table, select Load Color Table from the Color Table palette menu. You can load a color table from an .act file or a GIF file (to load the file's embedded color table). Once you load a new color table, the colors in the optimized image change to reflect the new color table.

3 Select the Image Size tab and type **128** into the Width text field under New Size. Click Apply.

Note: The file format, size and download time are listed in the lower left of the optimized preview pane. The download time calculation settings can be changed using the palette menu at the top of the Save for Web window.

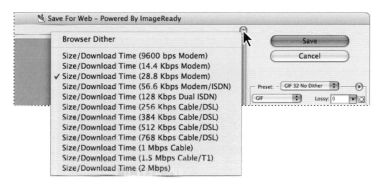

4 Click the Save button at the top of the Save for Web window. When the Save the Smart Object target file window appears, leave the name unchanged and click on the Site Folder button (⬜,) at the bottom of the window. Select Root (Windows) or Root folder (Mac OS); this directs you to the web-content folder of the image.site. Click Save. The logo now appears on your page.

5 Choose File > Save and keep the file open.

Using variables

Use variables to edit text in images directly in GoLive. In this example, you will take an Adobe Photoshop file whose topmost layer is a text layer and place it as a Smart Object on your page.

Have the index.html page open for this lesson.

1 Drag and drop the Smart Photoshop Object from the Smart section of the Objects palette to the grid area beneath the large image.

2 Click on the Browse button to the right of the Source text field. When the Open dialog window appears, browse to the Lesson07 folder. Open image > web-data > SmartObjects and select the generic_text.psd file. Click Open.

GoLive recognizes the topmost text layer and opens the Variable Settings window.

3 Check the box under the Use column and type **See the campus** in the lower section of the window. Click OK.

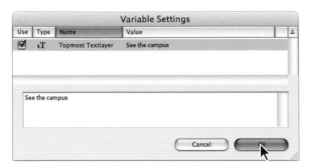

The Save for Web window appears with your text applied.

4 Since it is important that the transparency in the shadow remains, choose PNG-24 from the Presets drop-down menu.

5 Click the Save button at the top of the Save for Web window. When the Save the Smart Object target file window appears, leave the name unchanged, as it is already appropriately named. Click on the Site Folder button (📁,) at the bottom of the window. Select Root (Windows) or Root folder (Mac OS); this directs you to the web-content folder of the image.site. Click Save.

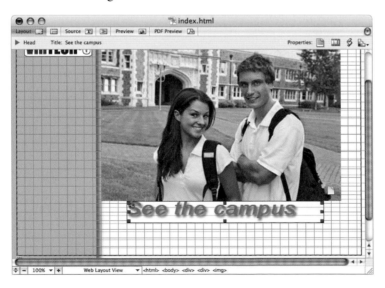

Note: You can click on the Variables or Settings buttons on the Smart Object Inspector at any time to change the optimization settings, or change your variable text.

6   Choose File > Save. Leave this file open.

Text to Banner

If you have a .psd image prepared with a top text layer, you can take advantage of the Text to Banner feature in GoLive. For this part of the lesson you will create a new blank page in which to experiment with this feature.

1   Choose File New. The New document window appears.

2   Select Web > Pages > HTML Page. Click OK.

3   Type **About Us** on the blank page.

4   Select the text and choose Special > Convert > Text to Banner. A window appears allowing you to select a Photoshop image whose topmost layer is a text layer. For this example, use the image named "button.psd" that is located in your Lesson07 folder. Click Open.

5   When the Variable Settings window appears, click OK.

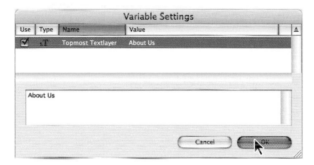

The Save for Web window appears. The "About Us" text is already inserted.

6   Choose GIF 32 No Dither from the Presets drop-down menu. Click Save.

7   When the Save the Smart Object target file window appears, select Root (Windows) or Root folder (Mac OS) using the Site Folder button (📁,) at the bottom of the window. Click Save. The image appears on the page with the About Us text.

8 Now Type **Contact Us** and repeat steps 4-7. Using the same Photoshop image, you can create as many buttons as you want.

Note: These buttons remain linked to the original. You can change the button or update the font, and the change will be reflected in all the buttons in GoLive.

9 Choose File > Close. Choose Don't Save for this document.

Aligning an image

In this next section you will add text and align the image to the text. This feature will get you about as close as you can get to the text wrap features you may be familiar with in page layout applications.

1 Using the Objects palette menu, choose Basic to return to the Basic section.

2 Select and drag the Layout Text Box object (▢) to the left side of the grid.

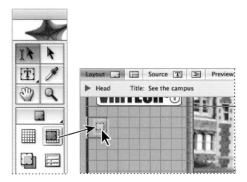

3   Using the Object Selection tool (↖), click and drag the middle right handle to extend the text box to the width of the blue background tint.

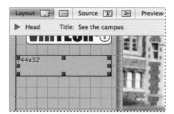

4   Choose File > Open and browse to locate the file named campus_copy.txt in the Lesson07 folder. Click Open.

5   Choose Edit > Select All and then Edit > Copy.

6   Choose File > Close.

7   Using the Standard Editing tool (↕↖), click to insert the cursor in the Layout Text Box and then choose Edit > Paste. The copy is now in the text box.

8   Click to insert the cursor at the beginning of the copy.

9   Double-click on the image object (▨) located in the Basic section of the Objects palette. The Image Object is placed before the start of the copy.

 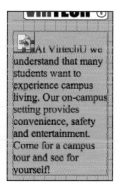

10   Use the Browse button in the Inspector to select the image named small_building.jpg from the image > web-content folder.

💡 *You can also select the image named small_building.jpg and drag and drop it into the Image Object.*

11 Select Right from the Alignment drop-down menu in the Image Inspector. The image moves to the right, text runs down the left side.

Default alignment.   *Change alignment to Right.*   *Result.*

Alignment settings

The Alignment drop-down menu in the Inspector for an image or other object provides the following options:

Default—Aligns the object with the baseline of text or adjacent objects in the line or the left side of the document window or container.

Top, Middle, or **Bottom**—Aligns the top, center, or bottom of the object with the top, center, bottom, or baseline of text or adjacent objects on the line.

Left or **Right**—Aligns the left or right side of the object with the left or right side of the line, document window, or container. Any text in the line moves to the left of the object. If there are no other objects or text in the line, the object aligns with the left or right side of the window or container.

Text Top—Aligns the top of the object with the top of text (the top of the tallest character) in the line.

Abs Middle, Baseline, or **Abs Bottom**—Aligns the center or bottom of the object with the absolute middle (half way between the top and the bottom), text baseline, or absolute bottom (including text descenders below the baseline) of text or objects in the line.

—From GoLive Help

12 Add space around the image by entering the value **4** into the HSpace (Horizontal) and VSpace (Vertical) text fields in the More tab of the Image Inspector. Press Tab.

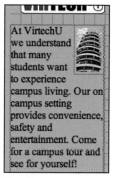

Enter values in VSpace
and HSpace.

Result.

13 Choose File > Save. Leave the page open.

Note: Adding images can add a considerable amount of data to a page. Check download time status of a page by choosing Special > Document Statistics. This will tell you how large the page is and the approximate download time. Try to keep your page download time at 10 seconds or fewer at 56 Kbps (the average speed of a dial-up Internet connection)

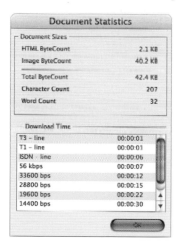

Cropping a Smart object

New in Adobe GoLive CS2, you can crop a Smart Object after it has been placed on a GoLive page.

1 Select the student_campus image on the index.html page that you have been working with.

2 Select the Crop button (✄) on the Smart Photoshop Inspector.

3 Click and drag to select the portion of the image that contains the two students. The area surrounding the crop area is dark, indicating that this part of the image will be removed.

4 Use the handles surrounding your crop area to adjust the size.

Cropping a Smart object in GoLive.

5 Press Return. The image is cropped. The original Photoshop file is left intact. Congratulations! You have finished the lesson.

Exploring on your own

If you have Adobe Photoshop you can take variables a little further with this exercise.

1   Have the image.site window used in this lesson open.

2   Create a new blank HTML page in GoLive. Select Web > Pages > HTML Page. Click OK.

3   Choose File > Save As and name the page **buttons**. Choose Root (Windows) or Root folder (Mac OS) from the Site Folder drop-down menu at the bottom of the Save As window.

4   Select and drag the Smart Photoshop object from the Smart section of the Objects palette onto the page. Position is not important for this experiment.

5   Browse to locate the native Photoshop file named "button" in the Lesson07 folder. Assign text to the topmost text layer, for example, Sales.

6   Choose to save the target file in the Root folder.

7   Repeat this two more times for a total of three buttons on the page. Assign different text to each instance. For example, Contact and About.

8   Double-click on any of the placed images to launch the original Photoshop file. If double-clicking does not launch Photoshop, you can choose to File > Open from within Adobe Photoshop. Browse to locate the file button.psd inside the Lesson07 folder.

9   Use the Type tool to change the font, choose File > Save.

10   Return to your GoLive page to see that the font has changed in every placed Smart Object.

Review

▶ **Review questions**

1 What file formats would work best for a photographic image?

2 What file formats would work best for an animated image with solid type?

3 What is alt text and why is it important?

4 What type of file will allow you to use the variable feature in GoLive?

▶ **Review answers**

1 Both JPEG and PNG-24 file formats work well with continuous-tone images. If transparency is necessary, choose PNG-24 as JPEG does not support transparency.

2 The GIF formats is best for images that have large spans of solid color. The GIF format supports transparency and animation. As a note, the PNG-8 format is also good for large spans of color but does not support transparency or animation.

3 Alt text is an HTML tag that provides alternative text when non-textual elements, typically images, cannot be displayed.

• Alt text is important because it is displayed when the viewer does not want or cannot see the images on a Web page.

• Using alt text that contains keywords can improve the search engine ranking of the page.

• Alt text assists in navigation when a graphics-intensive site is being viewed over a slow connection, enabling site visitors to make navigation choices before graphics are fully rendered.

4 The variable feature in GoLive works with Photoshop files that have a text layer as the topmost layer.

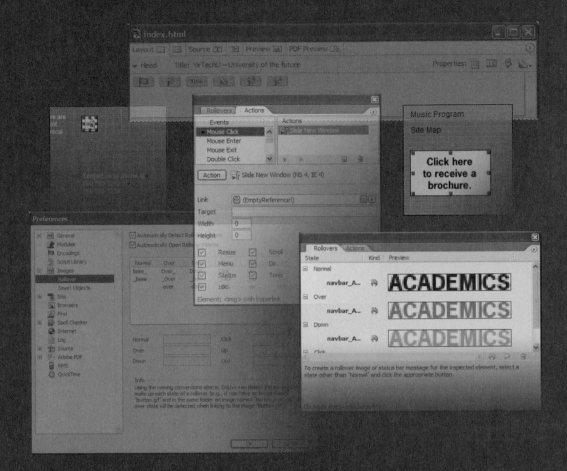

GoLive CS2 allows you to add interactivity to your Web sites in the form of rollovers and actions. Just as the design view generates HTML on the fly—as you add images, text and CSS—GoLive CS2 creates JavaScript when you add rollovers and actions.

8 Adding Interactivity: Rollovers and Actions

In this overview about adding interactivity in GoLive CS2, you'll learn how to do the following:

- Add layers to a page so that you can overlap objects.
- Create rollover buttons.
- Use the Detect Rollover Images feature.
- Add actions to rollover buttons for showing and hiding layers.
- Create an Open Window action.
- Apply the Browser Switch action.

Getting started

In this lesson, you will be working on the design for the VirtechU home page and two of its associated pages; events.html and contact.html. You'll create rollover images for the navigation bar, as well as remote rollovers for the events page. In the second half of the lesson, you will add JavaScript actions which allow you to trigger events, such as opening new windows, validating forms, and more.

1 To ensure that the tools and palettes function as described in this lesson, delete or deactivate the Adobe GoLive CS2 preferences file. See "Restoring default preferences" on page 3.

2 Launch Adobe GoLive CS2. Close the Welcome Screen if it appears.

3 Choose File > Open and locate the file lesson08.site in the Lesson08 folder, on your hard drive. Click open and the lesson08.site window appears.

4 In the site window, double-click on the file named lesson08_end.html. This document represents the final version of your file.

5   Preview the lesson08_end.html document in your Web browser by clicking the Preview tab in the document window. Mouse your cursor over the rollovers on the top and on the left to see how the rollovers function. When you are finished, return to the Layout Editor by clicking on the Layout tab. You can choose to File > Close the lesson08_end file, or keep it open for reference.

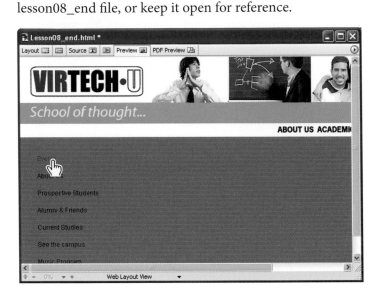

6   In the site window, double-click on the file named lesson08_start.html to open it. This document contains a partially completed page that you will complete.

7   Choose File > Save As and name the file **index.html**. Select the Site Folder (⬜,) at the bottom of the Save As window and choose Root (Windows) or Root folder (Mac OS). Then click Save.

Setting up your rollover buttons

Rollover buttons are buttons that change in appearance when your mouse moves over them or clicks on them (referred to as the Over and Down state in Adobe GoLive CS2, respectively). You can assign actions to rollover buttons that are triggered by mouse events. Examples of actions that you can assign to a rollover button are showing and hiding a layer or jumping to another destination.

In this exercise, you will be adding a table to place your images. Although there are automatic ways to add tables using Imageready for rollovers, this method will allow you to understand the process. In this example we place images inside a table, but you can also place buttons into layers, CSS layouts, or directly on a page.

1   Make sure that the Objects palette is visible; if it is not, choose Window > Objects. If you are not in the Basic set of your Objects palette, go there now by clicking on the Objects palette menu and choosing Basic.

2   Select the Standard Editing tool (↧) from the toolbox, and click inside the white row directly below the banner graphic. You will see a blinking cursor on the right side of the cell.

3   Hold down the Ctrl key (Windows) or Command key (Mac OS) and click and hold on the table object (⊞) in the Objects palette. A Rows and Columns pop-up will appear, allowing you to dynamically add the number of rows and columns to your table. Drag the cursor to the right to create 1 row and 2 columns.

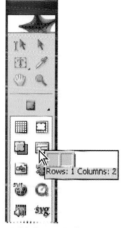

Hold down Ctrl or Command on the Table object.

4   Release the mouse and the table is inserted. The nested table is flush right because the original table had a horizontal alignment set to right.

5   Click and drag an Image object from the Objects palette to the first cell in the nested table to add an image placeholder.

6   Click on your site window or choose Window > lesson08.site to bring your site window forward. Arrange your site window and document window so that you can see both easily; you will be linking your rollover images using the Inspector palette and the two windows.

7   In the site window, expand the images folder. The images you will be using for the rollover navigation have been created and saved as GIF images.

8   In the document window, click on the Image object you added in Step 5. In the Source section of the Inspector palette, click and drag the Fetch URL button to the site window and select the about_us.gif image.

At this point you have added an image object and the image functions like any other image in GoLive CS2. In the next section you will learn about states and how they convert static images into images that react to the user's mouse behavior.

Creating self-rollovers

Self-rollovers are the most common of rollovers. The actions of the user's mouse trigger change between two or more image files. From the user's perspective, the change is usually instantaneous. Rollovers transform a static Web page into one more visually stimulating.

Rollovers require two or three similar images, which appear in the same spot on the page. The first image is the normal appearance of the rollover image, the way it appears when the user's cursor is somewhere else on the browser page. GoLive CS2 refers to this state as Normal. The second image is identical to the first in width and height, but differs visually in some way, usually a different color or perhaps an effect such as a drop shadow. GoLive CS2 refers to this state as the Over state and the image associated with this state appears when the user's cursor is on top of the rollover image. The third state is the Down state which is yet another image, also the same width and height, but different in appearance from the first two states. The Down state appears when a user clicks down on an image.

Note: There are additional states available, such as Click, Up, and Out. Although these states could add more dimensions to a rollover, they are not used as frequently.

You will now add two more states to the image you placed in the last exercise to create a visual effect on your Web page.

1   If it is not currently selected, click on the ABOUT US graphic.

2   Choose Window > Rollovers. The Rollover window displays your Normal state. Resize your window, if necessary, to see all the states in the window. At the top of the Rollover tab are three columns separated by divider lines: State, Kind, and Preview. These columns are resizable, which is useful especially for seeing the entire image within the Preview column. Place your cursor on the last divider line after the Preview column. Your cursor will change to a double arrow; click and drag to the right to expand the column and view more of the image.

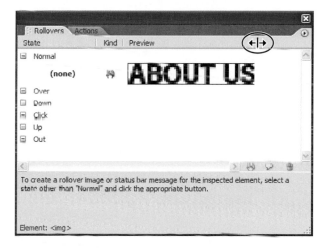

3   In the Rollover window, click on the Over state to select it. You will now tell GoLive which image to use for this state.

4   On the bottom right-hand side of the Rollover window, click on the Create new rollover image button (). GoLive adds the new state. Now you will link the new state with another image.

5   Reposition your Rollover window, if necessary, so that you can see your site window. Click and drag the Fetch URL button from the URL section of the Rollover window to the about_us-rollover.gif file in your site window. This links the Over state to the second image, which is orange.

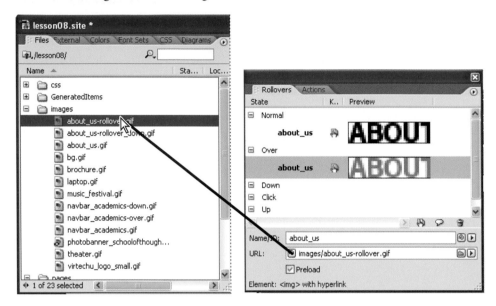

6   Expand your Rollover window, if need be, and then click on the Down state to select it. Click on the Create new rollover image button. Click and drag the Fetch URL button from the URL section of the Rollover window to the about_us-rollover_down.gif file in your site window. This links the Down state to the third image, which is blue.

7   Click on the Preview tab in your document window. Place your cursor over the ABOUT US graphic to see how the rollover reacts. Click and hold down on the button to see the Down state as it turns blue.

8   Click on the Layout tab to return to the Layout Editor.

Detecting rollover images

In the last exercise you manually determined the rollover states for the graphic about_
us.gif. However, there is a faster way to have GoLive CS2 create rollover images. This is
based on the file names of your graphics. Programs such as ImageReady and Photoshop
have the ability to export image files, and will automatically name the image files based
on standard file-naming conventions. When you import an image file that conforms to
specific presets into GoLive CS2, GoLive automatically creates the rollovers for you. For
this to work, the Detect Rollover Images feature must be turned on in the preferences.

1   Choose Edit > Preferences (Windows) or GoLive > Preferences (Mac OS). In the
Preferences window, expand the Images section and click on the Rollover section.
Make sure the two options at the top, Automatically Detect Rollover Images and
Automatically Open Rollover Palette, are checked.

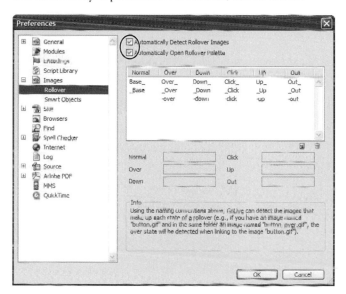

GoLive CS2 detects rollover images when you insert a graphic into your document. It
compares the filename of the graphic you add with other filenames in the same folder.
(This feature works only on images within the same folder.) It then looks for common
naming conventions in the other files and adds them if they match. For example, if
you add an image file named "graphic.gif" and there is another graphic in the same
folder named "graphic_Over," GoLive places the second graphic into the Over state
automatically.

The filename conventions GoLive uses are listed in the Rollover preferences and can be modified if desired. The images you added in the last exercise did not have the proper naming conventions; therefore, GoLive did not recognize them. The remaining images you will add were created and saved for the Web using Adobe Imageready—these images have the proper filename format and will be recognized by GoLive. For more information on formats suitable for the Web, see Lesson 7, "Using Graphics in GoLive."

2   Click OK to close the Rollover preferences window. Close the Rollover window as well, so you can see how GoLive automatically opens it when you add a new image.

3   Click and drag an Image object (⊞) from the Objects palette into the second cell of the table.

4   In the Source section of the Inspector palette, click and drag the Fetch URL button to your site window and select the academics.gif file. Your Rollover window automatically opens and the two remaining graphics are automatically placed into their correct states.

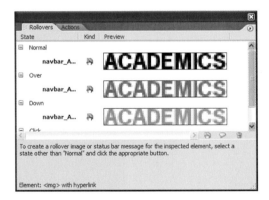

5   Click on the Preview tab and verify that the Academics rollover functions correctly.

Adding a link to a rollover

It is a simple matter to link the rollover images in GoLive CS2 to HTML documents, allowing your graphics to function as navigation.

1   Close or move your Rollover window as needed. Select the ABOUT US image. Before you link it to a HTML page, you will add Alt text, which will help identify the image for users who may be using a screen reader or turning off the browser preference to see images.

2   In the Alt Text section of the Inspector palette, enter **About Us**. Alt text should be added to all graphical elements on a Web page.

3   Click on the Link tab in the Inspector palette. Reposition the site window, if necessary. You may find it useful to close the images folder by clicking on the minus sign (Windows) or arrow (Mac OS). If your pages folder is not open, expand it now. You will be linking the about_us graphic to the about_us.html page.

4   Click on the ABOUT US image to select it. Click and drag the Fetch URL button from the Inspector palette to the site window and select the about_us.html file.

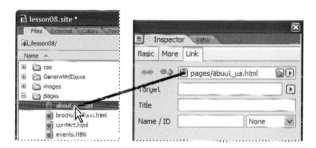

5   Click on the Preview tab. Click on the ABOUT US graphic and you will jump to the about_us.html page.

6   Click on the Layout tab to return to the Layout editor.

7   Choose File > Save to save your document.

Creating a remote rollover

A remote rollover takes the rollover concept a step further. The self-rollover uses at least two graphics of the same size and replaces the first image with a second to create an effect. Remote rollovers allow you to design elements of the page so that a user can mouse over one area of the page and trigger an image in another area. This can be a useful effect to liven up navigation, for example.

This exercise involves using the Actions palette in GoLive CS2.

In this exercise you will be linking the navigation on the left to the images on the right side of the screen so that different images appear when a user mouses over the navigation.

1   Open the contact.html file. You will be creating remote rollovers using the navigation on the left side of the screen to control images you will be placing on the right side.

2 Click and drag an Image object from the Objects palette onto your layout grid directly above the Contact us information. Align the left edge of the image object with the left edge of the Contact us text. Don't worry about the exact placement; you'll be repositioning the image at a later point.

3 Click on the Basic tab of the Image Inspector, then click and drag the Fetch URL button to your site window and select the image, beginning_image.gif, located in the images folder of your Lesson08 folder. This image will be the default image on your page. Reposition it, if necessary, to align with the Contact us text. Think of this image as being the Normal state. However, because this is a remote rollover, you need to give this image a unique name so that GoLive can identify what image it is going to swap out.

4 In the Name/ID section of the Inspector palette, click and hold down on the menu to the far right and choose the Name option. GoLive automatically fills in the name field with the text "beginning_image;" this name was chosen by GoLive by taking the name of the image file (leaving off the extension).

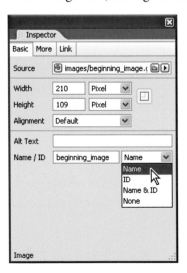

💡 *You can type in any name you choose if you do not like the name GoLive automatically assigns.*

Now that you have named the image, you will select some text and add an action to it, which will trigger another image to appear.

5   With the Standard Editing tool (⟨ɪ⟩), drag over the word "Events" at the far left to select it.

6   Choose Window > Actions to open the Actions palette. The Rollover and Actions palettes are stored in the same window because they are very closely linked. They both create JavaScript when applied in GoLive.

About actions

Adobe GoLive provides a complete set of pre-built actions—scripts triggered by events. These events may be browser-triggered, such as loading a page, or user-triggered, such as moving the pointer over an image. Actions also can be triggered by a point in time in a timeline sequence. To facilitate setting up actions, the Actions tab displays the selected item at the bottom (to ensure that you're working with the right tag), and the Action menu displays recently applied actions at the top (for quick selection).

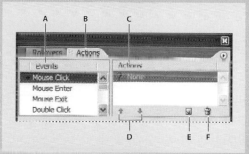

A. *Events (Triggers).* B. *Actions palette.*
C. *Actions Menu.* D. *Move Item Up or Down.*
E. *Create new item button.* F. *Remove selected items button.*

You should always preview actions in a variety of Web browsers and platforms to determine potential browser differences or incompatibilities. The earliest browser versions that support each action are displayed next to the selected action name in the Actions palette.

7   In the Actions palette, choose Mouse Enter from the Events list. Events in JavaScript are user actions, such as when the user places his cursor on a link or an image. Mouse Enter is the same as Mouse Over.

8   Click the Create new item button at the bottom of the Actions section. This tells GoLive that you would like to initiate a specific action when a cursor is placed over the object.

9   Click the Action button (⟨ Action ⟩) on the left side of the Actions tab to open a menu with a list of actions. These actions include pre-made JavaScript code that is included with GoLive. It is also possible to create your own actions using Javascript or to add actions that others have created.

10   From the Action drop-down, choose Image > Set Image URL. This action allows you to swap images with a named image on the page.

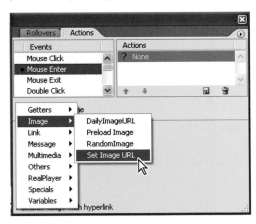

11 In the Image section of the Actions tab, click on the menu. The only option there is beginning_image, which is the name you specified for the graphic. If you had not specified a name for the graphic, you would not be able to use this action.

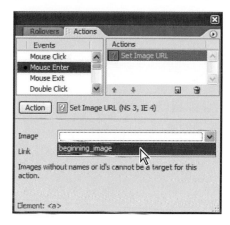

12 In the Link section of the Actions tab, click and drag the Fetch URL button to your site window and select the events.gif file in your images folder.

13 Click the Preview tab of your document window and place your cursor over the Events navigation. The events.gif image will appear in the specified location, but when you move your cursor off the text, the original image does not reappear. This is because you need to add another action specifically instructing the beginning image to be triggered when the user leaves the Events link. You need to be very specific when working with actions and tell GoLive exactly what you want to happen.

14 Click on the Layout tab of your document window and again select the text, Events. In the Actions palette, click on the event Mouse Exit (you can also think of this as Mouse Out) and then click the Create new item button.

15 Click the Action button. Notice at the top of the menu that Set Image URL is located first in the list. GoLive CS2 places the last-used action at the top of the menu so you do not have to look for it. Choose Set Image URL.

16 In the Image field drop-down, choose beginning_image. In the Link field, click and drag the Fetch URL button to the site window and choose the beginning_image.gif. This instructs GoLive to display the original image whenever the mouse leaves the word "Events."

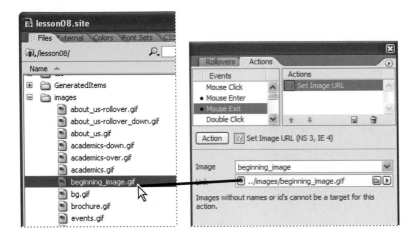

17 Click on the Preview tab and mouse over the Events text. The events image displays only when the cursor is directly above.

18 Click on the Layout tab and choose File > Save to save your document.

Adding an Open Window action

In addition to rollovers, another useful action is the Open Window Action. In this action, when a user clicks on a link or an image, a new window is created. The JavaScript code behind this action allows the designer to designate the width and height of the window, and even determine certain attributes, such as whether or not the window has an address bar or page controls.

In this exercise you will add an action to an image on your page so that when a user clicks on the image, a small pop-up window appears in the corner of the screen, allowing the user to fill in information and submit it in order to receive a brochure for the school.

1 If the contact.html file is not still open, open it now. On the left-hand side, below the navigation text, is a graphic with the text "Click here to receive a brochure." Click on this to select it. Currently this is a static image; you will add an action.

2 Choose File > Open and select the brochure_form.html from the pages folder on your hard drive. This is the page that will be used as your pop-up window. Notice that there is no navigation on this page. This is because, as a standalone page, it is outside the normal structure of the site navigation. Choose File > Close.

3 You should still have the image selected on the contact.html page. Select the Link tab in the Image Inspector. Click once inside the link text field and type the # sign and then press Return or Enter. This character is treated specially by your Web browser and allows an action to be activated on the page.

4 If it is not currently open, choose Window > Actions to open the Actions palette. The next step is to determine what event needs to take place for the action to occur.

5 Click on the Mouse Click event. Then click on the Create new item button (■). This event will occur when a user clicks on the image. Now you will choose the action that will take place with the mouse click.

6   Click on the Action button (Action) and choose Link > Slide New Window from the menu. The fields beneath the action become active. Next to the Slide New Window action in parentheses it reads (NS 4, IE 4). This refers to the lowest browser version that can use the JavaScript behind this code.

Certain actions will work successfully only on more modern browsers—it is important to check the compatibility of actions with the browsers of your target audience.

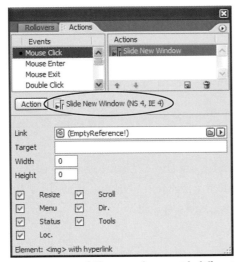

Browser compatibility may change with different actions.

7   In the Link section of the Actions palette, click and drag the Fetch URL button to your site window and choose the file, brochure_form.html. This completes the action so that a user who clicks on the brochure.gif graphic will trigger a window to open with the brochure_form.html document.

Note: *In this example, the Slide New Window action creates a new window with the HTML document inside; however, you can also open a new window which contains just a graphic.*

8   Preview your document in a browser by clicking the Preview in Browser button in your Main toolbar. It is best that you choose an actual browser to test scripts as the GoLive Preview will not consistently run all scripts. In your browser window, click on the graphic, "Click here to receive a brochure." This causes a new window to open.

About scripts in browsers

Certain operating systems and modern browsers have built-in protections against running JavaScript code and may actually prevent scripts from running in the browser without the user's consent.

For example, if you are running Internet Explorer with Windows XP SP2, when you visit a page which has active content, you may see the following message: "To help protect your security, Internet Explorer has restricted this file from showing active content that could access your computer. Click here for options..."

If you are certain that you want to allow the page to run scripts and ActiveX controls on your computer, follow the steps below:

 1 *Click the Information Bar at the top of the window.*

 2 *Click Allow blocked content from the options presented.*

Additionally, it is possible to turn off JavaScript within most browsers.

The window that was created may be the same size as the original window. You may have to click and drag the title bar of the new window to see the original window beneath. The action created a new window, but to make it more effective you will set the width and height of the new window using the controls in the Actions palette.

9 Close the brochure_form.html window and return to GoLive. Reselect the graphic if necessary. In the Actions palette, fill in the fields for Width and Height. Enter **300** for the width and **400** for the height. Press Tab.

10 If necessary, click and drag the bottom right corner of the Actions palette to expand it. There are several checkboxes which allow you to control which elements of the pop-up window will be visible when opened. Deselect all options except Resize. Keep this option available in case the content overflows the window. This allows the user to enlarge or reduce the window size, if necessary.

11 Choose File > Save to save your document, and then preview it in your browser by clicking the Preview in Browser button. Click on the graphic and a new window, 300 pixels wide by 400 pixels high, will slide in from the side of the screen into the center. Close the window. Return to GoLive by closing your browser and clicking on your GoLive document.

Note: Create a Close Window action in the "Exploring on your own" section of this lesson.

Creating head actions

The actions you have been applying up to this point in this lesson can all be categorized as "on call" actions; the behavior of the action takes place in response to a specific action by the user, such as clicking an image or a link. A head action is a script which is inserted into the header of your HTML page and is run as soon as a user opens or loads the page. When a browser opens a HTML page, it "reads" the code from top to bottom; therefore, code at the head of the document can be run before the page loads.

In this exercise you will create a browser switch action which provides designers a way to redirect users to an alternative page if they are using older browsers. Certain features and technology, such as layers, frames, and CSS, will not function correctly in older browsers. The browser switch action allows you to present alternative options for those users. The options may be as simple as a page stating that the site doesn't support their browser or as complex as directing them to an alternative site which does not make use of the newer technology. It is up to the designer to decide how important it is to present these alternative options.

1   Open the lesson08.site file if it is not already open, and double-click on the index.html file in the Lesson08 folder.

2   Click the triangle next to Head at the top of the document window to open the Head section of the page. This section shows a series of icons that represent the elements inside the head section, such as the Title and CSS code.

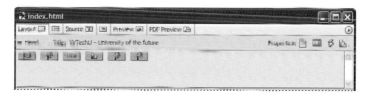

3   In the Objects palette, click the menu and select the Smart set. From the Smart set, drag the Browser Switch object to the Head section of the document window. Be sure you are placing it at the end of the current row of icons. The icon appears as a different color in the Head section to help you identify that it is code.

In the Browser Switch Inspector, there are a series of controls which allow you to specify the browsers that support the features on your page. In this lesson, you'll use the default Auto to have GoLive determine browser compatibility.

Note: You will have to research which browsers support certain features in your code. Advanced use of JavaScript and CSS will be less likely to function on older browsers.

4   In the Alternate Link section of the Inspector palette, type the # sign. Press Enter. This will function as a placeholder for now. If you had an alternate page designed, you could enter the page's name in the Alternate Link field. You could also place an absolute URL to a Web browser's latest download page, thereby encouraging a user to upgrade to a newer browser that would allow them to take advantage of your site's features.

5 In the Head section of the document window, click and drag the Browser Switch button to the left so that it follows the title icon. This ensures that the Browser Switch action runs before other actions on the page, which ensures that older browsers will be switched to an alternate page before the rest of the page loads.

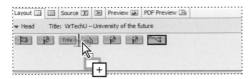

6 Choose File > Save and close your documents.

Congratulations! You have finished the lesson.

Locating and installing GoLive CS2 actions

GoLive Actions are nothing more than JavaScript code designed to work in GoLive as visual icons. This allows users who do not know how to write JavaScript to use these actions easily. As such, there are a number of third-party Actions available from authors who have created and distributed them. Sometimes these actions are free, but they are also commercially available. Users familiar with Adobe Photoshop plug-ins are probably familiar with the concept.

You should be somewhat careful with the actions you add to your system. The quality of JavaScript code will vary from author to author. One place to locate actions is at Adobe's Studio Exchange Web site which features user-reviewed actions which can be downloaded and installed on your system. At the time of this writing, the URL for the Studio Exchange is http://share.studio.adobe.com/.

A new action needs to be put into the proper location on your hard drive. To install an action, locate the GoLive CS2 application folder. The proper path is GoLive CS2 > Modules > Jscripts > Actions. There will be a series of subfolders there. You can place the action in one of the existing subfolders or create your own subfolder. After placing the action in the subfolder, you must restart GoLive to have access to the new action.

Exploring on your own

Experiment with the existing pages and images in your lesson08 site to help you feel more comfortable with Rollovers and Actions. Use a menu to jump between pages.

Creating a Close Window action

As a courtesy to your viewer, you may wish to add a Close Window action to the form page which pops-up as a separate window.

1   Open the brochure_form.html file.

2   Using the Standard Editing tool, insert the cursor after the Submit button.

3   Type **Close Window**.

4   Select the text "Close Window."

5   In the Text tab of the Table Inspector, type # in the link field. Press Enter.

6   In the Actions palette, choose Mouse Click and select the Create new item button.

7   Select the Action button and choose Link > Close Window.

8   Test in your browser.

Review

▶ **Review questions**

1   What is the purpose of the Rollovers tab in the Rollovers & Actions palette? What is the definition of a state?

2   What is the difference between a self-rollover and a remote rollover?

3   How do you assign an action to a link?

4   What is a Head action, and how do you add one in GoLive CS2?

▶ **Review answers**

1   You can use the Rollovers tab in the Rollovers & Actions palette to specify different images for different states of a rollover image. The three most common states are the Normal state, which is how the button appears by default, the Over state, which is how the image appears when the user places their cursor over the graphic, and the Down state, which is how the image appears when the user clicks on an image.

2   A self-rollover is when there are two virtually identical images which are swapped within the same location to create a visual effect when the user interacts with the image. A remote rollover is when a user interacts with one area of a Web page (such as mousing over a link) and creates the appearance of an image in a remote part of the page.

3   You assign an action to a link by selecting it and assigning an action using the Actions tab in the Rollover & Actions window.

4   A Head action is code which exists in the Head section of an HTML and is called before the HTML page loads. You create a Head action by dragging a Head Action object from the Smart set of the Objects palette to the Head section of a document.

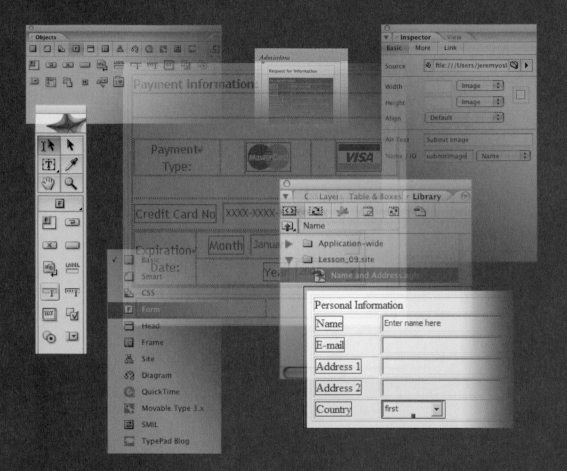

Forms are interactive elements on a Web page that allow users to send data from their browser to the author of the site. In this lesson, you will create forms allowing users of the site to request information from a university and send in an application online.

9 | Creating Forms

In this overview of creating forms in GoLive CS2, you'll learn how to do the following:

- Place form fields on a page.
- Add fields to a page, including text fields and pop-up menus.
- Add radio buttons, clickable images, and input buttons.
- Work with list boxes.
- Define the tab order of your form fields.

Getting started

In this lesson, you will be working on an application form for the fictional university, VirtechU. You'll create a section of the form that allows visitors to enter personal information. You will add a variety of form elements to the form, including radio buttons, a clickable image, and a Reset button.

1 To ensure that the tools and palettes function as described in this lesson, delete or deactivate the Adobe GoLive CS2 preferences file. See "Restoring default preferences" on page 3.

2 Launch Adobe GoLive CS2. Close the Welcome Screen if it appears.

3 Choose File > Open and navigate to the Lesson09 folder, locate the Lesson_09.site file. Click Open.

4 In the lesson09.site window, double-click on the file named lesson09_end.html to open it. This document represents the final version of your file.

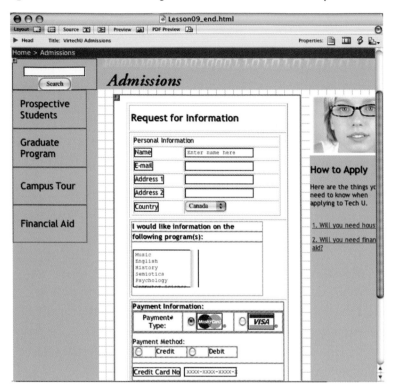

5 Preview the lesson09_end.html document by clicking the Preview in Browser button (📷.) in the Main toolbar.

If you have no browser defined you will see a GoLive CS2 alert window. Click OK. Then choose the Add button and navigate to locate the browser of choice. Check the browser and choose OK.

Make sure you have assigned the browser of your choice to preview your form throughout the lesson.

6   Once in the browser, experiment by filling out the form and entering information into the text fields. Also try the pop-up menus and radio buttons. When you are finished, close the browser window and return to GoLive.

7   You can choose File > Close to close this file, or keep it open for reference.

8   In the Lesson_09.site window, double-click on the file named lesson09_start.html to open it. This document contains a partially completed page with a form. You will add information to this form.

9   Choose File > Save As and name the file **admissions_form.html**. Click on the Site Folder (🗀) at the bottom of the Save As window and select Root (Windows) or Root folder (Mac OS), then click Save.

About forms

Forms in GoLive CS2 are created by dragging form elements from the Objects palette onto your page and using the Forms Inspector to set options for the elements. Although you have great flexibility when it comes to designing forms in GoLive, the act of submitting and collecting the information from forms is handled not by GoLive, but by the configuration of a Web server.

To submit and collect information from a form over the Web, you often use a Common Gateway Interface (CGI) application on a Web Server to collect and route the data to a database. The names of the form fields (such as an address line) must match those set in the CGI application. Keep in mind that CGI scripts must be built outside of Adobe GoLive CS2 and require some knowledge of computer programming. CGI applications are usually set up by a Web server administrator. Your Internet Service Provider (ISP) may also offer "canned" CGI scripts for use by customers with hosted sites. Be sure to check with your ISP about the availability of CGI scripts for handling forms.

In this exercise, you will be creating a form for personal information and then placing the form into the Snippets section of the Library palette. Snippets allow you to place common elements of a Web site, such as a form or a logo, and reuse them on numerous pages.

1   Choose File > Open. Navigate to the Lesson09 folder, choose the file form.html, and click Open. This page has a table with six rows and two columns already added for you. You will be adding form elements to the various cells, allowing users to enter personal information to submit to the university.

In order to add form elements to a page, you need to access the form objects in the Objects palette.

2   Click and hold down on the Palette menu button (⌄☰) at the bottom of the Objects palette and select Form.

Select Form from the Objects palette menu.

Form objects appear.

The Form Objects palette contains the form elements that can be dragged into GoLive CS2 documents. All form elements support HTML 4.0 standards and are backward compatible with the HTML 3.2 specification. The Objects palette appears as a separated palette below.

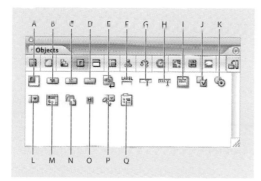

A. Form. B. Submit Button. C. Reset Button.
D. Button. E. Form Input Image. F. Label.
G. Text Field. H. Password. I. Text Area.
J. Check Box. K. Radio Button. L. Popup.
M. List Box. N. File Browser. O. Hidden.
P. Key Generator. Q. Fieldset.

3   Drag the Label Object (📋) from the Objects palette to the left cell of the second row of your table (underneath the Personal Information header). The Label object inserts a text-based label for identifying the purpose of an adjacent form element.

4   Double-click the default text "Label" and then type **Name** to change the label text.

5   Click in the right cell of the second row. Double-click on the Text Field object (⬜) in the Objects palette. This inserts a text field where your cursor was located.

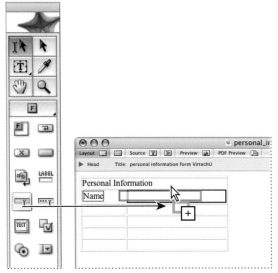

You can also drag and drop a Text Field Object to the cell.

6   In the Inspector palette, locate the Name section and replace the default textfieldName by highlighting it and typing **nameField**. It is very important to accurately name the elements in your forms because the name of the element is used to identify it and distinguish it from other elements.

7   In the section Value (Windows) or Content (Mac OS), type **Enter name here**. Notice the text is being filled out in the text field area in your document window. The value of the text field is the text located inside it; in this case, the value is being used to prompt the end user to enter their name.

Note: An initial value is useful for users but not required when creating text fields.

8   In the Visible text field, highlight the default value and type **20**, then press Enter. This controls the number of characters that can be displayed in the field.

9   In the Max text field, type **40**, then press Enter. This defines the maximum number of characters that can be entered into the field.

10   Choose File > Save to save the document.

Adding e-mail and address fields

You will now fill out the rest of the form by adding e-mail and address fields. Although you could duplicate the steps from the last exercise, it is sometimes faster to duplicate previously created form elements and then modify them.

1   Position the cursor over the left side of the row containing the label and text field. Click when the arrow appears. This selects the row.

2   Choose Edit > Copy.

3   Position the cursor on the left side of the row directly beneath the row you just copied. When the arrow appears, click then choose Edit > Paste to paste the contents into the row directly beneath.

4   Repeat step 2 two more times to duplicate the form content for a total of four rows. Now you will modify the duplicated fields.

5   Highlight the text "Name" in the second duplicated row, and change it to **E-mail**; highlight the text label in the third duplicated row and change it to **Address 1**; highlight the text label in the fourth duplicated row and change it to **Address 2**.

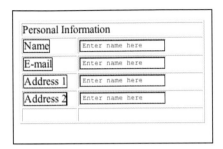

6   In the E-mail row, click on the text field to select it. In the Value field (Windows) or Content field (Mac OS) of the Form Text Field Inspector, highlight the current text and press the Delete key to remove it. This removes the initial field value, or content, from your e-mail text field. It is generally not necessary to put values in every form field. In the name section, rename the text field **emailField**.

Note: Every form field should always have a unique name. When you copied the form fields using the copy and paste technique, you also duplicated the original name. If you did not rename the subsequent form fields, this could lead to confusion.

7   In the Address 1 row, click on the text field to select it. In the Value field (Windows) or Content (Mac OS) of the Form Text Field Inspector, highlight the current text and press the Delete key to remove it. In the name section, rename the text field **Address1Field**, press Enter.

8   In the Address 2 row, click on the text field to select it. In the Value field (Windows) or Content (Mac OS) of the Form Text Field Inspector, highlight the text and press the Delete key to remove it. In the name section, rename the text field **Address2Field**. Press Enter.

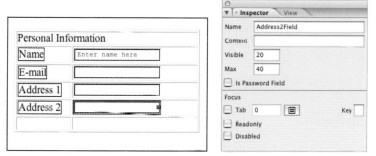

The name of the text field is unique for each element.

9   Choose File > Save to save your work.

Linking labels to text fields

Now you'll link each label to its corresponding text field on the page. When labels are linked to a text field, users can activate the text field by clicking its label. For example, users can click the "Name" label to insert a cursor in the text field for entering their name.

1   Position the cursor on the edge of the Name label; click when the cursor changes appearance (). The Inspector becomes a Form Label Inspector.

2   In the Form Label Inspector, click and drag the Fetch URL button () to the text field to the right of the "Name" label. The Reference text box automatically generates a number which associates the text field and the label.

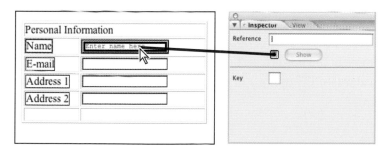

3   Select the "E-mail" label and link it to its corresponding text field using the Fetch URL button in the Property Inspector.

4   Link the "Address 1" and "Address 2" labels to their corresponding text fields using the Fetch URL button.

5   Select the Preview tab to view your page in the Preview Editor. Click on the E-mail or Address text to see it activate the corresponding text field.

6   Click on the Layout tab to return to the Layout Editor.

7   Choose File > Save to save your document.

Creating a pop-up menu

Pop-up menus provide viewers with multiple options from which they can choose. Now you'll add a pop-up menu that viewers will use to choose their country of origin.

1   Drag a Label object from the Objects palette to the first cell in the last row of your table.

2   Double-click the word Label to select it. Then type **Country** to change the label text.

3   Click in the second cell of the last row and drag the Popup object (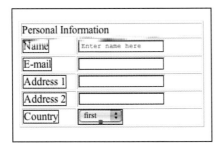) from the Objects palette to your last cell. The pop-up menu placeholder appears in the last cell.

4   In the Name section of the Form Popup Inspector, rename the pop-up menu **countryPopup**. Notice in the bottom section of the Inspector palette that there are default labels and values for the options in the pop-up menu. You will now modify these to add Country names.

5   In the Label section in the bottom half of the Form Popup Inspector, click on the text "first." A text field becomes active at the bottom of the Inspector; highlight the text and type **Canada** to replace it. Press the Tab key to jump to the Value field. Enter **country_Canada** and press Enter or Return. This replaces the text "one". Notice the label and value in both the Inspector and your document have been updated.

6   Select the second item ("second") in the Label section of the Form Popup Inspector. Change the label name to **France** and the value to **country_France**.

7   Select the third item ("third") and change the label name to **Germany** and the value to **country_Germany**.

8   Now you'll add a fourth value. Click the Create new item button (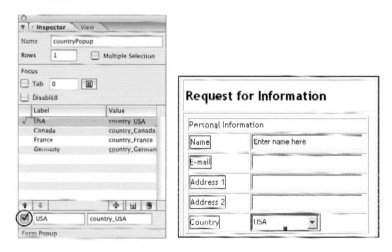) at the bottom of the Form Popup Inspector. Then enter **USA** as the label and **country_USA** as the value. Select the checkbox to the left of the label to mark this option as the default value in the list.

Notice that USA now appears as the default selection in the form pop-up window.

9   Choose File > Save to save the page.

Adding the table to the Library palette

With GoLive CS2, you can store frequently used objects in the Snippets section of the Library palette. In order to use this personal information section on several different pages throughout your Web site—you would add it to the library for reuse. You will now store the table you just created in the Library, so that you can quickly add it to the membership application form.

1   Choose Window > Site > Library to open the Library. If you are not on the first tab, Snippets (⊡), select it now. There you see folders for Application-wide items and a folder for the currently open site.

The first time you open the Library palette while in a site, GoLive CS2 needs to generate the default items in the Application-wide library; this can sometimes take a few seconds.

Note: The Application-wide library allows you to store commonly used items and share them between sites in GoLive CS2. You can find helpful pre-configured form snippets in the Form folder in the Application-wide snippets.

2   Click once in your document window and choose Edit > Select All to select the table and form elements in your document window.

3   Place your cursor on the top-left edge of the table. When the cursor changes appearance (⬐), click and drag the table from the document window into the Lesson_09.site folder in the Snippets tab of the Library palette. The form is added to the Library palette as "snippet.agls."

4 Click once on the text snippet.agls and rename it **NameandAddress** and press Return or Enter.

5 Choose File > Close to close the form.html document. Because you have saved the form as a snippet, you do not need the original file.

6 Choose Window > admissions_form.html to bring the document forward. If it is closed, choose File > Open and locate admissions_form.html in the Lesson_09 folder inside the Lesson09 folder.

7 Drag NameandAddress.agls from the Snippets tab of the Library palette to the empty table cell directly below the words "Request for Information." The form information you created is placed on the page.

8 Choose File > Save to save the page.

Modifying a list box

A List Box object (▦) is a form element, located in the Form section of the Objects palette, that you can use to create a list that allows users to select only certain choices. When the form is submitted, only the selected values are passed to the form recipient. The list box in this example is a list of various university programs in which a user may be interested. You'll now make several changes to the list box; the first step will be to add a sixth item to the list of five.

1   Click in the list box underneath the section, "I would like more information on the following program(s)" to select it. Notice, in the Form List Box Inspector, that each of the five listed items has a label and a value.

First you'll make the list box into a multiple selection form field so users can select more than one item on the list.

2   Select the Multiple Selection checkbox in the Inspector palette.
Now you'll add an item to the list box.

3   In the Rows section of the Inspector, enter **6** to increase the number of rows (or items) visible in the list box.

4   Click the Create new item button (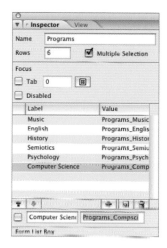) at the bottom of the Form List Box Inspector. In the left text box at the bottom of the Inspector, delete the default text "item," and type **Computer Science**. Press the Tab key and then type **Programs_Compsci**, and press Enter or Return.

Now you'll preview the page in a browser to verify that the list box works as it should.

5   Click the Preview in Browser button (📷.) in the Main toolbar. Click on a list item to select it. Ctrl+click (Windows) or Command+click (Mac OS) to add additional items to your selection.

6   Choose to close the browser window when you are finished and return to GoLive.

7   Choose File > Save to save your work.

Adding radio buttons

In this exercise you'll add payment information to a part of a form that will allow users to apply to a program online. This form has been partially created for you and is located at the bottom of the form you have been working in. You will add a group of radio buttons to this section.

Note: Radio buttons are generally used when only one item in a section is to be selected. The Check boxes are used when multiple items are to be selected.

1 Drag the Radio button object (⊙) from the Objects palette to the empty table cell located to the left of the MasterCard image.

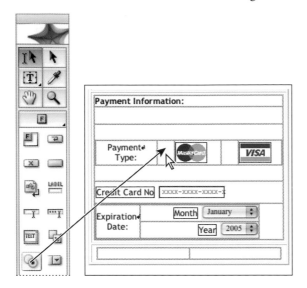

2 In the Group section of the Inspector palette, enter **paymentType** for Group. This names the group of radio buttons.

You'll use the same group name for the second radio button that you'll add to the page. Using the same group name for the two radio buttons ensures that users can select only one option from the group.

3 In the Value text field of the Form Radio Button Inspector, enter **mastercard**. This is the value that will be returned to the form recipient when a viewer chooses to pay with MasterCard. Press Tab.

4   Check the Selected option. This makes MasterCard the preselected option, although this is not a requirement.

Now you will copy the radio button that you just created.

5   Now Ctrl+drag (Windows) or Option+drag (Mac OS) the radio button to the empty table cell next to the Visa image. This keyboard shortcut allows you to copy selected objects in GoLive CS2.

6   In the Value section of the Form Radio Button Inspector, change the value to **visa** but leave the Group value unchanged. Uncheck the Selected option.

Now you will add a separate radio group.

7   Insert the cursor in the empty table cell to the left of the cell containing the word "Credit."

8   Double-click on the Radio Button object in the Objects palette. The Radio Button object is inserted into the table cell.

9   In the Form Radio Inspector, type **methodType** into the Group text field.

10   In the Value text field, type **credit**.

11   Ctrl+drag (Windows) or Option+drag (Mac OS) the radio button to the empty table cell next to the cell containing the word "Debit."

12 Change the Value to **debit**. Press Tab.

Note: If unique groups were not created, selecting MasterCard would deselect the choice of Credit or Debit. By establishing separate groups, you can use radio buttons throughout a form without conflict.

13 Select the Preview tab to enter the Layout Preview. Click on the radio buttons and note that only one can be selected in each group. Select the Layout tab to return to the Layout Editor.

14 Choose File > Save to save your work.

Adding a Submit button

After a form is complete, add a Submit button to send the information to the recipient of the form data. Both the Submit button and the Reset button are generic form objects which are rendered by the browser. In this exercise you will learn how to add a Submit button as an image file, in the form of a button.

1 Click in the last row of your table (beneath the Expiration date) to place your cursor inside.

2 Drag a Form Input Image object (🖼) from the Objects palette to the last row of your table. A Form Input Image placeholder is added to the row.

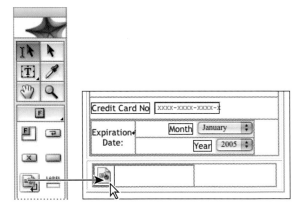

3 Click on the Browse button (🗁) in the Source section of the Form Input Image Inspector and navigate to the Lesson_09 folder. Select the submit_button.gif file in the images folder and click Open or OK. The submit application image is added to the row.

Note: You also could have used the Fetch URL button feature of the Inspector to link the form input image to the submit_button.gif file in the site window.

4   In the Alt Text box in the Inspector palette, enter **Submit Image** as an alternative text message for the image. Alt text allows users who may not be able to display images to understand the content of the image.

5   In the Name / ID area, click the drop-down box and choose Name.

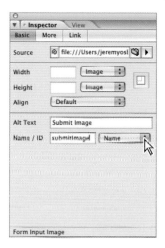

The text **submit_button** is automatically added to the Name field. This names the Form Input Image.

6   Click the More tab in the Inspector. Select the Border checkbox. The value 0 is assigned to prevent a border from being added to the image.

7   Choose File > Save to save your work.

Adding a Reset button

In the last exercise, you added an image for the Submit button and linked it to your form. Now you will add a Reset button, which can reset the data a user has added.

1 Drag a Reset button object () to the right of the Submit Application image.

The options for the Reset button are available in the Input Button Inspector, including the ability to change the button from a Reset button to a Submit button.

You can replace the "Reset" and "Submit" text on the Reset and Submit Button objects with your own by selecting the Label checkbox in the Input Button Inspector and typing new text.

The settings for the Reset button.

2 Select the Preview in Browser button. Change the value for the credit card expiration date and then click the Reset button and notice the values change back to the defaults.

3 Click the Submit button and you will receive an alert. This is because there is an empty reference linked to the Submit button. At this point, to make the form functional, you would need to contact your ISP or IT department to link the Submit button to a valid URL.

You can replace an (EmptyReference!) with the "#" symbol until you have valid URLs for your form to avoid link errors.

4 Close the browser window and return to GoLive. Choose File > Save. Leave the file open.

Setting the tabbing order

You can make your forms easy to navigate by specifying a tabbing chain. A tabbing chain lets you define the order in which form elements are selected when the Tab key is pressed.

1   Choose Special > Forms > Start Tabulator Indexing.

Small yellow index boxes appear on top of, or inside, form elements that can be tabbed, and a pound sign appears next to the index form element pointer when it's over a form element.

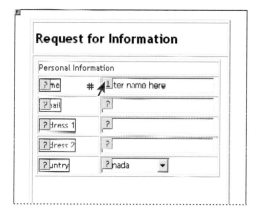

2   First, click the nameField text field that is to the right of the Name label. A number appears.

3   Then, click each element successively in the order as they appear until you reach the address2Field, located to the right of the Address2 label. A tab index number appears in each index box and in the Tab box of the Form Text Field Inspector.

Note: In this example, the form is not complex, but tabbing order is helpful when there are multiple columns of form elements.

4   When you have specified the tabbing chain, choose Special > Forms > Stop Tabulator Indexing, or click the Start/Stop Indexing button (⊞) in the Inspector.

Test the result in a Web browser. Tabbing is not supported in the GoLive Preview or Live Rendering.

Note: You can also assign the tabbing order by selecting each form element individually and entering a number in the Tab box in each element's Inspector. Form elements that support tabbing have the Tab option in their Inspector.

Congratulations! You have finished the lesson.

Exploring on your own

1   Create a new page and add a Form object. Using snippets, add the Name and Address data that you created earlier in the chapter into the form.
Open up existing files, and experiment by creating additional snippets of text and images and renaming them in the Library palette.

2   In your new document, experiment with the other form objects in the Forms palette to get an understanding of other forms concepts such as check boxes, the file browser, and the Popup objects.

For more information about using the objects in the Form section of the Objects palette, see "Creating Forms" in the Adobe Help Center.

Review

▶ **Review questions**

1 What are form fields?

2 Why does a Form object need to encompass all form elements?

3 How can you add a clickable image to a form?

4 Why would you link a Label object to a form element, such as a Text Field object?

▶ **Review answers**

1 Form fields are elements that you can add to forms, such as text fields, radio buttons, or list boxes. Users can interact with form fields by entering information, clicking items, or selecting items.

2 Dragging the Form object from the Objects palette creates the container for the form and allows the form to display and function properly in a browser. The Form object is where the URL for data submission is provided, as well as the method in which the data will be encoded.

3 To add a clickable image to a form, you can do one of the following:

- Drag a Form Input Image button from the Forms set of the Objects palette to the form and use the Browse button in the Inspector palette to browse for an image file.

- Drag a Form Input Image button from the Forms set of the Objects palette to the form and use the Fetch URL button in the Inspector to connect the placeholder to a file in the site window.

- Drag an image file directly to the Form Input Image placeholder in the form.

4 By linking a Label object to a form element, it makes it easier for users to select the coinciding field. Labels also tell screen readers which text to associate with which input field, thereby making your forms easier to fill out for the visually impaired.

GoLive offers several features that help you to update your Web site easily, as well as create a consistent look to your Web pages.

10 | Using Stationeries, Components, Page Templates, and Snippets

In this lesson about helpful site features you will learn how to do the following:

- Use components to place dynamic elements on your pages.
- Use the Library palette.
- Use snippets to store frequently used code.
- Save and use stationery files.
- Create a page template.
- Assign template regions.

Use the component, stationery, snippet, and page template site features in GoLive to speed up Web site creation, provide a consistent look to a Web site, and allow for automatic updates across multiple pages.

What is the difference?

A **Component** is a file that can be embedded into multiple pages. A component can contain anything that you can put on a page, such as text, rollovers links, and images. Components do not embed head information, such as keywords or scripts.

Components are useful for buttons, logos, headers, mastheads, or other common navigation elements that you want to use throughout your site. When you add a component to a page, the component remains linked to its source file until you detach it.

A **Stationery** file is used to create pages. The page can contain any elements typically placed on a page, such as layers, tables, and images. Stationery files can also contain head items, such as meta tags and keywords. Stationery files provide a base from which to build a page, but this base is not dynamic. Changes to a stationery file will not be reflected in the pages created from it.

Snippets allow you to store frequently used elements, such as tables, images, or copy. You can store these snippets specifically for a site or make them available application-wide. Library snippets are not dynamic and will not update if the original snippet is edited.

A **Page Template** is a feature that allows you to build a page with defined, editable regions. When a page template is opened as a new page, the user can edit only the defined regions; all other regions are locked. Like a stationery page, page templates can contain elements built into the head section of the page, such as page background, keywords, and scripting.

If a change is made to the original page template file, all pages created from it are updated.

Getting started

In this lesson you will work on a Web site for the athletic department of VirtechU. You will create library items to be stored for later use, a stationery file, and a page template.

Before you begin, restore the default preferences for Adobe GoLive CS2. Then open the finished site file for this lesson to see an illustration.

1   To ensure that the tools and palettes function exactly as described in this lesson, delete or deactivate (by renaming) the Adobe GoLive CS2 preferences file. See "Restoring default preferences" on page 3.

2   Launch Adobe GoLive CS2. Close the Welcome Screen if it appears.

3   Choose File > Open, and open the lesson10_finish.site file in the lesson10_finish folder inside the Lesson10 folder on your hard drive. You can use this site as a sample, as it contains the finished pages for you to use as a reference.

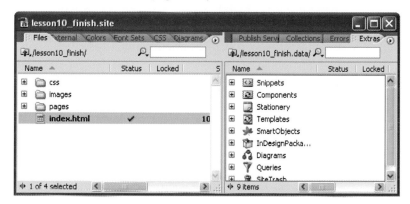

4   Double-click on the index file to open the page that you will create using the stationery and component features in GoLive.

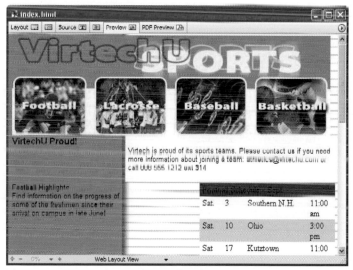

This page was created using the template feature, and contains components as well as items that are stored as library items.

5   Choose the Preview tab, and select the sports names from the header to link to the other pages in this site.

As you link to other pages, note their similarity. The first part of the lesson will be to create one consistent look for the individual team pages by creating a component for the navigational graphic.

6   Select the Layout tab to return to the Layout view in GoLive.

7   Choose File > Close. Repeat this for any open documents. Close the lesson10_finish.site window, and click OK when the Adobe GoLive CS2 warning window appears.

Creating a component file

In Lesson 4, "Creating Navigational Links," you created a simple text component. In this lesson, you will take the component feature a step further by integrating an image map and using the crop text feature. Start by creating and placing a component on several of the existing pages. For the remainder of this lesson you will be completing a site which has been started for you.

1   Choose File > Open and navigate to locate the lesson10_start.site file, inside the lesson10_start folder located in the Lesson10 folder. Click Open.

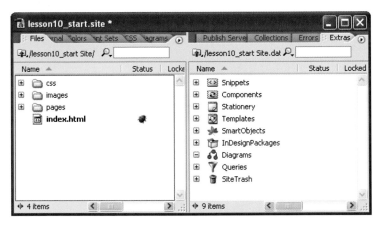

This is the start of a site that you will complete. Ignore any link warning icons (🔆); you will correct them as you add additional content to this site.

2   Double-click on the index.html page. The image map at the top of this page is to be used repeatedly throughout the site. It may frequently change, as sports are added or deleted. You will turn it into a component and place it on multiple pages.

3   With the Standard Editing tool (I↖), click to the right of the small M icon (M) underneath the navigational image. This icon represents the code necessary to create the image map and must travel with the image if the clickable regions are to function.

4   Choose Edit > Select All, or Ctrl+A (Windows) or Command+A (Mac OS).

Insert the cursor after the   Select All.
image map M icon.

5   Select Edit > Cut, or Ctrl+X (Windows) or Command+X (Mac OS).

6   Choose File > New. When the New options window appears, choose Web > Pages > HTML Page and click OK. The new page appears.

7   Choose Edit > Paste, or Ctrl+V (Windows) or Command+V (Mac OS). The artwork complete with the image map appears.

8 Choose File > Save. Select Components from the Site Folder (▱.) drop-down menu in the lower section of the Save As window. Name the file **navbar** and click Save.

9 When the Set Title alert window appears, type **navbar** in the "Enter a new title" text field. Click Set.

Note: You are setting a title on this page to conform to HTML standards, but since a component does not read page information, it has no relevance when embedded on another page.

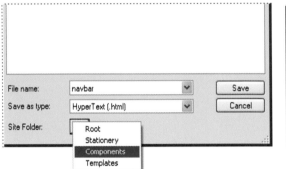

Save the page into the Components Folder.

Assign a title.

💡 *If the title is to be the same as the document name, you can check the "Set title to document name" checkbox.*

Placing a component

1 Choose File > Close to close the navbar.html page.

2 Return to the index.html page.

There are several methods you can use to place a component. For this lesson you will use the Component Object and navigate to your site data folder.

3   Using the Object palette menu, select Smart. Select the Component Object () and drag and drop into the top cell that previously held the image map.

Note: When placing components, it is best to drag the component into a table cell, layer, or layer grid; otherwise, the component will span the width of the entire page.

4   Click on the Browse button (📁) in the Component Inspector and locate the component you saved. The path is Lesson10 > lesson10_start > lesson10_start Site.data > Components > navbar.html. Select navbar.html then select Open or Choose.

💡 *You can also drag and drop the navbar component from the Extras tab in the site window directly to the cell on your page.*

The navbar appears on the page. The icon (⊘) in the upper left corner indicates that this element is placed as a component

5   Choose File > Save. Leave the index.html page open.

Editing a component

You will now add a line of text to the component.

1   Double-click on the placed navbar component. This opens the original component page.

2   Using the Standard Editing tool (➤), click to the right of the M icon (Ⓜ).

Note: The image map M icon is visible only in the Layout view.

3   Type **VirtechU Athletics Department**, then choose File > Save.

Add text to the original component.

4   Choose File > Close and return to the index.html page. The placed component is automatically updated.

5   Choose File > Save. Leave the index.html page open.

Cropping text in a component

You can crop text in components you've added to Web pages, removing characters, words, or paragraphs. If you use one component on multiple pages, you can crop each instance uniquely, creating text content-specific to each page design.

1   Select the navbar component on the index.html page.

2   In the Component Inspector, click the Crop Text button

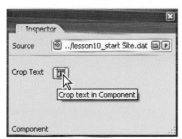

Crop text in individually placed components.

3   From the Crop Text By menu in the Main toolbar, select Words.

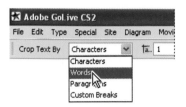

Note: To use custom breaks, you must first add <agl:custombreak/> in the source code of the component to specify break locations.

You will now drag to select the text you want to retain.

4   Starting to the right of Athletics, click and drag to the left and up over the graphic images in the placed navbar component.

Click and drag over the elements you want to retain in the placed component.

5   In the Main toolbar, click the Accept Crop button (✔). The text Department is removed from the component placed on this page but will remain in the original component file. If the text is not removed with the first click on the Accept Crop button, click it again.

Note: You can cancel the crop without applying it by clicking the Cancel button (✖).

6   Choose File > Save then File > Close.

Using snippets

In this next section you will use the Library palette to create a snippet of a table that is used repeatedly in the sports site.

1   Choose File > Open. Browse to locate the file named lesson10_table.html located in the Lesson10 folder. Click Open.

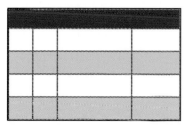

This table will be saved as a snippet.

2   Choose Window > Site > Library to open the Library palette. As a default it is docked at the bottom of the Color and Swatches palette. Click and drag in the Library tab to separate it from the other palettes and make it more accessible.

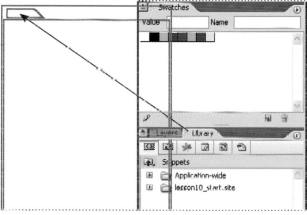

Click and drag the Library tab to separate the Library palette.

3   Make sure the Snippets tab (▦) of the Library palette is selected. There are two snippets already listed in this palette.

4   In the document window, move the cursor over the top-left edge of the table until the pointer changes to the Table Selection pointer (⬉), and then click and drag to the lesson10_start.site folder in the Library palette. The snippet is added to the Library palette.

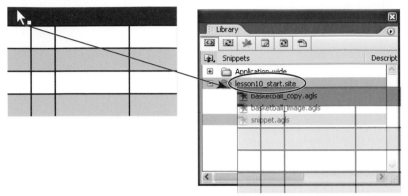

Drag the table to the Snippets tab in the Library palette.

Note: Site-specific snippets are stored in the site's web-data/snippets folder and appear in the Snippets tab in the Library palette and the Snippets folder in the Extras tab in the site window.

5   Click once to select, then again on the snippet.agls. Change the name to **table.agls** and press Enter.

6   Choose File > Close to close the lesson10_table.html file.

Collecting and organizing snippets

You collect snippets in the Snippets tab of the Library palette. When you save a site-specific snippet, GoLive adds a corresponding source file to the site's web-data folder and displays it in the site-specific section of the Snippets tab in the Library palette and in the Snippets folder in the Extras tab in the site window. Snippets are not limited to HTML. For example, you can drag image files from the site into the Snippets tab of the Library palette.

GoLive includes many preset snippets for common Web design tasks. These presets are organized in the application-wide group in the Snippets tab of the Library palette.

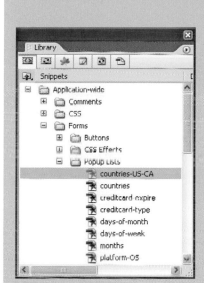 

Preset snippets in the Snippets tab of the Library palette.

—From GoLive Help

Placing the snippet

You will now use the table several times on the index.html page.

1   If the index.html page is not open, double-click on it to open it now. Click on the table.agls snippet listed under lesson10_start.site. Drag it to the right cell opposite the cell containing the Football Highlights copy.

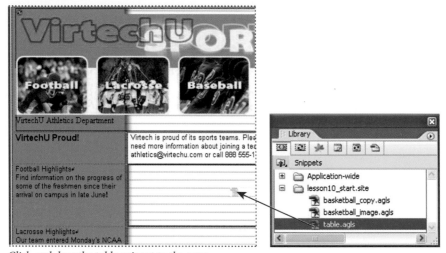

Click and drag the table snippet to the page.

The table appears in the cell. You will now import a text file into the table.

2   Using the Standard Selection tool (▮↖), click to insert your cursor in the top cell of the table.

3   Press Ctrl+Enter (Windows and Mac OS) to select the cell.

4   Choose Edit > Select All or Ctrl+A (Windows)/Command+A (Mac OS) to select all the cells.

5   Choose Special > Table > Import Tab-Delimited Text. Browse and locate the file named football_schedule from the Lesson10 folder. The text is entered.

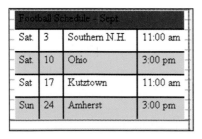

6   Repeat steps 1-2, placing the table in the cells opposite the highlights for Lacrosse, Baseball, and Basketball.

7   Repeat steps 3-5, importing the appropriately named text files, lacrosse_schedule, baseball_schedule and basketball_schedule in the Lesson10 folder.

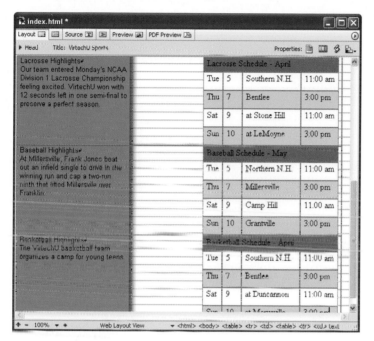

8   Choose File > Save and File > Close.

Creating a stationery file

In this next section you will create a base file using your component and snippet files and save it as a stationery file.

1   In the lesson10_start.site window, open the pages folder and double-click on the baseball.html file to open it.

2   If it is not visible, choose Window > Library to show the Library palette. Remember that it may appear at the bottom of your other palettes, and may need to be dragged up to be visible.

3 Click on the Components tab (▣) in the Library palette. If the lesson10_start. site folder in the Components tab is not open, open it now by double-clicking on it or clicking on the plus sign (Windows) or arrow (Mac OS).

4 Click and drag the navbar component that you created earlier up to the topmost cell. The navbar now appears on the baseball.html page.

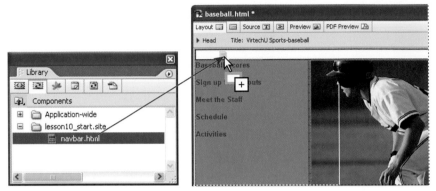

Select the navbar component.   Drag to the topmost cell.

5 Choose File > Save. Leave this document open.

Saving the stationery file

This document is the standard for which you are going to build another page. You will first delete any page-specific information, then save the page as a stationery file.

1 With the baseball.html file still open, click in the left cell that contains copy. Choose Edit > Select All, then Edit > Delete (Windows) or Edit > Clear (Mac OS).

2 Click on the image of the baseball player in the right, cell and choose Edit > Delete (Windows) or Edit > Clear (Mac OS).

3   Click in the title area and delete the copy, "–baseball."

Delete any page specific information.

4   Choose File > Save As. Choose Stationery from the Site Folder drop-down menu at the bottom of the Save As window. Change the name to **team_page.html** and click Save.

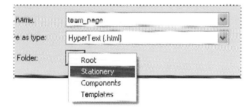

The file is now saved as a stationery file. Now you will use this file to create a new page.

5   Choose File > Close.

Creating a page from a stationery file

Now you will create a new page for the basketball team using the stationery file you just created.

1   Click on the Extras tab on the right side of the lesson10_start.site window.

2   Expand the folder named Stationery.

3   Double-click on the team_page file listed in the Stationery folder. When the Adobe GoLive alert window appears, choose Create to build a new page from this file. An untitled page is created from the saved stationery file.

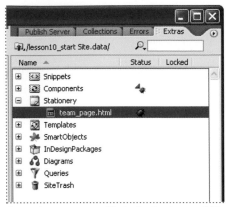

Open the team_page file in the Stationery folder.   Choose Create to build a new page from it.

Note: You would click Modify to update the saved stationery file.

4   Click in the Title text field and add –**basketball** to the end of the title and press Enter.

You will now add some information that has been saved as snippets to this page. Make sure that the Library palette is visible. Choose Window > Site > Library to open or bring the palette forward.

5   Select the Snippets tab of the Library palette. If the lesson10_start.site folder is not open, expand it now.

6 Click and drag the snippet called basketball_copy.agls to the left cell, underneath the navbar component. The copy appears.

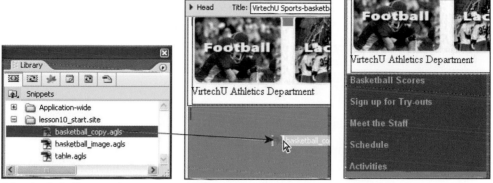

Select basketball_copy.agls.   Drag snippet to the left cell.   Result.

7 Click and drag the snippet named basketball_image.agls to the right cell, opposite the copy. The image snippet appears.

Drag the basketball_image.agls snippet into the right cell.

8 Choose File > Save. Select Root (Windows) or Root folder (Mac OS) from the Site Folder drop-down menu (📁) at the bottom of the Save As window.

9 Name the file **basketball.html** and click Save. Choose File > Close.

Saving a page template file

In this section, you will turn one of your team pages into a page template, restricting the user from editing certain elements in the page and allowing automatic updates to locked regions.

First, using the Library palette, you will add the navbar component to the page.

1　Double-click on football.html, located in the pages folder of the lesson10_start.site window.

2　If the Library palette is not visible, choose Window > Site > Library.

3　Click on the Component tab and click and drag the navbar component from the Library palette to the topmost cell on the football page. The navbar is added to the page.

Add the navbar component to the football.html page.

4　Choose File > Save.

Now you will make an edit to the placed component to see how changes are updated throughout a site.

5　Double-click on the navbar component to open the original page.

6 Carefully delete the text VirtechU Athletics Department, making sure that you do not delete the image map M icon. Choose File > Save.

Delete the copy in the navbar page.

An Updating Component "navbar.html" window appears. This window indicates which pages the navbar component is placed on. You can uncheck any pages that you do not wish to update. For this example, leave all pages checked. Click OK.

7 Click OK on the next Updating Component window. The text is now removed from all the components.

8 On the football.html page, click in the title area and delete the copy -football.

9 Choose File > Save. Leave football.html open.

10 Choose File > Close to close the navbar.html page.

Defining template regions

Now you will define what will be left as editable regions on this page. Remember, you can save any page as a page template. Any part of the page template that is not defined as an editable region is automatically locked. New pages based on a page template are automatically updated whenever you make changes to the template; content in the editable regions is not affected.

1 Using the Standard Editing tool (↖), click to insert the cursor in the left cell containing the text in the football.html file.

2 Press Ctrl+Enter (Windows and Mac OS) to select the cell.

3 Choose Window > Template Regions.

4 Click on the Create new editable paragraph region button (¶) at the bottom of the palette. The cell is highlighted.

Select the cell.

Define it as an editable region.

💡 *To change the highlight color of editable and locked regions, choose Window > View. Expand Highlight Colors, and click the color field for the Locked Regions or Editable Regions, and then select a new color. You can also drag a color slider to adjust opacity. To see the color highlighting applied to the locked regions in the template, choose Special > Template > Lock Page, or choose Lock Page from the Template Regions palette menu.*

5   Now click on the football image that is opposite the copy.

6   Click on the Create new editable inline region button (**I**) at the bottom of the
Template Regions palette.

7   Change the name of the region by clicking once on the default Region name in the
Template Regions palette. Wait a short while after clicking, then type **image** when the
text name becomes editable. Press Enter.

*Click once on a region name to
change it.*

8   Choose File > Save As. Click on the Site Folder drop-down menu and select
Templates. Name the file **team** and press Save.

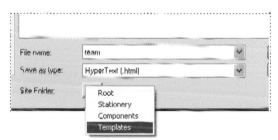

9   Choose File > Close.

Creating a page template

You use the Template Regions palette to mark regions of the page as editable. You can create two types of editable regions: paragraphs or inline selections within a paragraph. When a region is marked as an inline text style, you can't insert paragraphs in the region—in other words, you can type in the region but you can't press return to start a new paragraph.

You can lock or unlock everything in the template that is not marked as an editable region and use the Highlight tab of the View palette to set the color highlighting for locked and editable regions. (Regardless of whether or not you lock the uneditable regions in the template, these regions are automatically locked in all pages created from the template.)

Use Smart Objects for images in your page templates. If you resize a Smart Object in a template, GoLive automatically resizes and optimizes its Web image in every page that's connected to the template.

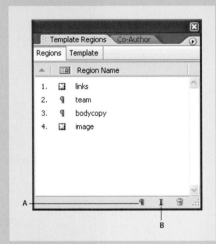

A. Paragraph region. B. Inline text region.

—From GoLive Help

Using the page template

There are several methods that you can use to take advantage of a saved page template. For this exercise you will use the Library palette.

1 Have your lesson10_start.site window open and also the Library palette. If the Library palette is not visible, choose Window > Site > Library.

2 Select the Template tab of the Library palette and expand the lesson10_start.site folder. Your team file is visible.

3 Click and drag the team file from the Library palette to the pages folder in the Files tab section of the lesson10_start.site window. A new_from_team.html file appears, ready to be renamed.

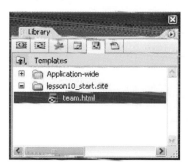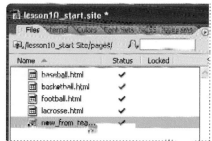

4 Type **soccer** and press Return.

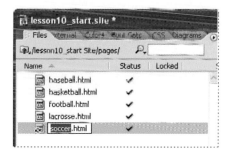

💡 *You could also drag the Page Template from the Templates folder on the Extras tab to the pages folder in the Files tab of the site window.*

5   Double-click on soccer.html to open it. Notice that all the fields outside the editable regions that you defined are locked.

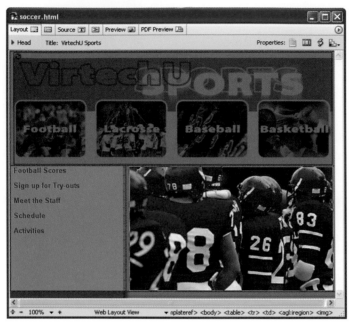

The editable regions are clear.

Building from the page template

You will now add text and an image to the new soccer page you created.

1   Using the Standard Editing tool (⬉), select the word "Football" in Football Scores.

2   Type **Soccer** to replace Football Scores with Soccer Scores.

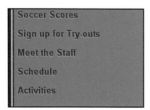

3   Use the Select window button (⬚.) to bring the lesson10_start.site window forward. Expand the images folder.

4   Position the site window so that you can see the soccer.html page at the same time.

5   Drag the image named soccer_ball.jpg directly on top of the football image already placed on the page. The football image is replaced with the soccer ball image.

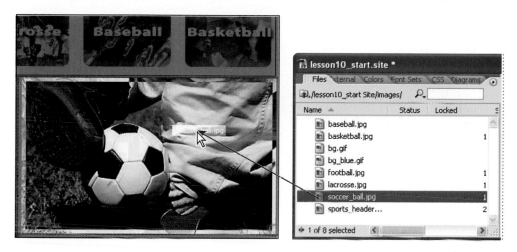

6   Click on the soccer.html page to make sure it is forward, then choose File > Save and File > Close. Leave the lesson10_start site open for the Exploring on your own section.

Congratulations! You have finished the lesson.

Exploring on your own

If your lesson10_start.site is no longer open, choose Open Recent and select the lesson10_start.site from the list, or choose File > Open and browse to the lesson10_start folder inside the Lesson10 folder.

Practice with components

Open the page lacrosse.html. Using what you have learned in this lesson, place the navbar component into the top cell of this page. Choose to close and save.

Take it further by opening the original component, adding text, and saving the changes.

Practice with snippets

Now that you have the basic concept of how snippets are used, you will take some copy from the index page and turn it into a snippet.

1   Double-click on the index.html page.

2   Select all the copy in the second cell down from the top on the right side. This is the contact information text.

3   Drag the selected copy to the Snippets tab of the Library palette into the Lesson10_start.site folder.

4   Drag the snippet from the Library palette onto the lacrosse.html page underneath the existing copy in the left cell.

Review

1   Although components and page templates are dynamic, what are the major differences between the two?

2   How would you store a logo that you want available site-wide?

3   What is the difference between a stationery file and a component?

▶ **Review answers**

1   The major differences between a component and page template are:

- A component cannot store page information, such as scripts, meta tags or page background images or color, whereas a page template can.

- A component cannot have regions within the page locked. A page template can lock user-defined regions on a page using the Template Regions palette.

- A component can be placed as an element on several pages. A page template is to be used as a page.

2   Store frequently used elements, such as a logo, by selecting the logo, then dragging it into the .site folder in the Snippets tab of the Library palette.

3   The difference between a stationery file and a component is that a stationery file is not dynamically linked to the pages created from it. Many users choose to place components on stationery files to add some dynamic elements to the page.

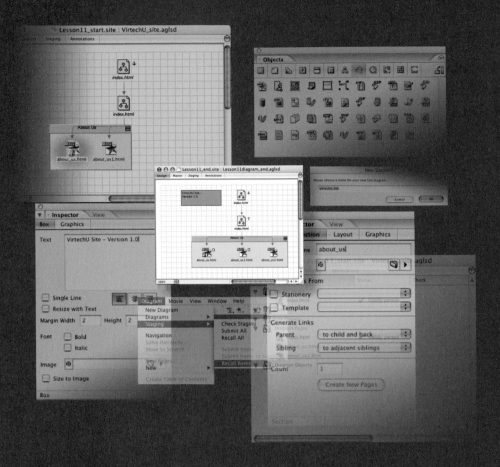

An organized Web site requires extensive planning but provides a positive experience for viewers. Use the Site Diagram feature in GoLive CS2 to create the flow from one page to another before submitting your diagram to become live pages.

11 | Using Site Diagrams

In this overview of using site diagrams in GoLive CS2 you'll learn how to do the following:

- Create a site diagram.
- Create pages, sections and elements.
- Move, distribute, and align elements in a site diagram.
- Create logos and elements on the master page.
- Submit a site diagram to convert the pages to editable HTML.

Getting started

In this lesson, you will create a site diagram. A site diagram is similar to a flowchart and allows you to organize your Web site visually. Site diagrams allow designers to plan the structure of the site before they begin building the content of the pages.

1 To ensure that the tools and palettes function as described in this lesson, delete or deactivate the Adobe GoLive CS2 preferences file. See "Restoring default preferences" on page 3.

2 Launch Adobe GoLive CS2. Close the Welcome Screen if it appears.

3 Choose File > Open and locate the file lesson11_end.site in the lesson11_end folder, in the Lesson11 folder. Click Open and the Diagram tab of the lesson11_end.site window appears.

Note: Ignore any link warnings that appear in this practice site.

4   If you are not in the Diagrams section of the site window, click on the Diagrams tab. Then double-click on the Lesson11diagram_end.

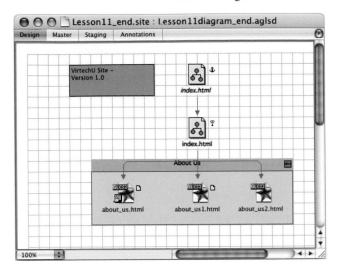

This is the final version of what you will be building. You can keep this site open if you wish to reference the diagram throughout this lesson, or close the diagram and site window now by choosing File > Close for each one.

5   Choose File > Open and navigate to the lesson11_start folder and choose the lesson11_start.site file. Click Open.

Note: You must be working in an active site to use the site diagram feature.

Creating a new site diagram

Using the diagram feature in GoLive CS2 involves working in a separate Diagram interface. The diagram feature allows a designer to conceptualize the flow of a site, dictating which pages link to each other, what the sections of the site are, or to visually indicate that a page links to a database. When the overall navigation and hierarchy are decided, GoLive generates the HTML pages based on your structure. You can even place elements such as text or images on each page. In this exercise you will be creating the About Us section of the VirtechU site using sections, pages, and groups.

Setting up diagrams

When setting up a diagram, use this general workflow:

1 *Set up the diagram.*
Open a new diagram and use the View palette to set page, grid, and canvas options for the design view, and to specify the appearance and labels of objects in the diagram.

2 *Develop the structure of the diagram.*
Add objects to the design view. You can add objects that represent pages or sections (subtrees of pages), and link them in a hierarchy to other pages or sections.

3 *Prepare the diagram for presentation.*
In the design view, you can add annotation objects to provide text commentary, or add level objects to display brackets indicating levels of the site. To make objects appear on each page of a multipage diagram, drag them to the Master tab of the diagram window. To present the diagram to reviewers, print it to paper or export it to Adobe PDF or SVG format.

4 *Submit the diagram.*
Submit an entire diagram or selected items. Submitting converts pages in the diagram to real pages in the site, and creates scratch files for custom objects.

—From GoLive Help

1　Select the Diagrams tab of the lesson11_start.site window. Currently it is empty because you have not created a diagram file.

2   Choose Diagram > New Diagram. In the New Diagram window, type **VirtechU_ site** and click OK.

A file named VirtechU_Site.aglsd appears in the Diagram window. You can have numerous site diagrams (with the extension .aglsd) in a GoLive site.

3   Double-click the VirtechU_site.aglsd file. This opens the site diagram window in the Design view. There are four tabs at the top of the site diagram window: Design, Master, Staging, and Annotations. You select these tabs to perform different functions in the Diagram window.

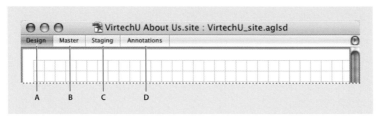

A. Design. *B. Master.* *C. Staging.* *D. Annotations.*

•   Design—This view is where you will be doing the bulk of your work. Think of it as dynamic graph paper. You will be adding page objects in this view and creating links between pages with the tools available to you.

•   Master—This view allows you to place objects on a "master page" which will then be applied to all pages of the diagram. A good use for this would be common elements of a page, such as copyright notices or logos.

•   Staging—The Staging view is where you will validate the links, pages, and folders in your diagram before you convert the diagram to a site.

•   Annotations—This view allows you to create notes relevant to the diagram, which allows you to document the diagram process for yourself or someone collaborating on the site.

Anchoring a diagram to a page

Although you can use your diagram as a visual representation of the site, you can also take it a step further in GoLive CS2 and convert the abstract structure of your diagram into a collection of HTML files which will constitute a site (or a section of a site). When you create a new site, GoLive creates an index page by default. You will now anchor your index page to your diagram. Anchoring the index page to the diagram ensures that the pages that will eventually be created are properly organized and linked to the site folder.

1   Position your site window and your diagram window so that both are in view. Click on the Files tab to view the root folder of your site.

2   Click on the index.html file in your site window and drag it into the diagram window; make sure you are placing it toward the top of the page. The index.html page is added to the diagram window as a page icon; the small anchor symbol confirms that it is an anchor.

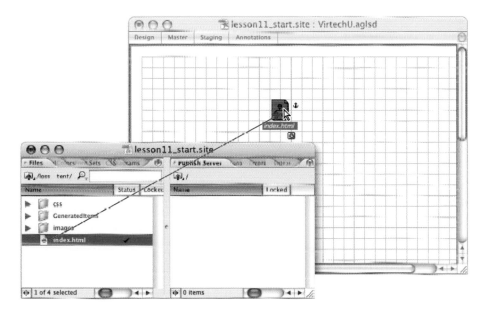

Note: It is not required that you anchor pages in your diagram; however, it is recommended. Pages in a diagram which are not anchored to a site are referred to as scratch pages and will exist as independent objects with no relation to your GoLive site. If you are not planning to convert your diagram to a working site, it is not necessary to anchor pages.

Adding Sections, Pages, and Groups

You have added your first page to your diagram. The index.html page can be considered your home page; all subsequent sections of the site will be linked to this main page. GoLive CS2 provides a number of different objects for you to use in diagrams. The ones you will likely use most often are sections, pages, and groups.

1   If the diagram window is not forward, select it now. Then position the window at the top of your screen, with the lesson11_start.site window positioned below.

2   Choose Diagram from the Object's palette menu. The diagram objects in this palette are all draggable, and can be added to your design view.

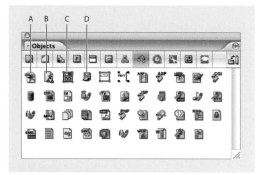

The Diagram section of the Objects palette.
A. Page. B. Section. C. Group. D. Annotation.

Note: *The Object palette shown above has been separated from the toolbox and expanded. You can investigate the other objects in the Diagram palette by placing your cursor over them to view the tooltips. In the toolbar view, click on the arrow at the bottom of the palette to scroll down and view the additional diagram objects.*

3   Click and drag the Section object (⬛) from the Objects palette over the index.html file in the diagram window. Release the mouse when you see a line appear underneath the index.html page. A link is created from the index page to the section.

A section is defined as several pages which are connected by theme or organization. Often times in the organization of a site, sections are defined by folders. For example, in the University site you would have an About Us section, an Academics section, an Admissions section, and so on.

4   Click on the Section tab of the Section Inspector. Enter **about _us** in the New Filename text field, press Enter. This designates the parent file (which is the index.html file) for this section. Additional pages in this section are called child pages and will inherit the about_us filename. For example, the first child page will be about_us.html, the second about_us2.html, and so on.

5   In the Folder text field in the Section Inspector, enter **about _us**, and press Enter. When submitted, GoLive will generate a folder with this name and put the associated section pages into this folder.

Note: If you have existing folders that you would like to place the section files into, you can browse or use the Fetch URL button to point to the selected folders.

6   In the "Create Pages From" section of the Section Inspector, click and hold down on the drop-down menu to the right of Template. A page template, virtcchu_template. html is available, but do not choose it; leave the selection at "None." Both GoLive stationery and page templates can be used to generate files in the diagram window. For more information on how to create stationery and template files see Lesson 10, "Using Stationeries, Components, Page Templates, and Snippets."

7   In the "Generate links" section of the Section Inspector, make sure the Parent menu is "to child and back" and the Sibling menu is "to adjacent siblings." Keep in mind that you are creating a diagram at this stage, so links specified here are not hyperlinks on a page, but are visual links (represented as arrows) which indicate hierarchical relationships between pages.

8   In the Count section of the Inspector palette, enter the number **2**. Press Tab.

9   Press the Create New Pages button at the bottom of the Section Inspector. Two pages are created in the Diagram window and linked to the index page.

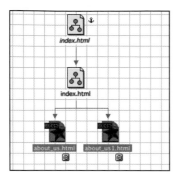

Creating a group of pages

When working with a diagram, you should organize the visual space. When you create a group of pages, you ensure that they are treated as a unit. Objects in a group can be moved, copied, and deleted as one.

1   If they are not currently selected, select the about_us and about_us1.html pages in your diagram view by Ctrl+clicking (Windows) or Shift+clicking (Mac OS) the icons in the window.

2   Choose Edit > Group to add a bounding box around the objects.

3   Resize the bounding box by clicking the corner points and dragging them toward the center. Make the box small enough to fit around the two about_us icons.

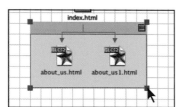

Group pages together in the diagram window.

4   In the "Group" section of the Group Inspector, type **About Us** in the Name text field, and press Enter or Return. This adds About Us to the title bar of the group box.

5   Click on the title bar and drag it down slightly to see how the newly formed group moves as a unit.

6   Click the Minimize button (▤) in the upper right corner of the group window to collapse it. Collapsing windows can help you keep the clutter of a diagram to a minimum.

7   Click on the Maximize button of the group window to expand it.

Adding annotations

When creating a site in the diagram window, you may wish to create notes for yourself or other members of your team. For example, you want to make a note that certain pages in a section already have artwork created; this can be done using the Annotation object.

1   If the Diagram section of your Objects palette is not visible, choose Diagram from the palette menu.

2   Click and drag the Annotation object (▤) from the Objects palette onto the about_us.html icon.

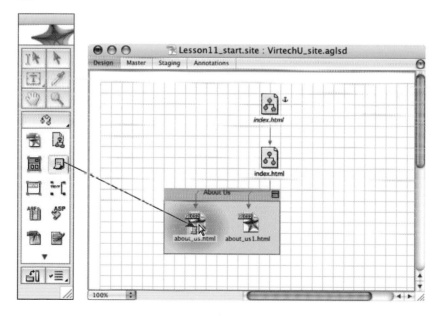

3   In the subject section of the Annotation Inspector, type **Need Artwork**.

4   Click in the text section. In the Text section, type **Dave will be sending the artwork for this section on 5/1**.

5   Select the checkboxes for "Display Subject" and "Display Text" and the annotation appears in the form of a "note" in the design window. You may want to display annotations only for the most important notes in a diagram, as too many annotations create clutter.

6   Deselect the "Display Subject" and "Display Text" checkboxes to turn off the annotation display.

💡 *If you have multiple annotations in a diagram, they can be viewed collectively in the Annotation tab of the Diagram window.*

Adding text and images to your diagram pages

Diagrams are more than just abstract views of your Web sites. You can access the pages that you create in the diagram and add content. A designer could add basic page elements at this stage, such as changing the background color to indicate different sections of the site, or adding simple text navigation.

1   Double-click on the about_us index.html page to open the page.

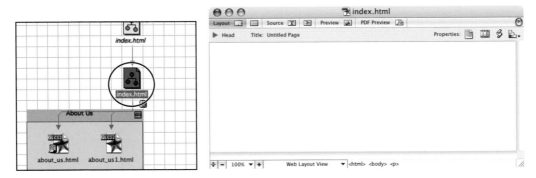

2   Choose Basic from the Objects palette menu, then click and drag an Image object (🖼) from the palette to your document window.

3   In the Image Inspector, click on the Browse button (📂) and navigate to the Lesson11 folder. Select the aboutus_heading.gif image by following this path; Lesson11/lesson11_start/web-content/images. This graphic appears on this page only when you publish the site. Select Open or Choose.

4   Click on the background of your document window to deselect the image. Press the Return or Enter key to go to the next line. Type **About Us Page**. You may want to keep a bare bones structure to your pages at first. When the site is published, you can expand the design by adding layout grids, tables, and/or CSS elements.

5   In the Title section of your document window, change the Untitled Page text to **VirtechU-About Us**. Press Tab to commit the change.

6   Choose File > Save but do not close the document.

Using the staging tools to create site pages

The final step in the site diagram process is to create the pages that you have been outlining in the Diagram design view. It is possible, however, that the structure you have created in the diagram may have conflicts, either with the creation of a new site, or more likely with the merging of an existing site. For this reason, you will want to check the status of your pages before you submit them.

There is the Check Staging command, which scans your site folder for possible conflicts; examples of conflicts might be a document which is currently open or a folder which has previously been created and has the same name as a section you are trying to create.

If your Check Staging process returns no conflicts, then you can progress to submitting the pages, which creates live pages and folders, and places them in your site folder.

1   If the index.html page for the About Us section is not currently open, double-click the index page in your diagram to open it.

2   Click on the diagram window and click on the Staging tab to view the current status of the diagram. GoLive CS2 organizes the site via folders; Diagram Objects and Pages show the current status of these elements.

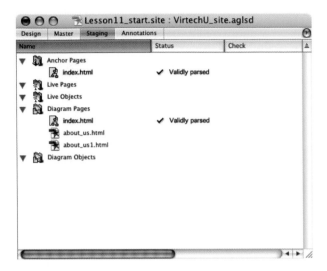

Live Pages and Objects appear when you submit a diagram. You can think of submitting as the process of converting diagram pages to pages that will be created and placed in the site folder. Currently, there are no pages in these folders.

Anchor pages were discussed earlier in the chapter; this is the page that GoLive builds the rest of the section around.

3   Choose Diagram > Staging > Check Staging. You should receive an error marked "file in use" indicated by a stop sign in the check column of the Staging window. Because your index.html file was open, this creates a conflict.

4   Click on the index.html file to select it and then close it. Choose Diagram > Staging > Check Staging again and the error should be replaced by a checkmark. You will now submit the site.

5 Choose Diagram > Staging > Submit All. GoLive will take a few moments and submit the pages you have created in the diagram view to the Live Pages folder. The Diagram Pages folder is now empty.

6 Click on the lesson11_start.site window to bring it forward, then click on the Files tab. The about_us folder was created for you in the submit process. Click on the plus sign (Windows) or arrow (Mac OS) to the left of the about_us folder to view the three pages within.

Note: *You may have noticed that about_us and about_us1.html have a Generic page icon rather than a Validly parsed icon. This is because you have not created HTML pages from these two pages; therefore, they remain generic pages. As soon as you open and save a generic page, it will automatically convert to a validated page.*

7 Click the Select window button (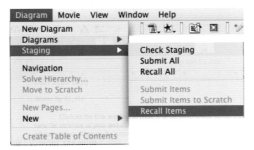) to bring your diagram window forward.

8 Double-click on the index.html file in the Live Pages folder to open it. The banner image and the text you entered were submitted and were included in the file.

9 Close the index.html file.

Recalling a diagram from a site

It is important to remember that the diagram pages are separate from the live pages, so if you wanted to rearrange a section of the site, you would have to remove the necessary pages from the Live pages of your site, update the diagram and then re-submit. For example, it is common to submit a diagram to your live pages to see how the links work in context and then to recall the site to work on the design or modify the hierarchy. To remove files from the Live pages section, you use the Recall command.

1 If you are not in the staging section of your diagram window, click on the Staging tab now.

2 Click on the about_us.html file and then Shift+click on the about_us1.html file. Although you can recall all the items in a diagram, you can also recall selected items, as in this example.

3 Choose Diagram > Staging > Recall Items. Notice that there is also an option for Recall All. After a few moments, GoLive returns the selected documents to the Diagram pages and removes them from the live pages.

4 Click on the Design tab to return to the design window. Choose Diagram from the Objects palette menu. Click and drag a Page object ( ) over the index.html page icon directly above the about_us group. Release the mouse when a bold line appears below the index.html page.

This adds an about_us2.html page to the group. You may need to expand the group box by clicking on the anchor points and dragging out.

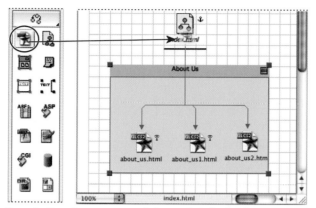

Drag the Page button on top of the words index.html.

5   Click on the about_us2.html file name in the design view and rename it **directions. html** and press Enter or Return. GoLive will automatically name additional pages, but you do not need to keep the assigned name.

6   Choose Diagram > Staging > Submit All to place the two about_us pages plus the new directions.html page into the Live pages.

Adding common elements using the Master tab

As you begin to build more complicated diagrams, you may find that additional diagram pages are needed. GoLive allows you to add commonly used elements to all pages in your diagram using the Master tab. A good use of this would be to put the version number of the diagram on each page. This way, as the site evolves and sections and pages are added or moved, you can keep track of the versions.

1   In the Diagram window, click on the Master tab to activate the master view. All elements that you add to this page will be placed in the same location on every page in the diagram.

2   If your Diagram objects are not visible, choose Diagram from the Objects palette menu. Click and drag the Box object (▣) from the Objects palette to the top left corner of your diagram.

3 In the text section of the Box Inspector, type **VirtechU site - Version 1.0**.

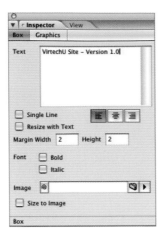

4 Click on the Graphics tab and double-click the color swatch to the right of "Fill Color." The Color Picker appears. Choose a light shade of red and click the Tab key and then OK.

5 Click on the background of the diagram to deselect the box. Click on the Design tab to return to this view. The box with the site information appears in the same location in the design view. Any additional diagram pages would also have this master element.

Note: Even though the box was created in the master tab, it can still be selected and modified in the design view.

Exporting and printing your diagram

GoLive CS2 allows you to export your diagrams as a graphic or as a PDF. You can then print them for review. You can always print the current contents of your design window by choosing File > Print. Exporting the diagram gives you a few more options.

1 Choose File > Export > Diagram. The Export Options window appears.

2 In the "Export Diagram As" drop-down menu, select PDF.

3 Click on the option for "Make Diagram Objects Into Links." This option allows you to click the links on the PDF and open the associated files. You must link the source file to make it work.

4 In the "Root URL For Links" section, click and drag the Fetch URL button to the index.html document at the top of your diagram.

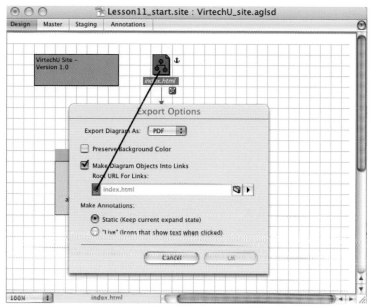

Click and drag from the Fetch URL button to the index.html page.

5 Click OK to export the document. Rename the file **virtechu1.pdf** and save it to the Lesson11 folder. Open it in Acrobat Reader to see the results. Close Acrobat Reader.

6 In GoLive, choose File > Save.

Congratulations! You have finished the lesson.

Exploring on your own

1 Try creating a new section, naming the new section **Academics**. Include four pages and then submit the pages to your live site.

2 Try adding the different elements in the Diagram master to see the different options available to you.

3 Add annotations to various pages in a diagram and export a diagram with the Annotations feature enabled.

Review

▶ **Review questions**

1   What are some of the reasons for using site diagrams?

2   How do you convert the site diagram to HTML pages? Where do the HTML pages you create go?

3   How do you add pages and elements to a site diagram?

4   Why should you check the staging of a site diagram?

▶ **Review answers**

1   A site diagram lets you lay out the structure of a site before you create pages, and helps you maintain the site creation process. You can use multiple prototype diagrams as you build or revise a site, creating and testing designs for review. You can present site diagrams in print or online in Adobe PDF or SVG format. When you are ready to create new pages, you can automatically do so.

2   The submit process allows you to convert diagram pages to real, editable HTML pages. The site pages are placed in the web-content folder of your site folder.

3   There are several ways to add pages and elements to a site diagram. You can drag diagram objects from the Diagram section of the Objects palette to your diagram window. After you add a page, you can also add pages and objects using the context menu. Right+click (Windows) or Ctrl+click (Mac OS) on a page or object in the diagram window, and choose from the Insert Object menu or the New menu.

4   Checking the staging of a site diagram lets you determine whether all of a site's pages are connected by links to an anchor page and whether there are folder or filename problems. Checking the staging allows you to correct errors before submitting the design.

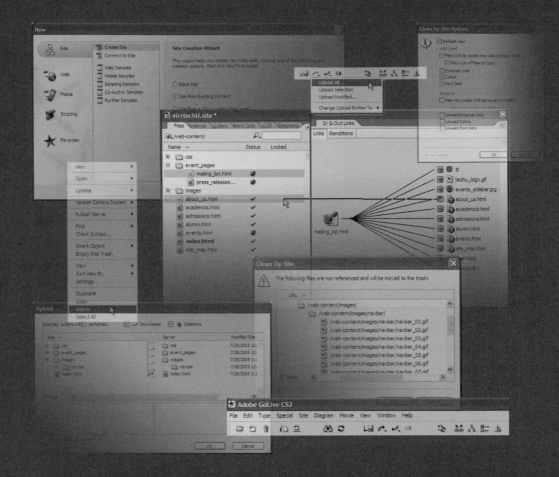

Adobe GoLive CS2 provides powerful site management tools which allow you to manage folders, files, and links; you will learn how to import sites into GoLive and upload your site to a Web server.

12 | Managing and Publishing Web Sites

In this overview of publishing Web sites in GoLive CS2, you'll learn how to do the following:

- Import an existing Web site into GoLive.

- Correct errors in a site.

- Manage folders in a site.

- Change links and file references.

- Clean up a site before uploading it to the Web.

- Upload a site with FTP.

GoLive site management and publishing

In this lesson, you will be working on a completed site for the fictional university, VirtechU. You'll check the site for errors, clean up the site, and then walk through the steps to publish it on the Web. The key to using GoLive's site management tools effectively is to make sure that you understand the organization of the site window and the site asset files that GoLive creates.

Note: The second half of this lesson walks through the steps for publishing a site on the Web. This section proceeds on the assumption that a user has a hosting provider which allows them to upload files on the Web.

Getting started

All of the previous lessons in the *Classroom in a Book* have allowed you to become familiar with GoLive's site window and the principles of site management. You will learn how to use some additional tools to resolve common problems in Web sites.

1   To ensure that the tools and palettes function as described in this lesson, delete or deactivate the Adobe GoLive CS2 preferences file. See "Restoring default preferences" on page 3.

2   Launch Adobe GoLive CS2; close the Welcome Screen if it appears.

3   Choose File > Open and locate the lesson12_end.site file in the Lesson12 > lesson12_end folder. Click Open.

This is the how the site window will appear when you are finished organizing and cleaning the provided site in this lesson.

4   You can leave the site window open for reference, or choose File > Close to close the site.

Importing an existing site into GoLive CS2

It is common for Web designers to work on files which have been created by another person or persons in another application. The first step when working on a previously created site (rather than creating one from scratch) is to import the collected files into GoLive.

1   Choose File > New.

2   In the New window, choose Site > Create Site and choose "Site from Existing Content." Click Next.

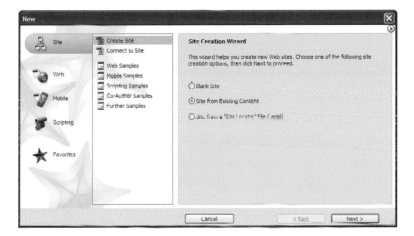

3   Choose "Create a site from a Local Folder of Existing Files." Click Next.

4   In the "Selecting a Local Folder of Existing Files window," click the Browse button in the Folder section and navigate to Lesson12/lesson12_start and click on the virtechu folder. This is a collection of previously created .html, and image files. Because this folder has an index.html page, GoLive automatically recognizes this as the home page. Click OK (Windows) or Choose (Mac OS). Click Next.

5   In the "Specifying a Site Name and Location" window GoLive automatically places the additional folders and site asset files next to the original folder.

6 Click Finish. GoLive imports the files into a virtechu.site window. There will be link warnings on most of the files at this time. Click on the Extras tab to view all the folders, files, and other site assets.

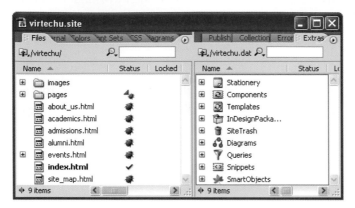

Converting the site into GoLive structure

GoLive maintains the original name of the folder, "virtechu," thus the name of the site is virtechu.site. However, in previous lessons you should have noted that when you create a new site, GoLive creates a series of site assets folders named "web-data," "web-content," and "web-settings." To reduce confusion, you can convert the folders created using a simple command.

1 Choose Site > Convert Site to New Structure.

2 You will be asked to confirm that you would like to convert the site to the new structure. Click Yes. GoLive will rename the folders to their familiar names.

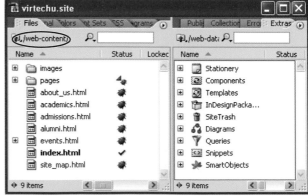

Folder name before converting site to new structure.

Folder name after converting to new structure.

Note: This does not change the site name or any of the content. It merely renames the folders.

This process makes working with sites more consistent, especially if there are multiple authors working in the site.

Correcting errors

Upon importing a site into GoLive, you can visually check the site for errors simply by looking at the site window. If all the pages have check marks (✔) and no bug icons (✱) next to them, then all the files have been declared valid by GoLive. Valid pages are defined as those in which the hyperlinks point to other files or images which have been located by GoLive. Note that in your site there are errors on all of the pages except the index.html page and the press_releases.html file in the pages folder.

The two main categories of errors: orphan files, links to files outside the root folder of your site, and missing files; it is crucial to resolve all issues with these files. A Web site which was put on a server with orphan or missing files will make links on the site "broken" and not function.

1　In the virtechu.site window, click on the Errors tab to view the list of errors. The two main categories are shown here as folders: Orphan Files and Missing Files.

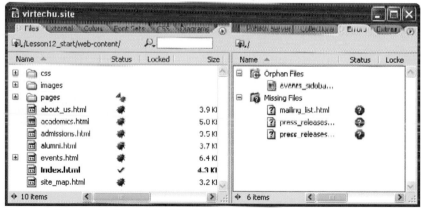

Errors are listed on the Errors tab of the site window.

2   In the Errors tab, click on the events_sidebar.jpg file. In the URL section of the File Inspector palette, the path is pointing to /../../events_sidebar.jpg. Each of the sets of dots followed by the forward slash indicate that GoLive is looking up one level in the directory. The image is loose in the Lesson12 folder. This is outside of the folder that you selected to be the root of your Web site.

3   Click and drag events_sidebar.jpg from the Orphan Files folder to the images folder. This copies the file from the Lesson12 folder to your site's root folder. The Copy Files window appears, informing you that the events.html file needs to be updated. Click OK. GoLive copies the image file and automatically updates the events.html document to updates the link's location.

Note: *When you drag or import files from other locations on your hard drive into the site window, GoLive creates a copy for you in the site folder.*

4   Click on the Refresh view button (⟳) at the top of the screen. This ensures that the assets in your site window are accurately displayed and removes the Orphan Files folder from the Errors tab.

Now you will fix the missing files in the Errors tab. Missing files are files which are referenced but cannot be found by GoLive. This could be because the files don't exist or the file names are misspelled. Another common cause of missing files has to do with Web site authors rearranging files and folders in the site without updating the links.

Two files are indicated as missing, mailing_list.html and press_releases.html. These two files are located in the pages folder in the Files tab of the virtechu.site window and need to be relinked.

5   Click on the mailing_list.html file in the Missing Files section of the Errors tab.

Note: As you may remember from earlier chapters, GoLive CS2 automatically updates links when you rearrange the structure. However, in this lesson, you are working with a Web site that you imported and the previous author may not have used GoLive.

6 Right-click (Windows) or Ctrl+click (Mac OS) on the mailing_list.html file and choose "Find" from the menu. The Find Site Assets window appears. The mailing_list. html document is selected; this first section is telling GoLive to "Find Item whose name contains mailing_list.html."

You could expand or narrow GoLive's parameters of search by clicking on the menus and changing these values. However, it is also important that you tell GoLive what type of file you are looking for. The Find Assets window can search for many types of objects, including colors and fonts.

7 Click on the "Search In" menu and select Files. Even if Files already appears in the "Search In" menu it is important to select it.

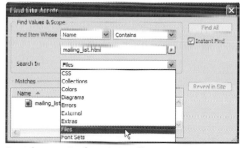

Search your site for missing files.

Selecting files results in a match, which is listed in the Matches section of the Find Site Assets window.

8 Click on the mailing_list.html name in the Matches section. The URL field in the Inspector tab becomes active and the file has been found in the /pages/ directory.

9 Click on the Reveal in Site button in the Find Site Assets window. The mailing_list. html file is selected.

10 Click on the virtechu.site window to bring it forward; click on mailing_list.html in the Errors tab.

11 If the Inspector is not visible choose Window > Inspector. Click and drag the Fetch URL button from Error Inspector to the mailing_list.html page in the pages folder in the virtechu.site window.

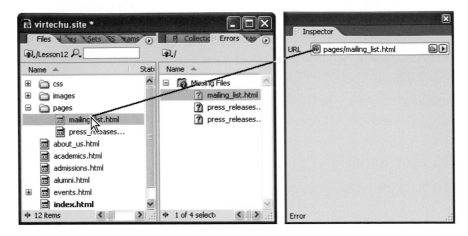

12 A Change Links window appears. Click OK to automatically update all pages referencing the mailing_list.html file to look in the new location. Click OK.

13 Close the Find Site Assets window.

Correcting the hypertext link error

In general, missing file errors can be resolved by fixing the broken reference. However, the cause for the broken reference may be different in many cases. In this exercise you will identify the broken reference to press_releases.html and then use the In & Out Links palette to fix it.

1   Double-click on the mailing_list.html file in your site window to open it.

2   Click on the Show Link Warnings (✱) in the Main toolbar to turn on the highlighting for the warnings. The link to Press Releases is highlighted. You will use the In & Out Links palette to repair this error.

3   Click on the virtechu.site window to bring it forward; the mailing_list.html file should still be selected. Click on the In & Out Links button (🖼) in the Main toolbar to open it in a separate window.

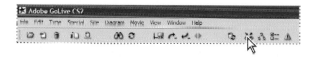

In the In & Out Links palette, the press_release.html file is identified as missing by the question mark. You will now relink it. For more information on the In & Out Links palette, see Lesson 4, "Creating Navigational Links."

4   If necessary, click and drag the In & Out Links palette to the right so you can see the Files tab in your virtechu.site window. In the In & Out Links palette, click and drag the Fetch URL button next to the press_releases.html link over to press_releases.html in the pages folder of the virtechu.site window.

Note: You may have had two press_release.html files in your Errors tab of the virtechu.site window, if so, repeat step 4.

5   When the Change Link window appears, click OK. This creates the proper hypertext link. This clears all your links and give you an error-free site.

6   When done, close the In & Out Links palette, then choose File > Save and File > Close for the mailing_list.html page.

Managing folders

You have seen in the last exercise how GoLive can change the links in a page without opening the page itself. The same principle applies to the structure of your site. Once the site has valid links throughout, you can move and rearrange files and GoLive will automatically update the links on all the pages that require it.

1   Click on the text for the folder "pages." (Not the folder but the name of the folder.) A tab field appears, allowing you to rename the folder.

2   Rename the folder **news_events** and press Enter or Return. GoLive opens a Rename Folder window and informs you that the mailing_list and press_releases.html pages need to be updated. Click OK. The links to these pages are automatically updated.

Note: *It is important that you never change the name of a referenced folder in the directory system of your computer, as it will not update paths to the links in the folder.*

Backing up and cleaning up your site

After you have fixed all the errors in your site, you should clean up the contents of your site. Cleaning up is the process of examining your site for files and objects which are not necessary for the functioning of your site. As sites get larger and evolve, it's important to make sure that only the pages which are necessary remain. Any unreferenced files should be removed, as they take up extra space on the server and potentially make the site more difficult to maintain.

You can view which files are being referenced by looking under the Used column in the site window. A bullet indicates that the file is being referenced.

Cleaning up a site can have drastic effects on reducing the size of your site because files are deleted from your site folder. Therefore, you should be careful. Because files can be removed permanently, you will make a backup of your virtechu.site folder. The simplest way to do this is to temporarily leave GoLive CS2 and duplicate the folder. This is not a required step, but it is recommended. After you are done, return to GoLive.

1   Choose Site > Update > Clean Up Site to open the Clean Up Site Options window. This window controls how GoLive cleans up your site. We will break down the window into two sections, Add Used and Remove.

2 If Refresh View and the checkboxes in Add Used are not selected, do so now.

The Add Used item is essentially a backup function. Checking these selections will add any items that are currently in your Web pages, even if they are not in the web-content folder. For example, earlier in this lesson, you found an orphan image file located outside your web-content folder and manually dragged it from the Errors tab of the site window to the images folder. If there are any additional orphan files they would be added automatically using this process.

The next three options are External resources, Colors, and Font Sets. Checking these ensures that these will be incorporated into your site as necessary.

3 Click on all the checkboxes in the Remove section. This command locates items not being used and place them into the Site Trash folder in your Extras tab.

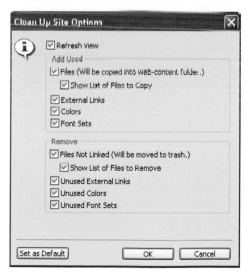

If you are comfortable with removing items every time you Clean Up a site, you can click the Set as Default button in order to avoid clicking the multiple checkboxes when you clean up.

4   Click OK. The Clean Up Site window appears with the techu_logo.gif file listed. Typically, you are familiar with your files enough to realize which ones you might need later, or where they are located, but in some cases you may want to do some more research before sending unused files to the Site Trash folder.

5   Click on the Show Folder Structure checkbox at the bottom of the window. This will format the window based on the structure of the site.

6   If necessary, click on the plus sign (Windows) or arrow (Mac OS) next to web-content and web-content/images and then web-content/images/navbar.

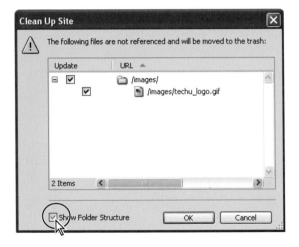

7   Click OK to remove the image and place it in the Site Trash folder. The larger the site you work on, the easier it is for files to become hidden and take up valuable space.

Working with Site Trash

Items which are deleted (either by the Cleanup Site or by deleting them in the site window) are not permanently deleted. There is a difference between GoLive's Site Trash and your system's Recycle Bin (Windows) or Trash (Mac OS).

1   Click on the Extras tab in the virtechu.site window and click on the plus sign (Windows) or arrow (Mac OS) next to the Site Trash. The items you removed in the last exercise are located here and will remain as part of the site file but not upload to the Web.

2   Right-click (Windows) or Control+click (Mac OS) on techu_logo.gif. A drop-down menu appears. Select the Delete option to permanently remove this file. If you are positive you want to delete an object, you can select the ones you want to permanently remove, while keeping the ones you may end up using in the Site Trash.

If you want to always delete your GoLive site files to the system trash choose Edit > Preferences (Windows) or GoLive > Preferences (Mac OS) and select Site. Choose "Move Them to the System Trash"(Windows) or "Move Them to the Finder Trash" (Mac OS) from the "When Removing Files Section."

Note: *If you later need a file located in the Site Trash folder, you can move it by clicking and dragging the file to the Files tab.*

If you are positive you want to delete everything, you can do that as well by right clicking (Windows) or Control+clicking (Mac OS) on the Site Trash icon. You would then choose Empty Site Trash. This will place the files into your system trash.

Setting up GoLive for FTP

FTP or File Transfer Protocol is the method for sending the files from your local machine to a server somewhere in the world. This process of sending files to a server is often referred to as uploading or publishing. Before you can publish your site on the Web, you must have the server space to do so, as well as the required information. Because there are so many variations of server space and options, these details fall outside the range of the *Classroom in a Book*. However, it's quite likely that the hosting provider which provides your Internet service also provides you with free (but limited) server space which will allow you to publish your site. You should contact your hosting provider customer service for more information.

There are essentially three required pieces of information which you will need to obtain:

- **A server address and directory**—This will often be a series of numbers or a domain such as ftp: adobe.com. Often the directory will be something like ~CIB, where CIB would be the owner of the account.

- **A User ID**—This is often the same ID you use when logging into your Internet account or checking your e-mail.

- **A password**—This may be the same as the password you use to access your e-mail, for example, but may also be something separate. Contact your service provider for details.

Configuring a publish server

In this lesson, you will navigate through the process of setting up GoLive CS2 for publishing sites to the Web. Again, keep in mind that different hosting providers may have slightly different settings from the ones you will see here.

1   Open the virtechu site if it is not currently open.

2   Choose Site > Publish Server > Set Up Server. The virtechu.site Settings window appears.

3   Click the New Server button to add a new site to the Publish Server. You can add numerous servers in this window if you have access to different sites.

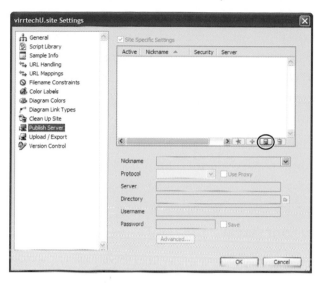

4   In the Nickname field, type **VirtechU**. The nickname is a way of identifying the site

5   Choose ftp protocol if it is not already selected. FTP is the most common method of transferring files across the Web.

6   Enter your server, username, and password information. This information needs to be provided by your ISP or other party. Click OK.

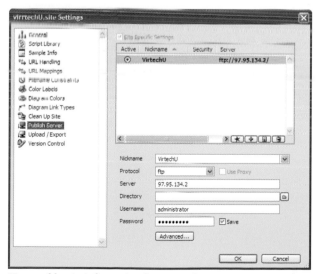

You need log-in information from your Internet service provider to publish from GoLive.

Note: The Directory field is not required on all servers, but certain servers may require you to add a directory to successfully access your server space.

If you have filled out the information correctly, you will return to the site window. If the information provided is incorrect, you will receive an error message. Often the error message will help you figure out which part of information is invalid or missing, such as "user and/or password incorrect."

You can return to the settings window by choosing Site > Settings. Reenter the missing information or contact your ISP for support if you cannot gain access to your site. When you have filled in the correct information, the right-side of the site window may display a list of files on the server. If the directory you are connecting to is empty, it may say "-empty-."

Uploading files via FTP to your server

In this part of the lesson you will need to have an internet connection and access to an FTP server. If you do not have access to a server, follow along by reading this section. Once you have successfully filled in your settings, the site will save them and you do not have to do it again. You are now able to upload your files using GoLive.

1 Click the Connect to publish server button (▉) in the Main toolbar. GoLive brings the Publish Server tab in the site window to the front and immediately attempts to connect to your server. You see the accessible directories on the right side of the site window if a connection is made, otherwise you will receive an error message.

If you receive an error message, click on the Open Site Settings dialog button (▤) in the Main toolbar and select Publish Server and verify your settings.

You can simply drag and drop files from the Files tab of the site window to the appropriate folders in the Publish Server tab or use some of the convenient server features explained in the rest of this lesson.

2   Click and hold on the Upload modified files button () in the Main toolbar. A menu appears, allowing you to choose various options. Choose the "Upload All" option to upload all the files in the web-content folder. Remember that the files being uploaded are only those in the web-content folder, not the entire site (which may consist of other assets such as components, smart objects, templates, etc.).

The Upload window appears with a list of the files in the site, and details which files will be sent to the server.

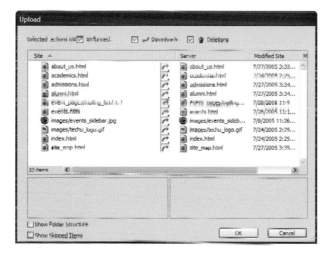

3   Click OK and the synchronize window appears as the files are sent via FTP to the server. This length of this process depends on the size of your site and the speed of your Internet connection. Once the files have been transferred, your site is live! Anyone with a Web browser can now go to the URL of your site.

Maintaining your site

After the site has been uploaded to the Web, you will essentially have two copies of the site. One will be on your local hard drive and the other will be online. Your goal will be to keep the two synchronized. As you change the content or redesign the pages in your site, you will have to make sure the online version is current with the changes. GoLive allows you to do this automatically by distinguishing between modified and unmodified pages.

1   Assuming you have uploaded the test files to a server in the last lesson, double-click the index page located in the Files tab to open it.

2   Using the Selection tool, highlight the word June and change it to **July**. Save your document and then close it.

3   Click the Upload Modified Files button (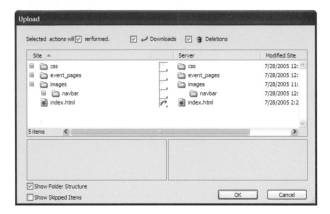) on the Main toolbar. In the Upload dialog box, note that the file you've just modified is marked with a green arrow, meaning GoLive will upload it to the publish server. Click OK to upload the modified file.

When GoLive uploads files, it saves the modification time for the local site files and the files on the server. When you perform a modified-item upload, GoLive compares the modification times and transfers only new files, and files that have been modified locally since the last upload.

Synchronizing files in your site

Occasionally, your site may get out of synch. This can happen if you or someone else moves, deletes or adds files without using GoLive. Additionally, if you rearrange your local site by rearranging files or renaming folders, you will want to make sure the online site is synchronized.

1   In the Files tab of the site window, select the site_map file and then click the Delete Selected Item button (🗑) in the Main toolbar. Click Yes to confirm the deletion.

2   Click the Synchronize With Publish Server button (◆) on the Main toolbar.

The Synchronize dialog box appears and displays files on the local site and on the publish server. The file you deleted locally is marked with a delete icon.

3   Select the file and cycle through the synchronization actions by clicking the Synchronization Action button displayed in the column next to the file. Click OK to delete the file from the publish server and synchronize the site.

Synchronizing a site ensures that the local site and the site on the server match. When you synchronize a site, you can upload files to the publish server, download them from the server to the local site, skip files completely, or delete them. You can exclude files from upload by setting their publish state to Never in the File Inspector.

Exporting a site

Exporting a site is a different concept from Publishing. Exporting is essentially the process of taking the contents of the web-content folder in the site window and saving it as a new folder. You may want to export sites for backup purposes or send the files to another person.

1   Open the virtechu site if it is not currently open. Choose File > Export > Site. The Export Site Options window appears. Make sure the following settings are set. In the hierarchy section: choose "As in Site". In the Honor Publish State of section, make sure both the Folders and Files options are checked. All other options should be unchecked.

The following options are available for site export:

Honor Publish State Of Files/Folders specifies whether to override individual publish state settings for files and folders, deselect the respective options.

Linked Files Only specifies whether to upload only those files that are part of the site hierarchy.

As In Site maps the hierarchy of groups, pages, and resources within your site window to the resulting root folder.

Separate Pages And Media creates a root folder that contains two subfolders for HTML pages and media, respectively.

Flat creates a root folder that contains all HTML pages and media, but no subfolders.

Folder Name entries apply to the Separate Pages And Media option. For files that are not in the site, the Folder Name entry applies only when you select the Export Linked Files That Are Not Part Of This Site option.

Export Linked Files That Are Not Part Of The Site specifies that the export will include orphan files.

Show Options Before Export displays these Export options at the time of each export.

Strip HTML Code For selects Comments or Space to streamline the source code without affecting the appearance of pages. Select Adobe GoLive Elements to remove GoLive tags and attributes that let you edit your animations, scripted actions, and so on.

Strip GoLive Data From Media Files checks all GIF, JPEG, PNG, SWF, and SVG files for data that has been added to those files to enable the Smart Object workflow. This data is added only to the target files of Smart Objects. The option then removes the data to make the files smaller.

Flatten Script Library scans all files that use the GoLive JavaScript library and rewrites the external files so they contain only the exact JavaScript needed for the site. This option is recommended.

Rewrite PDF Files scans all PDF files that are part of the site and optimizes them for quicker upload.

—From GoLive Help

2   Click Export and you will be prompted to create a Site Folder. Choose the desktop and create a new folder and name it **Virtechu_export**. Click the Save button and GoLive creates a copy of the files used in the web-content folder. When finished, a window appears, noting that the export was successful. Click Yes to see a detailed list of files (Windows) or Details (Mac OS).

An HTML page is automatically generated, listing the categories of files which were exported. You can use this page to make sure that only the files you wanted exported.

3   Close the HTML page that was generated.

4 Minimize GoLive and locate the Virtechu_export folder on your desktop. Double-click it to open. The HTML files, images, and any other files in your web-content folder have been copied to a standalone folder which can now be archived or sent to another designer.

Congratulations! You have finished the lesson.

To download sites from HTTP and FTP servers

Using the Site Creation Wizard, you can import an entire Web site into GoLive, including every linked page that branches out to multiple HTTP servers and every source file (such as images) referenced by the pages. Because large sites can take a long time to download, you can restrict the number of page levels in the page-link hierarchy to import.

Note: If you already have an ongoing workgroup project that employs version control, and you wish to continue the collaboration, connect to the existing site instead of using this procedure.

1 Choose File > New.

2 Select Site > Create Site.

3 Select Site From Existing Content, and click Next.

4 Select By Downloading Files From A Remote Server, and click Next.

5 Choose the server type (FTP or HTTP) from the Type Of Server menu.

6 If you are downloading from an HTTP server, specify the home page URL of the server in the URL box and then do one of the following:

• To download only the pages that are located in the same folder (or a subfolder) that contains the home page URL, select Only Get Pages Under Same Path.

• To download only those pages that are on the same server as the home page URL, select Stay On Same Server. GoLive downloads from other servers any source files that are referenced by the pages it downloads, whether or not this option is selected.

7 If you are downloading from an FTP server, enter the FTP server information. Click Advanced to set security and passive mode options. (See To set up access to a publish server.)

8 Click Next, and then specify a name and location for the downloaded files. To specify how the new site will handle encoding and case sensitivity checking in URLs, click Advanced. (See Advanced URL handling options.)

9 Click Finish.

GoLive imports only the pages on the levels you specify, and source files for images and other objects on those pages. GoLive converts any remaining page links that go to other levels into external URLs and lists them in the External tab of the site window. After you create the site, you can individually download the pages from these external URLs by choosing Download from a URL's context menu.

Exploring on your own

1 Make sure you understand how to import a site by choosing a folder of files from a previous lesson or from your own local machine.

2 Download an existing site from the Web by selecting Site > Create Site. Choose site from existing content and choose the download site from remote server option. Enter the HTTP address of a Web site you are familiar with. You should choose the Only Get Pages Under Same Path option until you are more familiar with this feature.

3 Contact your Internet Service Provider and request information for the server address. Upload practice files onto your site to get a sense of how GoLive's publish features work. Don't forget to delete them when you are done.

Review

Review questions

1   How do you import a collection of HTML pages and other assets as a site in GoLive and under what circumstances might you do so?

2   What is the definition of an "orphan file" and a "missing file?" Where would you locate them and why is it necessary to locate them?

3   What is FTP and how do you set up GoLive to use it?

4   When would you synchronize a site?

Review answers

1   You import a site by choosing File > New and then choosing the Site > Create Site from Existing Content. Importing a site is the process of creating a site from a previously existing folder of files and images. You might import a site if another author built HTML pages by hand or used another Web application.

2   An orphan file is a file which has been located by GoLive but is *not* located in the root folder of the Web site. A missing file is a file which has been linked to from a document in your site which GoLive cannot locate at all. A list of orphan and missing files can be found in the Errors tab of the site window. Orphan and missing files should be resolved before a site is put online, unresolved files may result in a "broken" site in which a user who clicks on a hyperlink may receive an error.

3   FTP is referred to as file transfer protocol and is the process by which you send the elements of your Web site from your local machine to a server, thereby making your site accessible on the World Wide Web. Choose Site > Publish Server > Set Up Server to access the setup screen. To successfully publish a site you need at least a server address, a user name and a password.

4   Synchronizing a site is the process of making sure that the files on your local machine and the files on a remote server are the same. You can synchronize your local machine to the remote server or vice versa. You want to synchronize your site when you make basic changes such as deleting or renaming files.

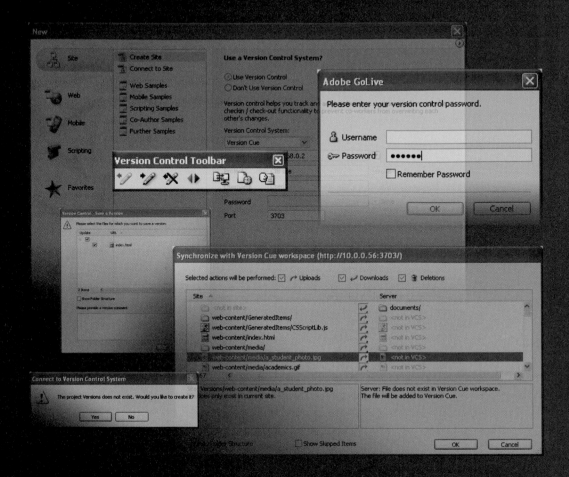

You can use Version Cue with Adobe GoLive CS2 to help manage Web site files and revisions. GoLive CS2 provides exclusive features designed to help manage the design process of complete Web sites.

13 | Using Version Cue and Bridge with GoLive CS2

This lesson covers the basics of using Version Cue CS2 and Adobe Bridge. After reviewing this section you'll learn how to do the following:

- Use Version Cue to organize and share projects.
- Create a Version Cue project.
- Add Content to a Version Cue project.
- Work offline when not connected to a Version Cue server.
- Use Adobe Bridge to access and organize files.

Note: This lesson is for users who have installed Adobe GoLive as part of Adobe Creative Suite 2. If you use Adobe Creative Suite 2, you have access to the full set of Version Cue features discussed in this lesson, including Version Cue Administration. If you don't have Adobe Creative Suite 2, you can gain access to the full Version Cue feature set by participating in a shared project; that is, if another user on your network installs Adobe Creative Suite 2 and gives you access to a Version Cue project in a Version Cue Workspace.

Getting started

Adobe Version Cue and GoLive CS2 provide unique capabilities designed to assist in building and managing Web content. Certain Version Cue features are unique to GoLive CS2, allowing you to create new Web site files or convert existing sites into Version Cue managed projects. Managed and non-managed projects are designed using the same tools, but managed projects contain additional options to help you work more effectively when revising sites or collaborating with other users on a project. This section contains no specific lesson files, and provides an opportunity for you to work with your own projects.

Working with Version Cue

If you own Adobe Creative Suite Standard or Premium, you can take advantage of Adobe Version Cue, an integrated workflow feature designed to help you be more productive by saving you, and others you work with, valuable time.

With Version Cue, you can easily create, manage, and find different versions of your project files. If you collaborate with others, you and your team members can share project files in a multi-user environment that protects content from being accidentally overwritten. You can also maintain descriptive comments with each file version, search embedded file information to quickly locate files, and work with robust file management features while working directly within each application.

Note: The Version Cue workspace is a feature of Adobe Creative Suite. If you purchased Adobe GoLive CS2 separately, and don't own Adobe Creative Suite, you can use the Version Cue feature in your Adobe CS2 application only if an owner of Adobe Creative Suite gives you network access to their Version Cue workspace.

If you previously installed Version Cue, it must be turned on. Open the Adobe Version Cue preferences from the Control Panel (Windows) or System Preferences (Mac OS), and choose On from the Version Cue drop-down menu.

What's inside a GoLive CS2 Version Cue project

When you create a Version Cue project in GoLive, the standard GoLive site folders (web-content, web-data, and web-settings) and a site project file (.site) are created on the Version Cue Workspace. The web-content folder is the root folder of the Web site and contains master files that are kept on the Version Cue Workspace.

Creating a new Version Cue project

You will create a new project and use it to explore the capabilities of Version Cue. The project will include a Web site and all the corresponding pages and images. You will then work with the Version Cue site management tools along with the methods for managing individual pages.

1   Choose File > New. The New window opens. Click the Site tab along the left side and then click the Create Site option in the center. Along the right side of the window, under the Site Creation Wizard heading, click the Blank Site radio button. This is the first step in creating a new, blank Web site.

2   Click the Next button and another window opens: the Specifying a Site Name and Location window.

3   In the Specifying a Site Name and Location window, locate the Name field and type **CIB Site**. For the Save To location, click the Browse button. In the window that opens, navigate to the Lesson13 folder on your hard drive and click OK (Windows) or Choose (Mac OS) to save the new site to this location, then click the Next button.

4   Under the Use a Version Control System heading, choose Use Version Control, and from the Version Control System menu choose Version Cue.

5   From the drop-down menu to the right of Server, choose your Version Cue server name.

6   In the Project field, type **CIB site**. Leave the user name and Port unchanged, then click Next.

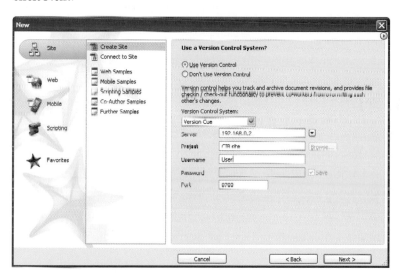

7   Click the Specify Server Later radio button as we will not be uploading these files to a server. Click the Finish button and a new, managed site is created. The CIB Project window opens.

Note: If a Connect to Version Cue window appears with the message: "Version Cue reported an error Could not connect to server," you may need to confirm that Version Cue is running correctly on your computer. Refer to the previous section or view GoLive Help for assistance.

*Note: You may be asked to log into the Version Cue Workspace when you use the GoLive Site Creation wizard either to create a new Version Cue project or to access an existing Version Cue project, even if the Version Cue project doesn't require users to log in. If you have a Version Cue user ID and password, enter them in the Username and Password boxes. If you want to log in as the system administrator, enter **system** in the Username box and the system password in the Password box. (The default system password is system). If you don't have a Version Cue user ID and password, enter the user name you use on your current computer and leave the Password box blank.*

Checking out a file for editing

After you have created a GoLive CS2 site that is managed by Version Cue, you will edit pages and add content to the site. To edit pages that are part of a site managed by Version Cue, you will check the files out for editing, which ensures that only one user will access each file at a time.

1   In the CIB site window, double-click the index.html file to open it.

Opening files managed by Version Cue is identical to the procedure for opening non-managed files. While you edit a file, your changes affect only the copy on your computer until you synchronize with the Version Cue workspace.

2   In the Title of the document, click the cursor to create an insertion point and type **CIB** to replace the Untitled Page title. An alert window appears before text is entered (Windows) or after typing and pressing Enter (Mac OS).

In the Version Cue – Mark in Use alert window, click Yes to mark the file in use. By marking the file in use, other users can see that you are editing the file.

When files are managed by Version Cue, you are reminded if files should be Marked In Use so that they are not modified by other users.

💡 *You can also mark a file In Use by clicking the Mark In Use icon in the Version Control toolbar or by choosing Site > Version Control System > Mark In Use.*

3   Continue to make the change to the title, entering the name **CIB** for the page title. Next, you will save a modified version of the file. Even though the modification is minor, with only the title changing, the process for saving versions is the same.

4   Click the Save a Version button (✐) in the Version Control Toolbar. Click OK if requested to automatically save a local file, and a version of the page is saved, while the original untitled page also remains available. The Version Control – Save a Version window opens.

5   In the Version Control – Save a Version window, confirm the name of the file being saved and click OK. Saving a version updates the master file on the Version Cue Workspace, making the file available for others working on the project. Saving a version also removes the lock, allowing others access to the file.

6   Close the file and the site window. It is not necessary to save any changes.

Note: You can also save a version of the file to the Version Cue Workspace by using the Site > Version Control System > Save A Version command.

Don't forget to also regularly save your files using the File > Save command. This saves your file locally on your computer (not using Version Cue).

Using the Version Control Toolbar

The Version Control Toolbar in GoLive gives you easy access to commonly used commands. You can mark files In Use, save a version, synchronize a file, view user activity, show information about all versions of a file, and compare the source code of Web page versions from the toolbar. If you don't see the toolbar, you can access it from the Windows > Toolbar menu.

The Version Control Toolbar contains the following buttons:

Mark In Use—Marks one or more selected files in use, or marks the currently open active document in use.

Save A Version—Saves the local version of a file as a new version to the Version Cue Workspace, and removes your ID from the file on the workspace.

Cancel Mark In Use—Discards any changes to one or more files, reverts the file to the most recent file version, and removes your user ID from the file's Version Cue edit status on the host Version Cue Workspace.

Synchronize With Version Control System—Synchronizes the working copy with Version Cue Workspace.

Compare To Latest Version On Version Cue—Reports that a working copy is identical to the file on the Version Cue Workspace or displays the source code for working and Version Cue Workspace file versions of a Web page in the Compare Local Version to Latest Version dialog box.

Versions—Displays a summary of a file's versions, including version thumbnails, version comments, and version authors. Also allows you to compare the source code of two versions of a Web page or a Web page version and a working copy, and create a new version based upon an existing version.

Show User Activity—Displays the User Activity tab in the Version Cue site window, which lists the project's users and any files each user is editing.

—From GoLive Help

About Version Cue Status

The status of files managed by Version Cue is displayed in the lower left corner of the document window. A checkmark icon (✔) indicates whether the document you are working with is Synchronized—meaning that the file on your system is identical to the Version Cue file. If you are working on a file and have made changes since opening it from the Version Cue project, the icon changes to a house (🏠), indicating that the file is in use by you.

The file status is also displayed in the site window under the Version Status column within the Files tab if the file is in-use.

Managing existing sites

Existing sites may need to have their structure changed to match the way Version Cue manages files. Here you will take an existing site, convert it so that it can be managed by Version Cue, and then create the Version Cue project.

1   Open a previously created GoLive site file.

2   Choose Site > Version Control System > Enable Version Control. The Settings window opens with data relating to this site.

3   In the Settings window, click the use Version Control check box. For Version Control System choose Version Cue. From the Server drop-down menu, choose your Version Cue server. Leave the other settings unchanged and click OK.

4   In the alert window that opens, click Yes to create the new project.

5   In the Synchronize with Version Cue workspace window that opens, keep the default settings and click OK. This causes GoLive to keep all the listed files and folders synchronized. Keep the site open.

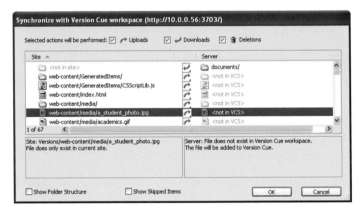

Note: *If you receive an error message, you may need to confirm that Version Cue is running correctly on your computer. Refer to GoLive Help for assistance.*

Note: *You may be asked to log into the Version Cue Workspace, even if the Version Cue project doesn't requires users to log in. If you have a Version Cue user ID and password, enter them in the Username and Password boxes. If you want to log in as the system administrator, enter* **system** *in the Username box and the system password in the Password box. (The default system password is system). If you don't have a Version Cue user ID and password, enter the user name you use on your current computer and leave the Password box blank.*

Adding files to a Version Cue site

Sites that are managed by Version Cue function identically to non-managed sites when adding content. When you add a graphic or a PDF document to the Web site, the files are added locally to the web-content folder. You must then synchronize the local site with the Version Cue site to ensure any files added to the site are also uploaded to the Version Cue project.

1   In the site window of the GoLive site you opened in the previous exercise, click the plus sign (Windows) or triangle (Mac OS) to expand the media folder, revealing its contents.

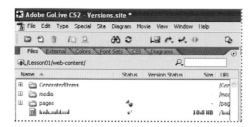

2   Locate and drag a new file such as a graphic or PDF file into the media folder in the site window. Note the icon that appears to the right of the file name, in the Version Status column. The Only Copy icon indicates that this is the only instance of the file that is known to Version Cue. There are no other copies available, and the file is not synchronized.

For more information about other status icons, see Version Cue File Statuses in GoLive Help.

3   In the Version Control Toolbar, click Synchronize With Version Control System (◀▶) to synchronize the entire project.

4   In the Synchronize with Version Cue workspace window that opens, confirm the file being synchronized and click OK, completing the synchronization process.

The file you have created is now part of the Version Cue project and available for others to use. Keep the site window open.

You can also synchronize individual files as they are added to a site by selecting the file or files, and choosing Site > Version Control System > Save An Initial Version. If you are part of a group sharing files using Version Cue, it is useful to synchronize on a regular basis. This provides you with the latest files that may have been uploaded to the workspace by other users, and makes your files available as well.

Working offline

GoLive maintains working copies of a site on your computer, so you can continue to work even if you are not connected to the Version Cue workspace. If you know you are going to be working offline, you should synchronize your project to obtain the latest files from the Version Cue workspace. If you want to indicate that you will be editing certain files, you can use the Mark In Use command to protect the files so that others do not unintentionally revise them.

1   Shift-click to select any files and folders that you will be using when not connected to the Version Cue server.

2   Click the Mark in use button (✏) in the Version Control Toolbar.

3   Choose Site > Version Control System > Work Offline.

When you are able to connect again to the Version Cue workspace, choose the same command to reconnect. You can then synchronize any files that have changed or save new versions to the Version Cue workspace.

Note: *While working offline, the Version Status information will not be displayed for any files being modified by other users, and you cannot change the status of any files that are a part of the Version Cue workspace. Your ability to add files to a specified Publish Server is not impacted by working offline as long as you still have access to the Publish Server.*

Working with Adobe Bridge

In this exercise, you'll use the Adobe Bridge to locate and access Adobe InDesign files. You will then create a Version Cue project and create multiple versions using Version Cue.

1   Start Adobe GoLive CS2.

2   Start Adobe Bridge by doing either one of the following:

• Choose File > Browse from within Adobe GoLive CS2.

• Click the Go to Bridge button (📷) in the GoLive Control palette.

The Adobe Bridge application starts, and a new window opens. The new Adobe Bridge provides a convenient, central location for accessing and managing your files and projects. With Adobe Bridge, you can easily locate, preview, and group your project files. Adobe Bridge also provides access to Version Cue's file tracking and organization tools.

Navigating and viewing files

1 Click Bridge Center in the upper left corner of the Bridge window, located under the Favorites tab. The Bridge Center window is displayed. Expand the size of the window to view all of the contents.

Use Bridge Center to easily access the Creative Suite 2 documents you've most recently accessed, including those from GoLive, InDesign, Illustrator, and Photoshop. These are displayed in the Recent Folders and Recent Files sections of this window.

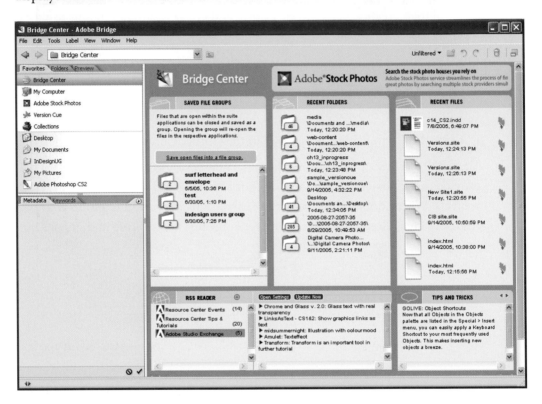

2   Click the Folders tab in the upper left corner of the Bridge window, and navigate to locate a folder that contains images, site files, or other content. You can select any folder on your computer or network.

All the files in this folder are displayed, including site files and image files. You can use Adobe Bridge to navigate. You can explore additional items by navigating into media folders located within the web-content folder in GoLive sites.

3   Click to select an object and note the Metadata that is displayed for the selected object in the Metadata tab.

4   Choose File > Exit (Windows) or Adobe Bridge > Quit (Mac OS) to close Adobe Bridge.

Congratulations! You have finished the lesson.

Index

A

absolute link paths 174
absolute URL 174
Acrobat 66
actions 49, 277–298
    actions, definition of 287
    browser switch 295
    close window 297
    locating and installing 296
    open window action 290
adaptive 262
adding components to a page 178
adding links to a graphic 175–176
Adding Sections, Pages, and Groups 360
Adobe Acrobat 66
Adobe Acrobat Reader 371
Adobe Bridge 10
Adobe Creative Suite 399, 400
Adobe Illustrator 240, 255, 261
Adobe InDesign 22, 78–79, 150, 409
Adobe Photoshop 87, 255, 265, 273, 296
Adobe Swatch Exchange format 236
alert, browser preview 303
alert, close site 115
alert, copy files 18
alert, empty reference 320
alert, error 119
alert, in use 402
alert, move files 104
alert, new project 406
alert, set title 85
alert, stationery 342
algorithm 262
align 29, 250, 268
alignment 52, 142, 147, 149, 152, 162, 165, 201, 210, 214, 270
align objects 122, 155
Align palette 250
alternate link 295

alternative text. *See also* alt text
alt text 34, 251, 252, 274, 319
anchors 182, 185, 359, 366
    creating 182–184
    testing 184–185
    using 185–186
annotations 358, 363, 371
assets, adding 16

B

background color 129, 223
    setting page background color with CSS 224
background image 23, 128, 253
backing up a site 384–386
backup 77
Basic Objects 21, 34
bitmap 244
blank site 15
block 210, 213
body 30
bookmark 18
border 35, 131, 136, 141, 142, 165, 319
border, image 319
border, selection 35
border, table 136, 165
Bringing objects forward. *See* layers
bringing objects forward. *See* layers
bring layers forward. *See* Z-index
broken links 172, 175, 192, 379
browser 31, 293
browser switch 295
button, reset 319
button, submit 319

C

Cascading Style Sheets 21, 29, 30, 77
    alignment 210
    applying 147
    applying CSS 211

class style 81, 147, 212
    Applying to a div 214
    block 213
    inline 213
default CSS file 83
exporting styles 67, 142, 144, 216
external style sheet 216
formatting body text 208
for hyperlinks 40
importing styles 217
internal style sheet 216
new style 208
paragraph formatting 204
selector 77
cell. *See* table cell
cell size 136–137
CGI (Common Gateway Interface) 174, 304
cleaning up a site 384–386
clickable images 301
clickable regions. *See* image map
close window action 297
CMYK 226, 229, 231
Collections 81
color 80
    broken links 192
    extracting color 235
    links 191–192
    template regions 346
color library 223
Color palette 205, 226
color picker 33, 128, 157, 191, 203, 210
    how to use 234
Color Reduction Method 262
Color tab 75, 110
Color Table 263, 264
columns 138–140
components 74, 176–181, 325
    adding 178–179
    creating 180–181, 328–330
    cropping text 333–334
    editing 332–333
    placing 330–332
converting a layout grid to a table 132–133

copy, files 269
copy, table 307
copy, text 200
copying classroom files 2
create site 15
cropping 272
CSS. *See* Cascading Style Sheets
CSS-based designs 114
CSS Editor 30, 40, 41, 161, 164, 204
CSS layouts 278
custom breaks 334
custom colors 236, 262, 264

D

description, meta 19
Design 358, 368, 370
detecting rollover images 283
diagrams 79, 81, 355, 356, 357, 364, 377. *See* site diagram
dimensions 87
distribute objects 122, 155
dither 26, 228, 262
div 153, 213, 214, 215, 218
doctype 30
Document Statistics 271
document window 58
down, rollover state 278, 282
download sites 395
Draggable Basic Objects 19
Draggable Head Objects 21

E

e-mail links 189–190
element 25, 30, 31, 40, 41, 370
emphasis 202
EmptyReference! 320
errors 81, 97, 379, 380, 381, 385, 397
events 29, 37, 38, 287–290
exporting a site 393–395
External CSS link 83
external links 186–189
External Style Sheet 29, 80
    exporting 216
    importing 217
Extras 78–80, 97, 105, 378, 387
Eyedropper 229, 235

F

favicon 9
Favorite 18
Fetch URL 38, 57, 248, 361, 371
Fetch URL button 382, 383
Files tab 80, 81, 85
File Transfer Protocol 388
Flash 74, 78
Flatten Script Library 394
folder 16
font family 31, 207
font properties 31, 41, 83, 207, 208, 209, 210, 214
font sets 80
font sets and color 127–128
forms 301, 303
    forms, definition of 304
    Label Object 306
    linking, labels 309
    list boxes 301, 314
    pop-up menus 301, 310
    radio buttons 301, 315
        group section 316
    reset button 319
    submit button 318
    tabbing order 301, 321
    text fields 301, 306
    Value 306
    Visible text field 306
Forms Inspector 304
form element 314
form fields 301
Form Label 309
Form List Box 315
Form Objects 305
frames 295
frames, text 27
Frame Editor 59
FTP 388, 389, 390, 395, 397
FTP (File Transfer Protocol) 16, 102
    importing sites 102

G

Generate links 361
GIF 26, 244, 261, 262, 264, 267, 274
graphics 243–247, 274
grayscale 227

grid text box 27, 28, 32
grouping pages 362
group section 316

H

h1 206
h2 210
h3 210
head 19, 295
Heading 1 206
head actions 294
Helvetica 31
hexadecimal color 33, 210, 226
    hexadecimal, defined 228
Hex Value. *See* hexadecimal color
home page 73, 74, 75, 76, 77, 102, 106, 360, 377, 395
href 40
HSB 226
HSpace 271
HSV 226
HTML 205. *See also* Hypertext Markup Language
HTML, importing pages 397
HTML tables 113, 114, 133, 134
HTTP (Hypertext Transfer Protocol) 102, 395
hyperlink 397
hyperlinks 37, 41, 176
hypertext link
    correcting errors 383
hypertext links 171–175
Hypertext Markup Language 22

I

image 23, 25, 34, 364, 365
    adding space around 271
    aligning an image 268
    placing 24, 247
Image Inspector 248
image map 248, 328, 345
import 246, 397
    files to site 17
importing an existing site 377
import images 118

import tab-delimited text 36
import text 143–145
InDesign 22
InDesign Package 9, 79
installing the program 2
internal style sheet 216
Internet Service Provider 304, 388, 389
In & Out Links palette 75, 194–195
  correcting errors 383
ISP 304, 388, 389
istockphoto.com 420

J

JavaScript 49, 277, 288, 290, 296, 394
JPEG 244, 257, 258, 274

K

keyboard shortcuts 52
keywords 19
Key Generator object 305

L

Label Object 306, 309
landscape 66
layers 25, 113, 150, 158, 223, 277, 278, 295
  adding 150–152
  aligning and distributing 153–155
  inserting objects into 152–153
  Layers palette 159
  organizing 157–158
  Z-index 158, 161
layout 21
Layout Editor 39, 58, 113
layout grid 22, 113, 114, 115, 116, 117, 118, 119, 120, 121, 122, 123, 124, 128, 131, 132, 133, 154, 165
  adding images 118
  aligning objects 120
  changing the background 128, 129
Layout Preview 59, 63
layout text box 124, 129, 131
Layout view 133, 185, 210, 216

Alignment
  Default
    Top
      Middle 270
Library palette 312, 325, 353
linking, labels 309, 323
linking, rollover 280
links 168–197, 171, 289. *See also* hyperlinks
  absolute paths 174
  adding links to a graphic 175–176
  broken 172, 175, 192
  color 191–192
  create 172, 173, 186–189
  e-mail 189–190
  external 186–189
  null 175
  remove 172
  using anchors for links 186
link warning 192–193, 328, 383
link warning icon 169
liquid layouts 113, 114, 161, 162, 164
List, Numbered 202
lists 202
  increase list level 202
  numbered list 202
  unnumbered 202
list boxes 301, 314
list boxes 301, 314
live rendering 9, 39
lossy 262

M

magnification 48
mailto: 190
maintaining a site 391–392
Main toolbar 29, 84
Map Area Inspector 250
Margin 210, 212
Markup Elements 206
master 358
media 80
meta 20
metadata 18
meta tags 326
missing file 379, 397
monitor size 22
mouse enter 288
mouse exit 289
mouse over 288
Movable Type 53

multimedia 1
Multiple Selection checkbox 314
M icon 329, 332

N

Name/ID 249, 286
navigational links 167–197
Navigation View 108
new folder 16
new page 85
null link 175

O

Objects palette 14
Object Selection tool 32
open window action 290
optimize 25
optimize the layout grid 131–132
orientation, page 108
orphan file 379, 397
Outline Editor 59, 61
over, rollover state 278

P

padding, cells 141, 210, 211, 212
PageMaker 22
page background 223
Page Properties 23, 223
Page Setup 108
page templates 74, 79, 361
  building from 350–351
  creating 348
  defined 326
  defining regions 346
  Library palette 349
  saving 344, 344–345
  using 349, 349–350
palettes 49
Pantone 232
Pantone Solid Coated 231
paragraph attributes 201
PDF 37, 74, 79, 357, 370, 372, 394
PDF Preview 66
perceptual 262
photographs 243
pick whip 131. *See* Fetch URL
placing text and images 146
plug-ins 5, 296

PMS, Pantone Matching System 232
PNG 244
PNG-24 244
PNG-8 244, 262, 264
positioning 113, 130, 153
preferences 4, 13, 67
preview 36, 39, 41, 63
Preview in Browser 39, 64, 65, 71, 164, 174, 176, 185, 190, 192, 292, 294, 302, 315, 320
project folder 77
publish server 81, 388, 390

Q

Queries 79, 252
QuickTime 53, 74

R

radio buttons 301, 315
Recall 368
Rectangular Map-area tool 249
relative path 174
remote rollover 286
remove link 172
resample, image 87
reset button 319
restrictive 262
RGB 226
rollovers 277
    Adding a link 284
    Creating self-rollovers 280
    detecting 283
    preview 281
    remote 285
    setting up 278
    state 281
rollover preferences 284
Root folder 27, 85, 132, 200
rows 138–140
rulers 120, 121

S

Save for Web 26, 27, 243, 244, 247, 254, 257, 259, 261, 263, 265, 266, 267
scratch pages 359
screen reader 284

scripts 293
search engine 18, 168
selective 262
selector 30, 83, 210
Select Map-area tool 250, 251
Select parent table button 138
select window 350
server address and directory 388
Settings8 4
Set Font Size 201
Set Image URL 288, 289
site 73, 76, 80, 109
    Adding existing files 86
    backing up and cleaning up 384–386
    color 73, 237
    configuring a publish server 388
    converting 378
    correcting errors 379–382
    correcting the hypertext link error 383
    download sites from HTTP and FTP servers 395
    exporting 393–395
    importing an existing site 377
    maintaining 391–392
    management and publishing 375
    managing folders 384
    new blank site 76
    setting up GoLive for FTP 388
    site file 77
    synchronizing files 392–393
    uploading files via FTP to your server 390–391
site colors 237
site diagram 365
    adding annotations 363–364
    adding sections, pages, and groups 360–362
    Adding text 363
    Adding Text and Images 364
    anchoring a page 359
    anchoring to a page 359
    creating 357–358
    creating a group of pages 362–363
    exporting and printing 370
    live Pages 366, 367, 368
    live pages 366
    master tab 357, 369
    recalling a diagram 368

    site pages 365, 372
    staging tools 365
    workflow 357
site folder 303
site preferences 79
site tools 75
Site Trash 78, 79, 385, 386, 387
site window 44, 45, 46, 55, 56, 57, 58, 168
Smart Favorite Icon 255
Smart Generic 255
Smart Illustrator 255, 261
Smart Objects 78, 79, 105, 247, 254, 394
    cropping 272
Smart PDF 255
Smart Photoshop 24, 255, 265, 272, 273
SMIL 53
snippets 313, 325, 335, 336, 351
    collecting and organizing 337
    defined 78, 326
    organizing and collecting 337
    placing 338–339
Source Code Editor 59
spanning rows and columns 138–140
Spot color 229
SSR 39
stacking order 157–158
Staging 358, 365, 366, 367, 368, 369
Standard Editing tool 29
stationeries 74, 78, 79, 326, 341, 342, 361
    creating 339–340
    creating a page from 341–343
    Library palette 340
    saving 340–341
Strip GoLive Data 394
strong 201
Studio Exchange 296
submit button 304, 318
SVG 6, 9, 245
Swatches palette 221, 229, 230, 231, 232, 233, 234, 235, 236, 239
    Toggle edit mode 233
SWF 245
synchronize 391, 392, 397
synchronizing files 392–393

T

tab-delimited text 144
tabbing order 321
table-based designs 114
tables 35, 114, 135, 136, 138, 141, 143, 146, 148, 279, 312. *See also* HTML tables
  cell 35
  column 37, 366, 384, 393
  padding, cells 141
  row 35, 36
  Select parent table button 138
  spanning 37
table attributes 142–143
table cell 136–137, 165
table style 142–143, 145–146, 165
tabulator indexing 321
tab order 301
target insertion point 123
template 79, 326, 346, 347, 348, 349, 353. *See also* page templates
template regions 346–347, 348
testing anchors 184–185
text 29
  alignment 201
  formatting 201
  importing 200
  increase list level 202
  remove color 203
  setting text color 203
  Set text color 33
text, formatting in HTML 201
text, importing 200
text area 32
text field 301, 306
text properties 210, 214
Text to Banner 243, 267
title 18
title bar 293
toolbars 14, 49
toolbox 51
tooltip 22
TypePad Blog 53

U

uploading files 390–391
URL (Uniform Resource Locators) 80, 102

Using classroom files 2

V

value 228, 306, 316, 317
variable 25, 26, 265, 267, 274
vector 244
Version Que 10
view 47, 48, 58, 59, 60, 64, 69, 70, 80, 91, 106, 107, 108, 110, 111, 120
VSpace 271

W

W3C 114
WBMP 245
web-content 27, 78, 81, 85, 169, 378, 385, 393
web-data 78, 81, 378
web-settings 80, 378
Web Colors 228
Web file format 244
Web Named Colors 223, 226
Web Settings 67
Web site 13
  backing up and cleaning up 384–386
  blank site, creating new 15, 245, 401
  configuring a publish server 388
  converting 378
  correcting errors 379–382
  correcting the hypertext link error 383
  download sites from HTTP and FTP servers 395
  exporting 393–395
  from existing files 100
  importing an existing site 377
  maintaining 391–392
  managing and publishing 375–397
  managing folders 384
  setting up GoLive for FTP 388
  synchronizing files 392–393
  uploading files via FTP to your server 390
Welcome Screen 13, 76
workspace 49, 50, 70
work area 46

World Wide Web 114

X

XHTML 80
XML 80

Z

Z-index 158–160
zoom 47, 48, 87, 138
Zoom tool 48

Production Notes

The *Adobe GoLive CS2 Classroom in a Book* was created electronically using Adobe InDesign. Additional art was produced using Adobe Illustrator and Adobe Photoshop.

Team credits

The following individuals contributed to the development of new and updated lessons for this edition of the *Adobe GoLive CS2 Classroom in a Book*:

Project coordinator, technical writer: Jennifer M. Smith

Additional technical writing: Jeremy Osborn, Christopher G. Smith

Production: AGI Training: Elizabeth Chambers

Artwork production: Lisa Fridsma

Proofreading: Jay Donahue

Technical Editors: Joda Alian, Cathy Auclair, Greg Heald, Robert Underwood

Typefaces used

Set in the Adobe Minion Pro and Adobe Myriad Pro OpenType families of typefaces. More information about OpenType and Adobe fonts is located inside the Studio folder on the *Classroom in a Book* CD or at Adobe.com.

Stock Photos

Stock Photos supplied by www.istockphoto.com. Photographers include the following: Oleksandr Gumerov (Man on laptop); Adrzej Burak (Woman with glasses); Kirk Peart (Female expressions); Sean Locke (Hanging on the quad); Oleg Prikhodko (Conference hall); Maartje van Caspel (Blackboard with hand); Jenny Schuck (The road ahead); Bill Grove (American football-handoff); James Boulette (Lacrosse tough guy); Ireneusz Skorupa (Students studying); Nancy Louie (Basketball coach); Nancy Louie (Casual Pals); Stefan Klein (Business woman); Jon McIntosh (Building with round front and Hospital entrance II); Diane Diederich (Woman with glasses); Rob Friedman (Baserunner and Teammates).